From International to World Society?

Barry Buzan offers an extensive and long overdue critique and reappraisal of the English school approach to International Relations. Starting on the neglected concept of world society and bringing together the international society tradition and the Wendtian mode of constructivism, Buzan offers a new theoretical framework that can be used to address globalisation as a complex political interplay among state and non-state actors. This approach forces English school theory to confront neglected questions both about its basic concepts and assumptions, and the constitution of society in terms of what values are shared, how and why they are shared, and by whom. Buzan highlights the idea of primary institutions as the central contribution of English school theory and shows how this both differentiates English school theory from realism and neoliberal institutionalism, and how it can be used to generate distinctive comparative and historical accounts of international society.

BARRY BUZAN is Professor of International Relations at the London School of Economics and a Fellow of the British Academy. He is the author, co-author or editor of over fifteen books and has published widely in academic journals.

T0381825

(List continues at the end of book)

From International to World Society?

English School Theory and the Social Structure of Globalisation

Barry Buzan

CAMBRIDGE
UNIVERSITY PRESS

CAMBRIDGE UNIVERSITY PRESS
Cambridge, New York, Melbourne, Madrid, Cape Town, Singapore,
São Paulo, Delhi, Dubai, Tokyo

Cambridge University Press
The Edinburgh Building, Cambridge CB2 8RU, UK

Published in the United States of America by Cambridge University Press, New York

www.cambridge.org
Information on this title: www.cambridge.org/9780521541213

First published 2004
Third printing 2006

A catalogue record for this publication is available from the British Library

Library of Congress Cataloguing in Publication data
Buzan, Barry.
From international to world society?: English school theory and the social
structure of globalisation / Barry Buzan.
    p. cm. – (Cambridge studies in international relations; 95)
Includes bibliographical references and index.
ISBN 0 521 83348 5 (HB) – ISBN 0 521 54121 2 (PB)
1. Globalization – Sociological aspects. I. Title. II. Series.
JZ1318.B89 2004
303.48′2 – dc22   2003055816

ISBN 978-0-521-83348-6 Hardback
ISBN 978-0-521-54121-3 Paperback

Transferred to digital printing 2010

To Richard Little

Contents

Figures and tables

Figures

Tables

Preface

This book started conscious life when I decided in the late 1990s to attempt a reconvening of the English school. Much of its agenda is already visible in a paper I wrote for the public launch of that project at the BISA Conference in 1999, and subsequently published in the *Review of International Studies* as part of a forum on the English school. That paper opens many of the criticisms of the English school classics, and some of the suggestions as to how to develop and apply the theory, that are followed up here. This book has deeper roots both in my earlier attempts to link English school ideas to American IR theory, which I extend here, and in my world historical writings with Richard Little, which point strongly towards the English school as an excellent site for developing grand theory. Its particular genesis was a growing feeling that a lot of the problems I saw in English school theory hinged on the concept of world society. World society occupied a key place in a triad alongside international society and international system, but was the Cinderella of English school theory, attracting neither consistent usage nor, and in contrast to international society, any systematic attempt to explore its meaning. The vagueness attending world society seemed to underpin a lot of the problems in English school theory about pluralism and solidarism, and how to handle the cosmopolitan and transnational aspects of international life. This dissatisfaction led me to apply for ESRC funding to look into world society. I originally offered an article, but as I dug into world society it quickly became obvious that I was writing a book, and that it would have to take on the whole body of English school theory. In that sense, writing this book has reminded me of the process of writing *People, States and Fear* twenty years ago – indeed, this book could be titled *Peoples, States and Transnational Actors*! Then I was trying to understand the concept of security, and had to follow the threads wherever they led without knowing what the whole thing would look like. Now I have pursued the threads opened by world society, and ended up focusing on institutions and the general theoretical framework of English school thinking.

I would like to thank the following for comments on all or parts of earlier versions of this work: Mathias Albert, William Bain, Chris Brown, Bruce Cronin, Thomas Diez, Tim Dunne, Ana Gonzalez-Pelaez, Stefano Guzzini, Lene Hansen, Andrew Hurrell, Dietrich Jung, John Keane, Morten Kelstrup, Bob Keohane, Anna Leander, Richard Little, Lene Mosegaard Madsen, Ian Manners, Noel Parker, Nick Rengger, John Ruggie, Brian Schmidt, Gerry Simpson, Hidemi Suganami, Ole Wæver, Adam Watson, Nick Wheeler, Richard Whitman, and several anonymous reviewers for the ESRC. My special thanks to Richard Little, Ole Wæver and the late Gerry Segal. Without my extensive collaborations with them I would never have learned half of the things I needed to understand in order to write this book. I dedicate it to Richard Little, who as well as being a good friend, has accompanied me on much of my intellectual journey towards the English school, and who has played a big role in the success of its reconvening.

I am grateful to the ESRC (award no. R000239415-A) for funding a two-year teaching buyout which enabled me to focus on this project, and to the University of Westminster, and then the London School of Economics, for giving me leave. I am also grateful to the late and much lamented Copenhagen Peace Research Institute (COPRI) for funding both my presence there, and a regular seminar at which many drafts related to this book received incisive criticism.

Abbreviations

ASEAN	Association of Southeast Asian Nations
BIS	Bank for International Settlements
BISA	British International Studies Association
CEO	Chief Executive Officer
CITES	Convention on International Trade in Endangered Species
COPRI	Copenhagen Peace Research Institute
CSD	Centre for the Study of Democracy
ECPR	European Consortium for Political Research
ESRC	Economic and Social Research Council
EU	European Union
FIDE	International Chess Federation
FIFA	International Federation of Football Associations
GATT	General Agreement on Tariffs and Trade
GCS	Global Civil Society
IAEA	International Atomic Energy Agency
IBRD	International Bank for Reconstruction and Development, aka World Bank
ICC	International Criminal Court
ICJ	International Court of Justice
IGO	Intergovernmental Organisation
IMF	International Monetary Fund
INGO	International Non-Governmental Organisation
IPCC	Intergovernmental Panel on Climate Change
IPE	International Political Economy
IPSA	International Political Science Association
IR	International Relations

ISA	International Studies Association
MFN	Most Favoured Nation

Montreal Protocol (1987) to the Vienna Convention for Protection of the Ozone Layer (1987)

NAFTA	North American Free Trade Association
NATO	North Atlantic Treaty Organisation
OECD	Organisation for Economic Cooperation and Development
OIC	Organisation of the Islamic Conference
PKO	peacekeeping operation
QUANGO	quasi-autonomous non-governmental organisation
TNA	transnational actor
TNC	transnational corporation
UN	United Nations
UNFCCC	United Nations Framework Convention on Climate Change (1992) and Kyoto Protocol (1997)
UNGA	United Nations General Assembly
UNHCR	United Nations High Commissioner for Refugees
US	United States
WHO	World Health Organisation
WSRG	World Society Research Group
WTO	World Trade Organisation

Glossary

Binding forces – coercion, calculation, belief

Interhuman society – social structures based on interactions amongst individual human beings, and in this book referred to as *first-order societies*, and mainly manifested as large-scale patterns of shared identity

International society has two meanings in this book:

(1) The classical English school usage: is about the institutionalisation of shared interest and identity amongst states, and puts the creation and maintenance of shared norms, rules and institutions at the centre of IR theory. I call this *interstate society*

(2) A more specific meaning developed along the way in this book to indicate situations in which the basic political and legal frame of international social structure is set by the states-system, with individuals and TNAs being given rights by states within the order defined by interstate society

Interstate society – see *international society* definition (1)

International system – refers generally to the macro side of the interactions that tie the human race together, and more specifically to the interactions among states. Its usage in classical English school thinking is close to that in realism, being about power politics amongst states within a political structure of international anarchy.

Montreal Protocol – (1987) to the Vienna Convention for Protection of the Ozone Layer (1987)

Pluralism – defines *second-order societies* of states with a relatively low degree of shared norms, rules and institutions amongst the states, where the focus of society is on creating a framework for orderly coexistence and competition, or possibly also the management of collective problems of common fate (e.g. arms control, environment)

Primary institutions – the institutions talked about by the English school as constitutive of both states and international society in that they define both the basic character and purpose of any such society. For *second-order societies* such institutions define the units that compose the society

Secondary institutions – the institutions talked about in regime theory are the products of certain types of international society (most obviously liberal, but possibly other types as well), and are for the most part consciously designed by states

Second-order societies – those in which the members are not individual human beings, but durable collectivities of humans possessed of identities and actor qualities that are more than the sum of their parts

Solidarism – can be used as a synonym for cosmopolitanism, but in my usage defines international societies with a relatively high degree of shared norms, rules and institutions among states, where the focus is not only on ordering coexistence and competition, but also on cooperation over a wider range of issues, whether in pursuit of joint gains (e.g. trade), or realisation of shared values (e.g. human rights)

State – any form of post-kinship, territorially based, politically centralised, self-governing entity capable of generating an inside–outside structure

The three domains – *interstate*, *interhuman* and *transnational society*

Transnational society – social structures composed of non-state collective actors

Vanguard – the idea common to both military strategy and Leninist thinking that a leading element plays a crucial role in how social movements unfold

World society – has two meanings in this book:

(1) the traditional English school usage takes individuals, non-state organisations and ultimately the global population as a whole as the focus of global societal identities and arrangements, and puts transcendence of the states-system at the centre of IR theory

(2) the usage developed in this book labelling situations in which no one of the three domains or types of unit is dominant over the other two, but all are in play together

Introduction

> The most fundamental question you can ask in international theory is,
> What is international society?   Wight (1987: 222)

After a long period of neglect, the social (or societal) dimension of the international system is being brought back into fashion within International Relations (IR) by the upsurge of interest in constructivism. For adherents of the English school, this dimension was never out of fashion, with the consequence that English school thinking itself has been somewhat on the margins of the discipline. In this book I will argue that English school theory has a lot to offer those interested in developing societal understandings of international systems, albeit itself being in need of substantial redevelopment.

International society is the flagship idea of the English school. It carves out a clearly bounded subject focused on the elements of society that states form among themselves. This domain has been quite extensively developed conceptually, and considerable work has also been done on the histories of international societies, particularly the creation of the modern international society in Europe and its expansion to the rest of the planet. *World society* also has a key place in English school theory, but is much less well worked out. While international society is focused on states, world society implies something that reaches well beyond the state towards more cosmopolitan images of how humankind is, or should be, organised. Quite what that 'something' that defines world society is, however, remains at best contested, and at worst simply unclear. Since world society can be (and is) easily cast as a challenger to international society, ambiguity about it is a major impediment to clear thinking about the social structure of international systems. A key cause of this problem is a widespread failure in English school thinking to

1

distinguish clearly enough between normative theory and theory about norms. It is a central focus of this book to address that problem. Fortunately, several other traditions of thought have grappled with world society, sometimes using that label, sometimes with variants such as 'global society' or 'global civil society'. Latterly, its popularity, or that of its synonyms, perhaps can be understood best as a way of getting to conceptual grips with the phenomenon of globalisation. These other bodies of thought provide useful insights applicable to English school theory.

Consequently, although this book is about English school theory generally, and will have a lot to say about international society, much of the argument in the early chapters will focus on trying to clarify world society. The concept of world society, and especially how world society and international society relate to each other, is in my view both the biggest weakness in existing English school theory, and the place where the biggest gains are to be found. John Vincent's (1988: 211) observation that the need to work out the relationship between cosmopolitan culture and international order was one of the unfinished legacies of Bull's work remains true today. English school theory has great potential to improve how globalisation is conceptualised, but cannot do so unless it finds a coherent position on world society. I plan to survey the basic ideas and approaches to world society, and to attempt a coherent theoretical construction of the concept. My starting position is that there is not much to be gained, and quite a lot to be lost analytically, from simply using world society as a label for the totality of human interaction in all forms and at all levels. Globalisation fills that role already. My initial strategy will be to construct world society as a concept to capture the non-state side of the international system, and therefore as the complement/opponent to the already well-developed idea of international society.

The book is aimed at two distinct but not mutually exclusive audiences. The narrower audience comprises those already working in the English school tradition plus followers of Wendt's mode of constructivism. For the English school people, it offers a comprehensive critique of English school theory and an ambitious, detailed attempt to address this critique by developing a more purely social structural interpretation of the theory to set alongside its existing normative and historical strands. For the Wendtians, the book offers a friendly critique, an extension of the logic and an application of the theory. I seek to create a synthesis between the structural elements of the Bull/Vincent side of English school theory about international and world society, and Wendt's (1999) social theory of international politics. I take from both sources a social structural reading of international society, and a methodologically pluralist rejection of the view that paradigms in IR are incommensurable. I insert into both two things that they ignore or marginalise: the international political economy, and the sub-global level. And I impose on both a more rigorous taxonomical scheme than either has attempted. The result is a radical reinterpretation of English school theory from the ground up, but one that remains supportive of, and in touch with, the basic aims of both English school and Wendtian theory – to understand and interpret the composition and the dynamics of the social structure of international politics.

The broader audience is all of those in IR who acknowledge that 'globalisation' represents an important way of labelling a set of substantial and significant changes in the international system, but who despair about the analytical vacuousness of 'the "G" word'. To them, I offer a Wendt-inspired social structural interpretation of English school theory as a good solution to the problems of how to think both analytically and normatively about globalisation. English school theory is ideally tailored to address this problematique, though it has not so far been much used in this way. The English school's triad of concepts exactly captures the simultaneous existence of state and non-state systems operating alongside and through each other, without finding this conceptually problematic. It keeps the old, while bringing in the new, and is thus well suited to looking at the transition from Westphalian to post-Westphalian international politics, whether this be at the level of globalisation, or in regional developments such as the EU. English school theory can handle the idea of a shift from balance of power and war to market and multilateralism as the dominant institutions of international society, and it provides an ideal framework for examining questions of intervention, whether on human rights or other grounds. Managing this expansion from interstate to world politics is important to IR as a discipline. IR's core strengths are in the states-system, and it needs to combine these with other elements of the international system, and to avoid ensnaring itself in the trap of unnecessary choices between state and non-state alternatives. In my view, English school theory shows how this can be done better than any available alternative.

This broader audience includes practically everyone engaged in the debates about IR theory. Some of them may baulk initially at the idea of wading through a sustained critique of what they may see as a somewhat marginal and traditional body of IR theory. Why, they may ask, should we bother with something so demonstrably flawed? They should take this book in three stages. First, it can be read as a relatively compact introduction to a stimulating and useful body of theory with which they may not be very familiar. Second, it is a sustained attempt to bring together the IR tradition of thinking about international society, and Wendtian constructivism, and to set both of these against more sociological thinking about society generally and world society in particular. Wendtian thinking is broadened out to include non-state actors, and English school theory is forced to confront neglected questions about the constitution of society in terms of what values are shared, how and why they are shared, and by whom. Third, it is about developing out of this conjuncture a theoretical framework that can be used to address globalisation as a complex social interplay among state and non-state actors mediated by a set of primary institutions. This interplay can be captured as a finite, though not simple, set of structural possibilities governed by a relatively small number of key variables. Using English school theory to address globalisation does not offer the predictive oversimplifications of neorealism and neoliberalism. But by opening the way to a wider historical interpretation, it does offer an escape from the Westphalian straitjacket. It gives powerful grounds for differentiation and comparison among types of international society, and ways of understanding both what Westphalian international society evolved from, and what it might be evolving into. In that mode, this book also speaks to those grappling with integration theory, and how to understand, and manage, developments in the EU.

The plan is as follows. Chapter 1 provides a quick overview of English school theory in order to set the context, and to note some of the problems that a more social structural interpretation might redress. Chapter 2 sets out a detailed exegesis of the world society concept in English school thinking, establishing the role it plays in the debates about pluralism and solidarism, the incoherence of its usage, and its importance to the whole structure of English school thinking. Chapter 3 surveys how others outside the English school have deployed the idea of world society, and looks for ideas there which can be applied to the English school framework. Chapter 4 engages four analytical tensions at the heart of English school theory (state versus non-state, physical versus social concepts of system, society versus community and individual versus transnational), and develops a revised framework for thinking about international and world society. Chapter 5 returns to the pluralist–solidarist debates, focusing on the neglected question of what counts as solidarism, and particularly the place of the economic sector. It reconstructs this debate as a way of thinking about the spectrum of interstate societies. Chapter 6 explores the concept of the institutions of international society in English school theory, relating them to usage in regime theory, and attempting a comprehensive mapping of them and how they relate to types of international society. Chapter 7 introduces geography, arguing that the traditional focus on the global level needs to be balanced by an equal focus on international social structures at the sub-global scale. Among other things, bringing in a geographic variable opens the way into understanding the dynamics and evolution of international societies through a type of vanguard theory. Chapter 8 uses the analytical lens developed in chapters 4–6 to sketch a portrait of contemporary international society, to look back at the institutional change of the last two centuries that brought us to where we are now, and to think about the forces driving it. The chapter concludes with a consideration of the likely directions of its development, and with proposals for the English school research agenda.

1 English school theory and its problems: an overview

> We need sharper analytical tools than those provided by Wight and
> Bull.
> Dunne (2001b: 66)

This chapter starts with a summary of English school theory as it is
conventionally understood. The second section looks at the different
strands, tensions and potentials within the school, and locates within
them the line to be taken in the rest of this book. The third section
reviews the main areas of weakness in English school theory that subsequent chapters will address and hopefully rectify. The fourth section tackles the question of whether English school theory is really
theory.

English school theory: a summary

The English school can be thought of as an established body of both
theoretical and empirical work dating back to the late 1950s (Dunne
1998; Wæver 1998; Buzan 2001). Robert Jackson (1992: 271) nicely sums
up the English school conversation by seeing it as:

> a variety of theoretical inquiries which conceive of international rela-
> tions as a world not merely of power or prudence or wealth or capa-
> bility or domination but also one of recognition, association, member-
> ship, equality, equity, legitimate interests, rights, reciprocity, customs
> and conventions, agreements and disagreements, disputes, offenses,
> injuries, damages, reparations, and the rest: the normative vocabulary
> of human conduct.

Two core elements define the distinctiveness of the English school: its
three key concepts, and its theoretically pluralist approach. The three
key concepts are: international system, international society and world

society (Little 1995: 15–16). Within the English school discourse, these are sometimes (and perhaps misleadingly) codified as *Hobbes* (or sometimes *Machiavelli*), *Grotius* and *Kant* (Cutler 1991). They line up with Wight's (1991) 'three traditions' of IR theory: *Realism*, *Rationalism* and *Revolutionism*. Broadly speaking, these terms are now understood as follows:

- *International system* (Hobbes/Machiavelli/realism) is about power politics amongst states, and puts the structure and process of international anarchy at the centre of IR theory. This position is broadly parallel to mainstream realism and neorealism and is thus well developed and clearly understood. It also appears elsewhere, as for example in Tilly's (1990: 162) definition that states form a system 'to the extent that they interact with each other regularly, and to the degree that their interaction affects the behaviour of each state'. It is based on an ontology of states, and is generally approached with a positivist epistemology, materialist and rationalist methodologies and structural theories.
- *International society* (Grotius/rationalism) is about the institutionalisation of shared interest and identity amongst states, and puts the creation and maintenance of shared norms, rules and institutions at the centre of IR theory. This position has some parallels to regime theory, but is much deeper, having constitutive rather than merely instrumental implications (Hurrell 1991: 12–16; Dunne 1995: 140–3). International society has been the main focus of English school thinking, and the concept is quite well developed and relatively clear. In parallel with international system, it is also based on an ontology of states, but is generally approached with a constructivist epistemology and historical methods.
- *World society* (Kant/revolutionism) takes individuals, non-state organisations and ultimately the global population as a whole as the focus of global societal identities and arrangements, and puts transcendence of the states-system at the centre of IR theory. Revolutionism is mostly about forms of universalist cosmopolitanism. It could include communism, but as Wæver (1992: 98) notes, these days it is usually taken to mean liberalism. This position has some parallels to transnationalism, but carries a much more foundational link to normative political theory. It clearly does not rest on an ontology of states, but given the transnational element neither does it rest entirely on one of individuals. Critical theory defines some, but not all of the approaches

7

to it, and in Wightian mode it is more about historically operating alternative images of the international system as a whole than it is about capturing the non-state aspects of the system.[1]

Jackson (2000: 169–78) puts an interesting twist on the three traditions by viewing them as defining the diverse values that statespeople have to juggle in the conduct of foreign policy. Realism he sees as giving priority to national responsibilities, rationalism he sees as giving priority to international responsibilities, and revolutionism (which he prefers to call cosmopolitanism) he sees as giving priority to humanitarian responsibilities. He adds a fourth, more recent value – stewardship of the planet – in effect, giving priority to responsibility for the environment.

The classical English school framework is summarised in figure 1 below. So far, the main thrust of the English school's work has been to uncover the nature and function of international societies, and to trace their history and development. The basic idea of international society is quite simple: just as human beings as individuals live in societies which they both shape and are shaped by, so also states live in an international society which they shape and are shaped by. This social element has to be put alongside realism's raw logic of anarchy if one is to get a meaningful picture of how systems of states operate. When units are sentient, how they perceive each other is a major determinant of how they interact. If the units share a common identity (a religion, a system of governance, a language), or even just a common set of rules or norms (about how to determine relative status, and how to conduct diplomacy), then these intersubjective understandings not only condition their behaviour, but also define the boundaries of a social system. Within the idea of international society, the principal debate has been that between pluralists and solidarists. This hinges on the question of the type and extent of norms, rules and institutions that an international society can form without departing from the foundational rules of sovereignty and non-intervention that define it as a system of states. Pluralists think that the sovereignty/non-intervention principles restrict international society to fairly minimal rules of coexistence. Solidarists think that international society can develop quite wide-ranging norms, rules and institutions, covering both coexistence issues and cooperation in pursuit of shared interests, including some scope for collective enforcement. As indicated on figure 1, pluralism and solidarism define the boundary zones, respectively, towards realism and revolutionism.

---

[1] I am grateful to Ole Wæver for this latter point.

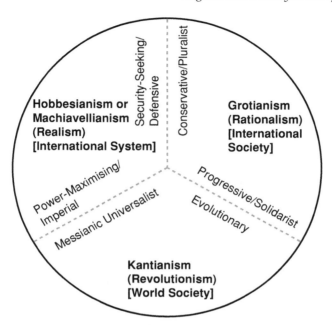

Figure 1. The classical 'Three Traditions' model of English school theory
Note: Titles in ( ) are Wight's labels; titles in [ ] are the analytical focus; titles along the border zones are where the traditions blend into each other

The main focus of English school work has centred on a synthesis of realism and rationalism. This focus is nicely captured by Bull and Watson's (1984: 1) classic definition of international society as:

> a group of states (or, more generally, a group of independent political communities) which not merely form a system, in the sense that the behaviour of each is a necessary factor in the calculations of the others, but also have established by dialogue and consent common rules and institutions for the conduct of their relations, and recognise their common interest in maintaining these arrangements.

This definition neatly demonstrates the combination of the Hobbesian/ realist element of international system, with the Grotian/rationalist element of a socially constructed order. It interleaves the logic of more material theories of the international system, driven by billiard ball metaphors, with the view that sentience makes a difference, and that social systems cannot be understood in the same way as physical ones.

9

But the pursuit of international society has obliged the English school to engage with the element of liberal revolutionism. Once the idea of society was conceded, one had to think not just of international society (amongst states), but also 'world society' (the idea of shared norms and values at the individual level, transcending the state). It is clear from figure 1 that world society is fundamental to the ability of English school theory to focus enquiry along these lines.

As captured in figure 1, the idea is that these three key concepts form a complete and interlinked picture of the IR universe. Although each element is conceptually and methodologically distinct, they blur into each other at the boundaries. In the English school perspective all three of these elements are in continuous coexistence and interplay, the question being how strong they are in relation to each other (Bull 1991: xvii–xviii; Dunne 1995: 134–7). The three key concepts thus generate the second distinctive feature of the English school, its theoretical pluralism. Little (1998, 2000) makes a strong case that the English school should be seen not just as a series of ontological statements about reality, but more as a pluralist methodological approach. By introducing international society as a third element, not only as a *via media* between realism and liberalism/cosmopolitanism, but also as the keystone to an interdependent set of concepts, English school theory transcends the binary opposition between them that for long plagued debates about IR theory. By assuming not only that all three elements always operate simultaneously, but also that each carries its own distinctive ontological and epistemological package, English school theory also transcends the assumption often made in the so-called inter-paradigm debate, that realist, liberal and marxist approaches to IR theory are incommensurable (McKinlay and Little 1986).

World society, and the problems and potentials of English school theory

As just noted, the foundation of English school theory is the idea that international system, international society and world society all exist simultaneously, both as objects of discussion and as aspects of international reality. This theoretically pluralist formulation takes the focus away from the oppositional either/or approaches of much IR theory (interparadigm debate, realism-idealism, rationalist-reflectivist, etc.) and moves it towards a holistic, synthesising approach that features the patterns of strength and interplay amongst the three pillars. But world society has been the Cinderella concept of English school theory, receiving relatively little attention and almost no conceptual development. To the extent that it gets discussed at all, it is in the context of other concerns, usually, but not always, human rights.

So long as day-to-day world politics was dominated by the international system and international society pillars, with world society only a residual element in the background, the English school could get away with treating world society as a Cinderella. But if, as many people think, the world society element is rising in significance, this neglect becomes untenable. There are at least three compelling reasons for giving priority to rectifying this weakness. First is that the English school needs to clarify the nature of its own claim to the idea in relation to the claims of others using the concept. Second is that English school theory itself cannot develop until the weak world society pillar is brought up to strength. Third, is that there is an opportunity to use English school theory to clarify the perennially unfocused, but politically central, debate about globalisation. This opportunity depends on the English school getting its own theoretical house in order. Even if the current assumptions about the rising importance of world society are wrong, the English school still needs to sort out the concept, partly in order to come to a judgement on the matter, and partly to move to completion in the development of its distinctive theoretical approach.

On this latter point, part of the case I want to make is that there is a pressing need for the English school to begin pulling away from its founding fathers. Manning, Wight, Bull, Vincent and others deserve much credit for originating an extremely interesting and already quite influential set of ideas. Krasner (1999: 46) acknowledges the English school as the 'best known sociological perspective' in IR. But as I hope to show, they also deserve criticism, both for not developing some of these ideas, and for steering them down a number of narrow channels that, while not dead ends, and still of interest and importance in themselves, have hamstrung the development of the theory. Among other things, I will show that some of the English school's founding fathers allowed their normative concerns with human rights to distort their theoretical reflections; were too much in thrall to universalist principles of order and justice derived from debates in political theory; and were too disinterested in international political economy. These shortcomings blinded them and most of their successors to much of the actual development in international and world society. The emphasis on universalism, and also on the high politics issues of human rights and (non-)intervention,

has strongly conditioned both the pessimism and the political pluralism that mark much of the school's 'classical' work, as has posing the
hard test of willingness to support the collective enforcement of international law as a measure of solidarism (Bull 1966a: 52). The potential of
English school theory as a basis for grand theory in IR (Buzan and Little
2001) will not be realised unless English school theory can be disentangled from its roots, and presented in a more systematically structured
way.

World society is the key to linking English school theory to the debate
about globalisation (Weller 2000: 47) and as well, to linking English
school theory to the debates about the European Union (Diez and
Whitman 2000). Scholte (2000: 8–9, 59–61) argues that globalisation is
defined by a deterritorialisation of social life which has created new actors and networks alongside the existing territorial ones: 'territoriality
and supraterritoriality coexist in complex interrelation'. The more sen-
sible globalisation writers all agree that there is no simple zero-sum
game between globalisation and the states-system. Both Woods (2000)
and Held *et al.* (1999) agree with Scholte's idea that the states-system
and the non-state system(s) coexist side by side, and argue that states,
especially the stronger states and powers, have played a major role in
bringing globalisation into being and steering its development. Some
even think that 'the word "globalisation" is really a contemporary eu-
phemism for American economic dominance' (Kapstein 1999: 468; see
also Woods 2000: 9). Either way, as argued above, English school theory is ideally tailored to address this problematique because of the way
in which it takes on board both the territorial and the non-territorial
elements.

By this point some readers will be shaking their heads in disapproval
on the grounds that I am misrepresenting the English school. They
have a point. It is possible to understand what English school theory
represents in at least three different (though potentially overlapping)
ways:

(1) as a set of ideas to be found in the minds of statesmen;
(2) as a set of ideas to be found in the minds of political theorists;
(3) as a set of externally imposed concepts that define the material and
    social structures of the international system.

Manning (1962) is the classical exponent of the first view. For Manning, the idea of international society was just that – an idea. What
was important for him was that this was not just any idea, or anyone's

idea. It was an idea incorporated in the official thinking of states about their mutual intercourse. It formed part of the assumption that was prevalent as orthodox among those who talked and acted in the names of states. For Manning, understanding world politics necessarily involved *Verstehen*, which meant, for him, that the analyst should understand the thoughts that underlie the actions of the states. Thus, for Manning, the idea of international society was not an analyst's idea, invented externally to the practice. Rather, the analyst reconstructs the idea of international society already contained in the practice.[2] The central subjects of study in this perspective are diplomats and diplomatic practice (see also Osiander 1994: 1–11).

The second view is most manifest in Wight's (1991) idea of the three traditions, but is also strongly present in the work of Bull (1966a, b, 1977a) and Vincent (1986), and many others who participate in the debates of the English school from the perspective of political theory (e.g. Rengger 1992, 1996, 1999; Brown 1998; Halliday 1992; Linklater 1998; Jackson 2000). Wight's three categories of international thought are extracted from writings by international lawyers, political philosophers, diplomats and statesmen. In this version, English school theory is a set of ideas which fill the minds of people as they think about and/or participate in world politics. The three traditions can be seen as a kind of 'great conversation' about international politics, setting out the primary positions that are always in some sense in play in discussions about foreign policy and international relations. The approaches and concerns of political theory are strong in this perspective. They inform not only the influential strand of normative theory in English school thinking, but also the disposition to think both in terms of universal principles, and in terms of a level of analysis distinction between individuals and the state. By 'universal principles' I mean here those principles whose validity requires that they be applied to all the members of a specified group. There is some tendency in this political theory understanding to treat English school theory as part of the history of ideas, and therefore as essentially a philosophical debate, as opposed to a discussion about the condition of the real world. The scope for normative positioning within this debate is large. At one end, much of English school writing about pluralist international society could be read from a progressive perspective as justifying the history of imperialism. At the other end, there is a strong and persistent progressive concern to improve the

---

[2] I am grateful to Hidemi Suganami for this formulation.

condition of world politics by getting practitioners to change their conceptual maps of world politics towards more enlightened forms. This normative approach to English school theory has been the dominant one, strongly influenced by the core questions of political theory ('What is the relationship between citizen and state?' 'How do we lead the good life?' and 'How is progress possible in international society?').

The third view sees international system, international society and world society as a set of analytical concepts designed to capture the material and social structures of the international system (Buzan and Little 2000). This is the one that I intend to develop in the chapters that follow. This view is strong in the work of Bull (1977), and even more so of James (1978, 1986, 1993), and is analogous to the structural approaches taken by non-English-school IR theorists such as Waltz (1979), who is only interested in material structures, and Wendt (1999) who sets up a social structural approach. This approach does not have any necessary normative content in the sense of promoting preferred values (though that is not excluded). Norms and ideas play their role here as different forms of social structure: not normative theory, but theory about norms. It is about finding sets of analytical constructs with which to describe and theorise about what goes on in the world, and in that sense it is a positivist approach, though not a materialist one. One illustration of its potential strengths is shown by Little's (2000: 404–8) discussion of how English school theory leads to a much different understanding of the balance of power than one finds in the purely mechanical idea of it in neorealism. As will become clear, I am less driven by taking sides on normative questions, or interpretations of political philosophy, and more concerned to put into place the building blocks for a methodologically pluralist grand theory of IR.

Delineating these different approaches to the English school raises the question of how the normative and structural strands within it, and the different goals they represent, interact. As a rule, they have been blended together, a practice most clearly visible in the works of Bull and Vincent, and one that has come at the cost of a lack of clarity and precision in the analytical framework. This is not to blame the normative theorists, for without them precious little analytical development would have taken place at all. But it is to assert the need to develop the social structural strand more in its own right, and less as an annex to human rights concerns. Whether the resulting conceptual scheme will make it easier or more difficult to pursue the traditional normative concerns of the English school remains to be seen, and the outcome either way is not a driving concern of this enterprise. My concern is to set up a social structural interpretation of English school theory by disentangling this approach from the Wightean one. In doing this, it is absolutely <u>not</u> my intention to question the validity of the normative approach. My aim is to set up the social structural interpretation alongside it as an alternative, parallel, reading of English school theory. Some people will prefer one approach, some the other, though I do hope that clarifying the social structural approach will challenge those in the Wightean track to reflect on the conceptual incoherence on which some of their ideas seem to rest. In addition, I hope to expose the dynamics and driving forces underlying international society more clearly, and to break out of the somewhat stultifying opposition between a self-paralysed set of pluralists, and a self-confined set of solidarists. Will this still be English school theory? Definitely, for it remains linked to the classic texts, the focus on international social structure and the methodological pluralism. But it will not be English school theory as we have known it so far.

One last point on the theme of social structure is to remind the reader that the term 'society' should <u>not</u> be read as in itself carrying any necessarily positive connotation. To say that society, in the sense of social structure, is more fully developed in one place or time than in another is not to say that this is therefore an improvement in some moral sense. As Luard (1976: 340) reminds us: 'a society may be closely knit yet marked by frequent conflict'. Many human societies have ritualised and institutionalised both intense violence (rituals of sacrifice, warrior cultures) and huge degrees of inequality (slavery; ethnic, religious, caste and gender discrimination). The English school has been admirably forthright about this, going so far as to classify war as an institution of Westphalian international society in Europe. Despite the warnings of history, it is nevertheless easy in a sustained abstract discussion of society to slip into the assumption that society is essentially good and nice, and that more of it is therefore better.

The main areas of weakness in English school theory

For all of its many attractions, English school theory is neither fully developed nor without problems, many of which hinge in one way or another around the weakly developed world society pillar. It would not be an exaggeration to say that English school theory is in serious need of a taxonomical overhaul. John Vincent (1988: 197; see also Richardson

1990: 178) said of Bull that 'his genius for making distinctions that went to the heart of a subject-matter constituted the essence of his contribution to international relations'. Bull's distinctions have indeed provided much of the analytical leverage that has made the English school an attractive and insightful approach. But in this book I want to argue that even Bull's distinctions are neither complete enough nor deeply enough developed to unleash the full potential of English school theory (see also Hurrell 2002b: xv–xxii). Bull was heading in the right direction, but he did not have time to do more than carve out the opening stages of the path. The areas of concern about the existing opus of English school theory can be organised under five headings: levels, sectors, boundaries, normative conflicts and methodology.

Levels

In much of both 'classical' and contemporary English school writing there is a strong assumption that the only relevant level is the system, or global one. This assumption applies to all three key concepts (international system, international society, world society). The general rule is that states are considered mainly as components of international systems and/or as members of international society, and that both international system and society are assumed to be global phenomena. Europe occupies a special place in this scheme because of its role as the original creator of what subsequently became the contemporary global international system and society. Since the modern international system is a closed one on a planetary scale, assumptions of universalism become assumptions of global scale, and vice versa. To the extent that this system-level assumption is breached, it is in the acknowledged historical process of the international system and international society becoming global during the few hundred years preceding the nineteenth century. Discussion of modern international society is almost wholly rooted in the assumption of a single, global phenomenon. Individuals, and therefore world society, are also treated as a collective whole – in effect, humankind.

There seem to be several reasons for this strong bias towards the system/global level. In relation to states, perhaps the main one is the dominance of a baseline story about the emergence of a distinctive European international system and society, its transformation into a global international system and society, and the ups and downs of that global international society since then. Whatever the past might have been, the assumption is that for the last two centuries, and for the foreseeable future, international system and society are global phenomena, and to be studied as such. Added to this is a strong normative disposition against subglobal developments of international society, seeing these as divisive, necessarily corrosive of global international society, and prone to generate conflict (Bull 1977a: 279–81; Vincent 1986: 101, 105). The system/global approach to individuals/humankind has a different source. Concern with individuals in English school literature largely focuses on the tension between human rights on the one hand, and the state, and the international society that legitimises the state and gives it primacy, on the other. In that context, the approach is predominantly normative, drawing on the debates from political theory. In those debates, the source of system/global assumptions is the idea, whether drawn from natural law or pragmatic reasoning, that the principles underpinning human rights must be universal (Vincent 1978: 30; Cutler 1991: 46–9). As Vincent (1986: 117) argues: 'What is right is something we seek one answer to, not several.' This line of thinking dominates his arguments despite his warning elsewhere (1986: 125) against the dangers of accepting 'any purportedly universalist doctrine'. Because the international system and international and world society are global, the referent group for universal principles must necessarily be humankind as a whole.

Although Vincent does not spell it out, one of those dangers is that both the possibility and the fact of regional level developments of international society get ignored. The main exception to this position is Wight, who took the view (1991: 49) that all known international societies have been subsystemic and therefore faced the problem of outsiders ('barbarians' in his language). But Wight can be dismissed on the grounds that he was mainly interested in looking back into history, before there was even a global international system, let alone society. Watson (1992) is also talking mostly about the self-contained sub-global systems of the past rather than about regional subsystems within a global system. Occasional hints can be found elsewhere that seem to admit at least the logical possibility of regional level developments in international society. Bull (1977a: 41), for example, when talking of the three elements of Hobbesian, Kantian and Grotian traditions, notes that 'one of these three elements may predominate over the others' in three different contexts: 'in different historical phases of the states system, <u>in different geographical theatres of its operation</u> [my emphasis], and in the policies of different states and statesmen'. But this opening is not followed up, and indeed actively discouraged for the reasons given above. To the extent that he thought about the European Community at all, Bull (1982) was mainly interested in getting it to play a great power role at the global level.

It seems to me that this rejection of regional level developments sets a standard for international society so demanding that by itself this factor can explain the pessimism and pluralism that dominate most classical English school writing. On the global level it is hardly surprising that international society strikes a fairly minimal lowest common denominator. It is much more likely that one might find solidarist developments within a civilisational community (such as in EU-Europe over Bosnia and Kosovo) than worldwide. The assumption that such developments must be at odds with the development of global international society needs to be questioned. Certainly they can be, as during the Cold War when the great powers were ideologically divided over the nature of international society. But it is neither necessary, nor even probable, that they must be. When the leading edge of international society is amongst a large majority of the leading powers, a case can be made – with realists from Carr (ideas as a form of power) to Waltz (socialisation and competition) in support – that this might well be the key to progress in development at the global level. This view is not out of line with the English school's own account of the expansion of international society (Bull and Watson 1984a). More on this in chapter 7.

I will argue that there is a lot of room for differentiating between global international/world society on the one hand, and subglobal, and particularly regional, international/world societies on the other. Neither 'international' nor 'world' in this usage necessarily implies global (just as Wallerstein's 'world-systems' and 'world empires' do not have to be global). The empirical record suggests that different regional international societies can build on common global international society foundations, as they have done in Europe, the Islamic world and Southeast Asia (and earlier amongst the communist states). Given the apparent regionalising tendencies in the post-Cold War international system (Buzan and Wæver 2003), the scope for sub-global developments, and their implications for global ones, needs to be investigated urgently. So too does the possibility for non-Western forms of international society, or fusions between Western and non-Western forms. Among other things, understanding the sub-global dimension of international society offers big insights into the problem of (non-)intervention.

Sectors

There are some similarities between the English school's problem with levels and its problem in sectors: both involve a missing element that plays a crucial role in 'really existing' international and world society. Whereas under levels, the missing element is sub-global or regional, under sectors it is the economy. Unlike with regions, there seems to be no reason in principle why the economic sector should not feature in discussion of international and world society, and this rather glaring omission is often pointed out (Miller 1990: 70–4; Richardson 1990: 148, 184; Hurrell 2002b: xvii). At various points along the way, English school writers have acknowledged the economic sector. Wight (1991: 7–8) talks of the rationalist position in terms of diplomacy and commerce. Bull (in Wight, 1977: 16) notes trade as one of the four institutions in Wight's understanding of a states-system, and mentions it in his theoretical discussion of rules about cooperation in society (1977: 70). He makes clear that the economy is a major part of contemporary international society (Bull 1990: 72–3) and his discussion of justice (Bull 1984c) rested heavily on the need for a more equitable international political economy. Although Bull (1991: xix–xx) is critical of Wight's disinterest in economics, he nevertheless failed to develop this aspect in his own discussions of international society. This is all the more surprising given that he made a feature of the economic sector in his critique of those who wanted to take a Hobbesian interpretation of international anarchy. Bull (1966b: 42) argued that 'trade, symbolic as it is of the existence of overlapping through [*sic*, though?] different interests, is the activity most characteristic of international relationships as a whole'.

Vincent, although critical of Bull for ignoring the economy as a major component of international order (Vincent 1988: 196, 204) also fails to develop the topic even though he does put it on the agenda in a major way. His book on human rights (Vincent, 1986) develops a case for making the right to subsistence the floor of a global human rights programme. He is fully aware that this implies 'a radical reshaping of the international economic order' and that such a project 'might require a radical shift in patterns of political power in order that resources can reach the submerged 40% in developing countries'. That he understood the political side of the international economy is clear from his statement that: 'in regard to the failure to provide subsistence rights, it is not this or that government whose legitimacy is in question, but the whole international system in which we are all implicated' (Vincent 1986: 127,

145). But as Gonzalez-Pelaez (2002) points out, this opening into international political economy (IPE) was not followed up either by Vincent or by his followers, who have focused instead on the more directly violent abuses of citizens by their states, such as torture and genocide. The one exception to this rule was James Mayall (1982, 1984, 1989) who did begin to think about economic liberalism in international society terms, and at one point (Mayall 1982) even argued for the existence of a sense of community in the economic sphere despite differences between North and South. Given that he was positioned at the LSE alongside Susan Strange, he was well placed to bridge between the English school and IPE. But he seemed to lose faith in his earlier interpretation (Mayall 1984). His more recent works (1990, 2000) have focused largely on nationalism, and see economic nationalism returning on the back of national security concerns in such a way as to undermine economic solidarism. This sidelining of the economic sector in representations of international society is surprising given both the enormous development of norms, rules and institutions (including ones with some powers of collective enforcement) in this sector, and the growth of IPE as a major branch of the study of international relations.

The English school's focus on the state might be one explanation. It is clear that the English school formulation explicitly privileges the states-system and international society on historical and pragmatic grounds as being the dominant form in the political sector. This produces an emphasis on the 'high politics' of collective security, diplomacy and human rights, which kept most classical English school writers quite close to realism. But the state focus is also apparent in IPE, so state-centrism is not an adequate explanation. Perhaps the main explanation is simple disinterest and lack of knowledge about the economy amongst the founding fathers. If so, there is no excuse for the perpetuation of this tradition. Indeed, there is an urgent need to reject it. Their disinterest in the economic sector may have been reinforced by the ignoring of the regional level, and certainly aggravated the drift towards a pessimistic and pluralist outlook in classical English school writing.

Boundaries

As sketched out in figure 1, the theoretical scheme of the English school generates three primary boundaries separating (or more loosely, delineating the frontier zones between) its three key concepts. Two of these do not seem problematic inasmuch as the concepts on either side of them line up clearly: defensive realism and pluralism make a good fit, as do power-maximising imperialism and messianic universalism. By contrast, the boundary between the solidarist side of international society and the evolutionary side of world society is both unclear and controversial. It is not at all obvious where solidarist international society ends, and world society begins. This problem relates to that flagged above about the weak development of the world society concept. As I will show in chapter 2, world society has functioned as a kind of intellectual dustbin into which all sorts of things have been thrown. The world society pillar contains Kantian conceptions of a homogenised system of states, transnational ideas about non-state actors, cosmopolitan ideas about identity at the level of individuals/humankind, and ideas about ideological crusaders wanting to impose their universal 'truth' on all of humanity. At a minimum, it has to be questioned how these things relate to each other within the world society pillar, and the possibility has to be investigated that they cannot, in fact, all be accommodated within a single concept.

Normative conflicts

There are two linked normative conflicts within the English school. One is between advocates of pluralist and solidarist conceptions of international society, and the other is between states' rights, or international society, and individual rights or world society. The essence of the matter is whether individual rights/world society necessarily conflict with states' rights/international society, or can be in harmony with them, an issue with some close connections to the debates in political theory between cosmopolitans and communitarians. In practice, these largely add up to a single dispute. Because of the boundary ambiguities between international and world society described above, it is not clear whether pluralism and solidarism apply only to international society, or whether solidarism somehow spills over into world society. Many of the key sources of solidarist thinking, such as natural law, humanism and cosmopolitanism are deeply rooted in world society. This ambiguity means that it is not immediately clear whether this sometimes quite heated dispute is real, or simply a product of unclear classifications and definitions. Is international society just a system for preserving the distinctiveness and independence of states within a limited framework of shared rules, or does it develop, as the practice of regimes and regional cooperations seem to suggest, into increasing degrees of harmonisation and integration? At what point does solidarism become so progressive that it calls into question the existence of a states-system, or is it the case that the understanding and practice of sovereignty evolve along with solidarism, continuously solving the contradiction as it arises?

Methodology

There are two problems here: first, the lack of any sustained attempt to construct a typology of international or world societies; and second, a lack of clarity in setting out exactly what is entailed in the theoretical pluralism underpinning English school theory.

Wight (1977: 21–9) made an early start on the classification of types of international society with his differentiation between states-systems based on mutual recognition among sovereign entities, and suzerain systems based on more hierarchical relations. He added to this the idea of secondary states-systems composed of relations among suzerain systems. Watson (1990: 102–6; 1992: 13–18) followed this up with his more elaborate idea of a spectrum of international societies ranging from anarchy, through hegemony, suzerainty and dominion, to empire. Both Wight and Watson were mainly looking backwards, aiming at classifications for comparative history. Except in the rather inconclusive work of Luard (1976), which was not part of the English school mainstream, this start has not been followed up by those more interested in contemporary and future international societies. One consequence of this neglect is that the Wight and Watson schemes overplay the coercive, and underplay the consensual, side of international society. There is not much room in Watson's spectrum for something like the EU unless one takes the implausible (but in some quarters politically popular) view that it is a species of German empire. The reasons that the English school has not developed a typology of international societies are not difficult to see. Because the school's mainstream writers locked themselves into concern with the single, global, modern international society; chose not to look at the regional level; and failed to consider economic developments; they did not have much reason to be interested in differentiating types.

Nevertheless, from a theory-building perspective, Wight's opening suggests that several obvious questions can and should be asked about international and world societies. What is their scale in relation to the overall system in which they sit? How loosely or tightly are they bound together? Is the nature of what binds them more rational, contractual and constructed (society, *Gesellschaft*), or more emotional, identity-based and historical (community, *Gemeinschaft*), or some combination of these two? Are the organising principles based on the idea of political equality amongst the units (Westphalian), or political inequality amongst the units (suzerain), or functional differentiation among the units (medieval or neomedieval)? These basic questions suggest not only a means for comparing instances of international society across history, but also for monitoring the development and evolution of the layered global and regional international society in which we currently live. If the key concepts of English school theory are to be understood as types of social structure, then a robust typology is a necessary condition for being able to monitor structural change.

The second methodological problem concerns the incoherence of ontological and epistemological differentiation within the theoretical pluralism of the English school framework. That there is significant ontological and epistemological differentiation amongst international system, international society and world society is not in doubt (Little 1998, 2000). But just what that differentiation is, is rather less clear. Much hangs on which reading of English school theory one wants to pursue. In Wightian (1991: 15–24) mode, the focus is on the three Rs, with realists proceeding on the basis of inductively arrived at laws of human behaviour, rationalists proceeding from ontological and teleological views about the nature of social reality, and revolutionists proceeding from ethical and prescriptive imperatives.

If one comes at this with a more structural approach, international system and international society are pretty solidly based on an ontology of states. World society, at least in its cosmopolitan aspect, is based on an ontology of individuals, but given the confusion about what world society contains one has also to think about non-state entities, and in some versions also states. The epistemological and methodological picture is even less clear. Little (1998: 74–5) sees international system as based on structural methodology and international society as based on agency-based methodology. But, as well as leaving out world society, this does not quite add up. International systems can certainly be studied using structural theory, but so can international and world societies, as Little himself shows in later work (Buzan and Little 2000; see also Wendt 1999), where constructivist elements are seen as structural. More promising is Little's idea (2000: 402), following from Linklater, that each of the English school's three key concepts is associated with a different methodological approach: international system with positivism, international society with hermeneutics and interpretivism, and world society with critical theory. The linkage of international system and positivism seems fairly uncontroversial. Less clear is why the interaction aspects of international and world society cannot also be studied using positivist methods. Similarly, international society can indeed be studied using hermeneutic and interpretivist methods, but it is not clear why these cannot also be applied to world society. Critical theory certainly captures the revolutionist aspect of world society, but it is less clear that it covers the cosmopolitan and Kantian aspects. Some of this confusion, perhaps a lot of it, reflects the incoherence of the world society pillar of English school theory.

One other problem, not of English school theory, but of this book, is of keeping consistency in the use of terms. The very nature of the taxonomical overhaul which is central to this book makes such consistency almost impossible. Readers are therefore warned to keep aware as they proceed. In the early chapters, my usage of terms such as international and world society reflects the usage in the existing literature. From chapter 4 onwards, I embark on a systematic critique and reworking of most of the basic concepts, bringing in some new usages, and attaching more specific meanings to old ones. Once this is done, my usage of terms will reflect the new meanings, though it will sometimes be necessary, such as in quotes from or references to the classical literature, to use terms in their older sense. I have tried to make my usage as consistent as possible, but I cannot avoid some risk of confusion in the presentation.

Is English school theory really theory?

One final issue is the standing of English school thinking as theory. I have already begun to refer to 'English school theory', and will do so throughout the book, but the question of what counts as theory is controversial, so the basis of my assertion needs to be explained. In the Social Sciences, the answer to the question of whether or not something qualifies as theory often depends on where it is asked. Many Europeans use the term theory for anything that organises a field systematically, structures questions and establishes a coherent and rigorous set of interrelated concepts and categories. Many Americans, however, often demand that a theory strictly <u>explains</u> and that it contains – or is able to generate – testable hypotheses of a causal nature. English school theory clearly qualifies on the first (European) account, but not on the second. In its Wightian, normative theory form, English school theory cannot (and does not want to) meet the criteria for positivist theory. But if the English school is presented not as normative theory but as theory about norms, there is some potential to close the trans-Atlantic gap. In the more social structural approach unfolded in this book English school thinking has as much of a claim to theory as Wendt's (1999) attempt to pose constructivism as a social theory of international politics. In this form, it provides social structural benchmarks for the evaluation of significant change in international orders (Holsti 2002); sets out a taxonomy that enables comparisons to be made across time and space; and provides some predictions and explanations of outcome, such as Watson's (1990, 1992) macro-level theory about the inherent instabilities of anarchy and empire.

The English school also has two other claims to theoretical standing. The first, and most obvious, is its importance as a self-conscious location for the practice of a methodologically pluralist approach to the study of international relations, and therefore as a potential site for grand theory. The assumption of incommensurability has been one of the main factors generating fragmentation in IR theory. Among other things, it made the idea of grand theory seem illegitimate or impossible. But incommensurability may have been more a temporary fashion in IR than an absolute epistemological judgement. For a time it suited the discipline to think this way, both to end pointless polemics amongst realists, liberals and radicals, and to establish the right to exist of paradigms other than realism. Now, however, incommensurability seems to be mainly a position of extremists, whether ideological or epistemological, who insist either that their own story is the only valid one, or that their way of telling a story is the only valid one. Some positivists and some postmodernists still take this position (or are accused by the other side of doing so), but doing so seems to be a preference rather than a logical necessity. As suggested by the 'neo-neo' synthesis, the fashion is swinging back to more tolerance of, or even enthusiasm for, theoretical pluralism, though debate will doubtless remain active as to whether a pluralist approach requires giving all the stories equal weight, or making some more equal than others. Wendt (1999: 90, 155) is clearly trying to construct a *via media* between positivist epistemology and post-positivist ontology. A more sophisticated set of paths around the incommensurability problem is sketched out by Wæver (1996: esp. 169–74). Having never surrendered to incommensurability, the English school is well placed to capitalise on this turn of intellectual fashion.

The second claim is equally interesting, but much less explored. It concerns an implicit, but seemingly unselfconscious, move into the novel domain of second-order societies. With this move, English school thinking has transcended the conventional boundaries of both sociology and political theory in one important way. Its main concept of international society has moved the idea of society out of the state, and away from individual human beings as members. International society is not based on the crude idea of a 'domestic analogy' (Suganami 1989) which simply scales the society within states up to the global level. Instead it argues for a new second-order form of society, where the members are not individual human beings, but durable collectivities of humans possessed of identities and actor qualities that are more than the sum of their parts. This move opens up an aspect of sociology that has not been much, if at all, explored by sociologists, but that should be the natural meeting point between Sociology and Political Theory on the one hand, and International Relations on the other. In what ways do such second-order societies and communities differ from the societies and communities composed of individuals, and how appropriate (or not) is theory derived from first-order societies to the study of second-order ones?

If English school thinking counts as theory in these senses it is nevertheless, for the reasons given above, imperfect theory. The next task is to address the weak pillar of world society, and to see how to repair it.

2 World society in English school theory

As Little (2000: 411) notes, world society is 'the most problematic feature' of the English school framework. Yet that world society is crucial to English school theory cannot be in doubt. If English school theory is to work as a vehicle for a methodologically pluralist approach to IR, then each of its three pillars must have the same clarity and the same standing as the others. Yet what world society means in relation to solidarism is far from clear, with a consequent blurring of the boundary between international and world society. In figure 1, the conjunction of international system and realism/Hobbes is wholly conventional, and that of international society and rationalism/Grotius poses no obvious difficulties (notwithstanding that there are substantial debates going on about how to interpret Hobbes, Machiavelli and Grotius). But the conjunction of world society, revolutionism and Kant rings several alarm bells. Revolutionism seems particularly out of line with most of what is currently discussed under the heading of world society, and it is not clear that Kant fits comfortably with either image. Transnationalism, cosmopolitanism and crusading universalist ideologies are implausibly crammed together in the world society segment. To make matters worse, the world society segment lacks a 'world system' counterpart: international system and international society compose a clear set, differentiating physical systems of interaction from socially constructed ones. World society is clearly aimed at socially constructed non-state systems, but what is its physical counterpart? Little (2000: 412–13) thinks that, for Bull, transnationalism related to world society as international system does to international society, but this was never worked out, and on the face of it does not look very plausible (more on this in chapter 4). Bull (1977a: 276–81) offers the idea of a *world political system* to play the physical counterpoint to world society, seeing this as the totality of state plus non-state interactions. Bull never worked up much enthusiasm for this idea, seeing the states-system as so dominant within it as to make the additional complication hardly worthwhile. Vincent and his followers did pick up some of this idea, but bundled it into an expanded concept of world society (or latterly, in the case of Dunne 2001b: 38, an expanded 'master concept' of international society). It is hard to escape the conclusion that the concept of world society has served as a residual category for many in the English school. Similar to the way in which the unit level served as a dumping ground for neorealist theory (Keohane and Nye 1987: 746), English school writers have used world society as a place to deposit all the things they did not want to talk about.

A further problem is the existence of a disagreement about the relationship between world society and international society. The more historical side of the school represented by Butterfield, Wight and Watson, think of world society (in the form of shared culture) as a prerequisite for international society. As Wight (1977: 33) puts it: 'We must assume that a states-system [i.e. an international society] will not come into being without a degree of cultural unity among its members.' Likewise, Bull (1977a: 16) accepts that a common feature of the main historical cases of international societies 'is that they were all founded upon a common culture or civilisation'.[1] Much of the historical record from classical Greece to early modern Europe supports this view, suggesting that a common culture is a necessary condition for an international society. As in the expansion of European international society, states from other cultures may then join this core (Bull and Watson 1984a; Gong 1984; Zhang 1998) raising questions about how the norms, rules and institutions of international society interact with the domestic life of polities rooted in different civilisations, and whether international norms are sustainable under these circumstances.

Those more concerned with the maintenance and development of international societies, rather than their origins, come from a different angle (though the two concerns meet on the ground where established international societies expand into areas with a different culture, as has happened in modern times). This second position is quite complicated, not least because most English school thinking about world society has taken place around the hotly contested subject of human rights. Perhaps the central issue is the possibility of an ontological tension between the

---

[1] According to Adam Watson (interview) this understanding of common culture as the starting point for international society derived from Heeren, and was influential in the thinking of the British Committee.

development of world society (particularly human rights) and the main-tenance of international society. On one side, the argument is that the development of individual rights in international law will undermine state sovereignty. The expansion of individual rights threatens exter-nal, or juridical, sovereignty both by facilitating grounds for outside intervention in the domestic life of the state, and by weakening the state's authority to act internationally. It threatens internal, or empiri-cal, sovereignty by restricting the rights of the state against its citizens. In other words, regardless of whether a measure of common culture is required as a foundation for international society, any serious attempt to develop a world society (by advancing a universalist human rights law for example), will tend to undermine the states that are the foun-dation of international society. Linklater (1981: 23–37; 1998), celebrates the potential of this assault on the Westphalian order, but Bull (1977a: 151–3; 1984: 11–18) is fearful of destructive dynamics between the two levels of society. On the other side, the solidarist argument seeks to link the right of recognition of sovereignty to some minimum observance by the state of the rights of its citizens.

Wæver (1992: 104–7) argues that the oppositional view of the rela-tionship between international society and world society has become rooted in English school thinking, and serves to cut off the possibility of positive interaction between them. This oppositional view departs from the Wightian historical perspective, and tends to construct plu-ralist, Westphalian-type international society as the defence against the dangers of both hard realism (power politics) and liberal utopianism (universal harmony of interest). Wæver agrees with Jones (1981) that this closure prevents the English school from moving into the inter-esting ground on which international society is 'an intermediary vari-able between the deeper liberal forces and international politics, i.e. the growth of moral awareness, of technological interdependence, of inter-national learning translated into a gradual maturing of international society which has in turn effects on the working of anarchy' (Wæver 1992: 107).

How did this confused view of world society develop, and what can be done about it? To begin answering this question, it helps to look at the intellectual history of world society within English school think-ing. Doing so makes clear that quite radical shifts of understanding of the basic elements of English school theory have taken place since the ideas were first stated in British Committee work. There are notewor-thy differences of understanding even among the founding fathers, and while there is certainly awareness of some of the key splits, no systematic attempt has been made either to track these or to sort them out. English school theory needs to decide whether international society and world society are mutually exclusive ideas (state sovereignty versus cosmopolitanism), mutually dependent ideas (the need for an element of solidarism to underpin international society; the need for a framework of political order to stabilise more liberal visions), or some mixture of the two. Or is world society simply a manifestation of hegemonic dominance (currently, Americanisation or Westernisation), and therefore simply an epiphenomenon of power structure?

The next section will trace the development of the world society concept in English school thinking from Manning and Wight through Bull to Vincent in terms of direct discussion about it in the classical literature. The second section will take an indirect approach, using the pluralist–solidarist debate to explore the boundary between international and world society. Readers not wishing to engage with a detailed exegesis of the English school classics can simply read the summaries at the end of the next two sections.

The intellectual history of world society within English school thinking

In the classical discussions of world society, many of the ideas came out of political theory and international law, and were strongly driven by normative agendas. None of the founding fathers of the English school, with the possible exception of Vincent, was particularly interested in world society as such. All of them were primarily concerned to develop the idea of international society. World society thus only got thought about on the margins: as an alternative to international society, or in the context of debates about solidarist versus pluralist international societies.

In thinking about all this it helps to keep in mind how the founders of the English school were trying to position themselves between liberalism and realism in the debates about IR. On one side was the liberal tradition summed up in Richard Cobden's famous aphorism that there should be 'as little intercourse as possible betwixt the Governments, as much connection as possible between the nations of the world'. This remark both established an analytical distinction between the world of states and the world of civil society, and staked out a clear position against international society and in favour of world society. On the other side was the cynicism of E. H. Carr (1946: 80–1) who saw international society as a deception practised by the powerful to legitimate their position and possession. On world society Carr was equally damning (1946: 162): 'There is a world community for the reason (and no other) that people talk, and within certain limits behave, as if there were a world community.' Carr saw this as a dangerous illusion given that this community is at best shallow and insubstantial, and not capable of supporting claims of morality because: '(i) the principle of equality between members of the community is not applied, and is indeed not easily applicable, in the world community, and (ii) the principle that the good of the whole takes precedence over the good of the part, which is a postulate of any fully integrated community, is not generally accepted'. The English school's founding thinkers had also to position themselves in relation to the great clashes between universalist ideologies that marked the twentieth century, and that were locked into the confrontation of the Cold War all around them.

Manning, though not a member of the British Committee, influenced the early thinking of Wight and Bull. His position on world society set the template that was to shape the ideas of Bull and Vincent, and through them more recent English school writers. Manning (1962: 177) wrote that 'Within, beneath, alongside, behind and transcending, the notional society of states, there exists, and for some purposes fairly effectively, the nascent society of all mankind.' This view is in pretty direct opposition to Carr's. It acknowledges some of the Cobdenite view, though not setting it in opposition to international society. But it does not say much about what the actual form and content of this 'nascent society of all mankind' might be. Neither does its rather convoluted spatial metaphor make clear whether Manning thought of international and world society as in any sense analytically separable.

This approach of talking about international and world society as somehow distinct, but not making any systematic attempt to specify them, was continued by Wight. Perhaps the most widely cited of Wight's remarks about world society is his proposition (Wight 1977: 33) that: 'We must assume that a states-system will not come into being without a degree of cultural unity among its members.' This remark was made in the context of a discussion about the origins of historical states-systems in classical Greece and post-Roman Europe. Although it does not mention world society, it clearly sets up the proposition that 'cultural unity' is something distinct from international society (and in the context of Wight's analysis, prior to it). It infers the idea that world society is defined by common culture shared perhaps at the level of individuals, and certainly at the level of elites, and that the development of international society requires the existence of world society in these terms as a precondition. As noted above, this position has become the counterpoint to that of Bull and others who worried that world society development would undermine the sovereignty foundation of international society. One of the differences between Wight's view and that of other English school writers is that he accepted that all known international societies have been subsystemic (Wight 1991: 49), whereas their focus was on global international societies (more on this in chapter 7).

But a closer look at Wight's writings on world society does not suggest that he had a clear or coherent view of it, and certainly not one that rested on this historical foundation (Keene 2002: 34). As James (1993: 277–8) observes, Wight uses 'common culture' so loosely that it is unclear whether he has in mind a deep, historic sense of culture, or the more superficial agreed rules that compose a contractual society. Wight's (1991: 30) definition of international society suggests a conflation of the state and individual levels: 'International society is, prima facie, a political and social fact attested to by the diplomatic system, diplomatic society, the acceptance of international law and writings of international lawyers, and also, by a certain instinct of sociability, one whose effects are widely diffused among almost all individuals.' Elsewhere, his idea of international society seems more clearly state-centred, as when he presents it as a second-order social contract amongst the several primary social contracts represented by states (Wight 1991: 137), or says that: 'The most essential evidence for the existence of an international society is the existence of international law' (Wight 1979: 107), or identifies the institutions of international society as diplomacy, balance of power, arbitration and war (Wight 1991: 141). These statements suggest a separation between the levels of states and individuals, along with an almost complete ignoring of non-state entities.

Another way to try to get at Wight's understanding of world society is through its position in his 'three traditions' approach to the study of IR. In the early versions of this approach, Wight (1987 [1960]: 221, 226) seems to hang between seeing the three traditions as 'component social elements' of reality, and seeing them as 'patterns of thought' about international reality. On the one hand, he sees a sovereignty/anarchy social structure, patterns of habitual intercourse (diplomacy, law, commerce) and patterns of moral solidarity. On the other, he sees modes of thought linked to Hobbes, Locke and teleological 'historicists' such as Kant, Toynbee, Hegel, Marx and Spengler, and finds 'all these three ways of thought within me' (Wight 1987: 227). In the end, Wight's approach through traditions puts the focus very much on the sources of ideas in political theory, and much less on the empirical realities of the international system. Bull (Wight 1991: xi) nicely characterises Wight's position on the three traditions as: realism is about 'the blood and iron and immorality men', rationalism is about 'the law and order and keep your word men', and revolutionism is about 'the subversion and liberation and missionary men'. Wight's view of realism is fairly conventional. For him 'Realists are those who emphasize and concentrate upon the element of international anarchy' (Wight 1991: 7), and who take a pessimistic view of human nature (1991: 25–9). Realist thinking allows civilisations the right to expand according to their power, to deny rights to barbarians, to exploit them and even to treat them as non-human (Wight 1991: 50–66). Realists see no international society because there is no social contract, only a state of nature, or a system; at best there are limited and temporary management agreements amongst the great powers. Only states are the subjects of international law (Wight 1991: 30–7).

Rationalism in Wight's view (1991: 268) adds 'a civilising factor' to the realist vision. 'Rationalists are those who emphasize and concentrate upon the element of international intercourse' (Wight 1991: 7) – by international intercourse here Wight means diplomacy, law and commerce. Rationalists have a mixed view of human nature, with reason as the key to dealing with the contradictions, and they see both states and individuals as subjects of international law (Wight 1991: 25–9, 36–7). They understand the state of nature as a 'quasi-social condition' created either by natural law or by limited forms of social contract: 'It might be argued cogently that at any given moment the greater part of the totality of international relationships reposes on custom rather than force' (Wight 1991: 39). For rationalists, civilisations have paternalistic, trusteeship-type obligations to barbarians, and an obligation to civilise them, and barbarians should be accorded rights appropriate to a ward or an inferior culture (Wight 1991: 66–82). Wight also notes (1991: 134) that rationalism 'makes a presumption in favour of the existing international society' and is therefore conservative. This view of rationalism does not immediately strike one as very representative of what has become the mainstream English school view on international society, but it is not substantially at odds with it either. Passages such as: 'in the last analysis, international society is a society of the whole human race'

(Wight 1991: 36) again suggest that Wight had not crystallised out the distinction between international and world society.

Wight's view of revolutionism is both interesting and very confusing. From the outset, initially classifying them as historicists, Wight's (1987 [1960]: 223–6) focus is on those who want to change the world, have an idea of how it should be, and (usually) have some mechanism in mind (commerce, enlightenment, revolution, war) that will bring their visions to reality. There is occasional incoherence, such as his worrying assertion that 'Revolutionists are those who emphasise and concentrate upon the element of the society of states, or international society' (Wight 1991: 7–8). This seems almost incomprehensible; the definition is a perfect fit with later interpretations of the Grotian, or rationalist position. But the rest of Wight's discussion does not go down this line. Instead, it unfolds a largely negative view of 'the subversion and liberation and missionary men'. Wight (1991: 268) acknowledged that revolutionism added 'a vitalizing factor' to international relations, but his main concern was to inveigh against those who wanted to impose ideological uniformity on the international system. For Wight, revolutionists were 'cosmopolitan rather than "internationalist"' . . . 'for them, the whole of international society transcends its parts' (Wight 1991: 8), meaning that they assigned a transcendent value to some social vision of humankind other than the existing states-system. They focused on the 'ought' side of politics, desiring an 'international revolution which will renovate and unify the society of states' (Wight 1991: 22; 1987: 223–6). Revolutionists have an optimistic, but fearful, view of human nature: what is 'right' is potentially achievable, but always threatened (Wight 1991: 25–9).

The key point for Wight was that revolutionists wanted to overcome and replace the states-system. They could do so in one of three ways (Wight 1991: 40–8): (1) by the creation of ideological homogeneity; (2) by a successful doctrinal imperialism leading to a world empire; or (3) via a cosmopolitan route 'producing a world society of individuals which overrides nations or states'. Linklater (2002: 323) characterises Wight's scheme as dividing revolutionism into three forms: 'civitas maxima' or world society of individuals; 'doctrinal uniformity' which is the Kantian vision of republican homogeneity and peace; and 'doctrinal imperialism' or 'Stalinism' which is the attempt by one power to impose its ideology onto the system. Who the agents are supposed to be in these transformations is left unspecified; they could be either or both of state or non-state actors. This view lines up badly with what is now thought of as world society. The cosmopolitan scenario is the closest to current understandings of world society, but sits in unreconciled tension with Wight's argument that shared cultures have to underpin international societies. Ideological homogeneity seems to depict a solidarist version of international society, and the Stalinist model seems to belong to the imperialist side of realism. What unites these is that all stand as alternative visions to the Westphalian society of states, and that all move towards the creation of the global equivalent of domestic politics, the question being whether the form is a stateless society, a (con)federation of some sort or an empire.

Wight's rendition of revolutionism is thus not an attempt to define world society as a non-state parallel to international society in any structural sense. His concern is much more with the ways in which systems of states as such might be overthrown, transcended or replaced. In that sense, Wight's revolutionism is about ideological rejection of the states-system. It consists of images of the future that can provide the basis for political action in the present aimed at solving the problem of the states-system (whether that 'problem' is seen as the propensity towards war of the states-system, or its dividing up of the unity of humankind, or its blocking of the 'right' universal truth).

So although Wight is the key mover in setting up the three traditions approach, his actual discussions fail to make any clear distinction between international and world society. In his thinking, perhaps reflecting its roots in political and legal theory, the world is composed of states and individuals, and his definitions often blend these two levels together, paying little attention to transnational actors. As noted in chapter 1, Wight's approach was more about identifying the core elements of a great conversation about world politics than it was about developing concepts aimed at capturing the social structures of the international system.

As becomes immediately apparent to anyone reading *The Anarchical Society*, Bull had much more inclination towards tidy classifications and structural modes of thinking than did Wight. Perhaps Bull's main accomplishment was to single out and clarify the concept of international society. In doing so he shaped much subsequent writing, and the nature of his contribution is comparable to Waltz's in singling out and clarifying international system structure, though Bull was always careful not to assert the necessary dominance of international society.

Bull's work provides a much crisper conceptualisation of international society than Wight's. It therefore helps to delimit world society, if only by exclusion, particularly by offering a clear sense of international society as being state-based, and world society as being to do with transnational actors (TNAs) and individuals. In his thinking about international and world society Bull seemed to link them to two different ontologies in relation to his central concern with political order. International society he based on an ontology of states, providing order top down in an 'anarchical society'. World society he based on an ontology of individuals, working towards order from the bottom up. This kind of thinking, like Wight's, drew heavily on political theory and international law, particularly in its use of a duality between state and individual. This dualism creates problems for conceptualising world society by leaving no obvious place for TNAs (more on this in chapter 4).

One of the central problems for Bull was the persistent, and not easily resolved, tension between the pragmatic and normative aspects of order. His interest in international society was largely pragmatic. As he saw it, the state-based approach provided both the only immediately available pathway to a degree of achievable international order, and also a valuable *via media* between the extremes of realism and liberalism. Bull shared Wight's view that the states-system represented a second-order social construct, underneath which lay a 'wider', 'more fundamental and primordial' world order that is a 'morally prior' phenomenon to international order (Bull 1977a: 22). In Bull's view, individuals are the ultimate, irreducible unit of analysis, and world order is the basic goal for which international order is only instrumental. He argues that the law and morality of states 'have only a subordinate or derivative value' compared to 'the rights and interests of the individual persons of whom humanity is made up' (Bull 1984: 13). The problem is, echoing Carr, that world society doesn't exist in any substantive form, and therefore its moral priority is unattached to any practical capability to deliver much world order: 'The world society of individual human beings entitled to human rights as we understand them exists only as an ideal, not as a reality' (Bull 1984: 13). Much of this argument stems from simple common sense: why do states exist if not, in the end, to serve the needs of their citizens? – an idea that later became a key element in the thinking of Vincent and his followers. The tension is between, on the one hand, the many imperfections of states but their actual ability to deliver some measure of world order, and on the other, the possibility of better, more just, systems of order that nobody yet knows how to bring into existence.

This dualism runs in parallel to the tension in Bull between natural law (the idea that law is inherent in nature, and specifically human nature, and like knowledge of the physical world, can be discovered by reason), out of which the primacy of the individual came, and positive law (that which is made by political process within and between states), which was very much a product of the states-system. Bull leaned strongly in favour of positive law as the foundation and expression of international society but could not abandon the moral primacy of individuals that came out of natural law. Wheeler and Dunne (1998: 47–50) point out that Bull's reason for rejecting the natural law position on world society (other than as a fundamental normative referent) was that such a society didn't exist in fact. Thus the states-system was *de facto* what one had to work with in pursuit of world order goals. As Wheeler and Dunne argue, the flaw in Bull's scheme is that it doesn't confront the potential (and actual) contradiction between states as the agents for world order, and individuals as the moral referent. How much can states misbehave towards individuals before forfeiting their moral and legal claims to sovereignty and non-intervention within international society?

Unlike Wight, Bull did make an attempt to deliver a clear conceptualisation of world society:

> By a world society we understand not merely a degree of interaction linking all parts of the human community to one another, but a sense of common interest and common values on the basis of which common rules and institutions may be built. The concept of world society, in this sense, stands to the totality of global social interaction as our concept of international society stands to the concept of the international system.
>
> (Bull 1977a: 279)

There are several things to note about this definition. First, it is consciously parallel to his definition of international society (Bull and Watson 1984a: 1) in which the physical interaction is taken as given, and on top of which states 'have established by dialogue and consent common rules and institutions for the conduct of their relations, and recognise their common interest in maintaining these arrangements'.

Second, it is clearly and explicitly linked to the distinction between the physical and social that underpins his distinction between international system (Hobbes) and international society (Grotius). Although confusingly put in the passage just cited, Bull does in fact (as noted above) draw a distinction between world society and the 'world political system' with the latter representing physical interaction. Indeed, Bull (1977a: 248–54) makes central to his whole analysis a general distinction between the physical aspect of systems (interaction amongst units more or less in the absence of social structure) and the social and normative elements which constitute the social order ('degree of acceptance of common rules and institutions'). One can see here Bull's step away from Wight's understanding of realism as a cast of mind, or an understanding of the human condition, towards a more structural view of it as the social (or rather asocial) condition of a system. Yet even though he explicitly draws a parallel in these terms between world society and international society (both representing the social dimension), Bull fails to give much guidance about what the physical counterpart to world society actually is. All he says is 'a degree of interaction linking all parts of the human community to one another' in which get included both layers of government above and below the state, and TNAs. His 'world political system' includes firms, states and intergovernmental organisations (IGOs), a bundling together which blurs any distinction between international and world system, and feels close to what Americans once labelled a world politics paradigm, and now goes more under 'globalisation'. And Bull (1977a: 270–3, 276–81) is anyway keen to downplay the idea of adding TNAs to the international system, seeing them as being nothing new, not necessarily generative of a world society, and not yet threatening the historical primacy of the states-system and international society. It remains unclear why the physical dimension gets no separate standing as 'world system', paralleling international system's pairing with international society. The logic of Bull's distinction between the physical and the social points towards a four-part scheme, with a separate quadrant for 'world system' rather than the traditional English school scheme of three pillars shown in figure 1. Is it that a world system without a world society is inconceivable in a way that a states-system without an international society is not? Bull does not develop this line, but I will return to it in chapter 4.

Third, it remains unclear from his definition exactly how Bull understands the connection between his conception of world society and Wight's Kantian tradition. Sometimes Bull depicts Kantianism in fairly neutral terms as being about 'the element of transnational solidarity and conflict, cutting across the divisions among states' (Bull 1977a: 41), leaving ambiguous whether this is about people or TNAs. But sometimes a more Wightian revolutionist view shows through, when Kantianism is said to be about 'the transnational social bonds that link . . . individual human beings', and revolutionists look forward to 'the overthrow of the system of states and its replacement by a cosmopolitan international society' (1977a: 25–6). Bull thus makes a considerable advance on Wight's development of world society, but he also leaves a lot undone, and still carries Wight's normative disposition against 'the subversion and liberation and missionary men'. Indeed, Suganami (2002: 10) offers the thought that Bull and most others in the rationalist tradition felt themselves to be distant from revolutionism, and that this explains why they did not devote much thought to the world society dimension of English school theory.

Also noteworthy is that Bull develops in his definitions a strictly globalist view of both international and world society. He dismisses regional and other transnational developments as not necessarily contributing to, and possibly obstructing, global developments (Bull 1977a: 279–81). With this move, Bull takes a quite different path from Wight. Bull was concerned mainly with the evolution of the global international society that developed out of European imperialism, and his gaze was thus fixed forward. Wight's view was more historical, making the idea of international and world societies as subsystemic phenomena unavoidable. The assumption of global scale became a strong element in the English school's thinking about international and world society. As will become apparent in the discussion of Vincent, the global scale assumption was also supported by some universal normative imperatives to do with human rights. The global scale assumption is, I will argue, one of the major wrong turnings in the development of English school theory. One of the curiosities here is that both the moral primacy of individuals and the assumption of universalism come out of the natural law tradition that Bull rejected, yet remained strong in his conception of international and world society.

The work of Watson does not touch much on the world society question. Watson was more concerned to apply Bull's ideas about international system and international society to the study of world history. In that sense, he was furthering Wight's project to develop the field of comparative international societies. Watson's significance here is that he explicitly sides with Wight's view that all known international societies originated 'inside a dominant culture' (1990: 100–1). Watson is keen to add the possibility that regulated, cross-cultural, *Gesellschaft* international societies might expand from such *Gemeinschaft* cores. By picking up this key idea of Wight's, Watson not only kept alive, but greatly strengthened, the idea that shared culture, in effect civilisation, was a key element in world society.

To the extent that any of the founding fathers of English school theory took a particular interest in world society, it was Vincent. His abiding concern with human rights focused his work precisely on the tensions between the individual and the state level, and therefore placed him in the boundary zone between international and world society. Like Wight and Bull, he drew heavily on political theory and international law. With his focus on human rights, Vincent was trying to advance beyond Bull's rather pluralist understanding of international society towards the more solidarist conception with which Bull seemed to be struggling in his later work.

In order to see why Vincent talks about both international and world society in the way he does, it helps to understand what he was and was not trying to do. Vincent was not trying to set out a new clarification or specification of English school concepts. His work is essentially a discussion of human rights, where these are seen as (a) challengers to pluralist international society (and therefore a moral and political problem *per se*), and (b) as representing the cosmopolitanism intrinsic to world society. World society gets discussed in this context, and Vincent does not make it an object of enquiry in its own right. For Vincent (1978: 40) it is the standing of individuals in Western thought that gives them the right to make claims against the state (international society), and, in the twentieth century, this way of thinking is embodied in the human rights discourse.

Vincent is searching for a way out of the pluralist frame set by Bull, particularly in seeking a way around Bull's concern that the cultivation of human rights law would almost inevitably be subversive of the key principles of international society (sovereignty and non-intervention) and therefore subversive of world order. His angle of attack hangs on the degree to which the rights of states derive from their being manifestations of the right of self-determination of peoples (Vincent 1986: 113–18). This right, in his view, requires that states have some minimum degree of civil relationship with their citizens. If a state is 'utterly delinquent in this regard (by laying waste its own citizens, or by bringing on secessionist movements)' (Vincent 1986: 115), and 'by its conduct outrages the conscience of mankind' (1986: 125), then its entitlement to the protection of the principle of non-intervention should be suspended. He qualifies such suspensions by saying that the circumstances triggering a right of humanitarian intervention must be extraordinary ones, not routine (Vincent 1986: 126), though it is unclear why, on moral grounds, routine large-scale violence by the state against its citizens, such as that in Stalin's USSR, or in Burma under the military junta, should be less of an offence against either the principle of a state's duty to its citizens, or the conscience of humankind, than one-off cases. In this

way, Vincent offers a possible solution to the tension between a pluralist international society (focused on sovereignty and non-intervention),
and the cosmopolitan or even revolutionist, world society implicit in a
doctrine of universal human rights. His idea is the development of a
more solidarist international society, in which states become more alike
internally, and therefore more likely to find common ground in agreeing
about when the right of humanitarian intervention overrides the principle of non-intervention (Vincent 1986: 150–2). In this context, Vincent
notes that 'the spread of a global culture makes international society
work more smoothly' (1986: 151), and takes hope in the historical record
by which the state has made deals with civil society 'coopting the ideology of individualism by translating human rights into citizens rights'.
With this line of thinking, Vincent begins to blend together a state-based,
solidarist international society, with an underlying world society of
common culture.

Within the framework of this discussion, Vincent offers various remarks about world society and international society. These go in several
directions, making different readings of his position possible (Gonzalez-
Pelaez 2002). Whereas Wight was more focused on revolutionists seeking to overthrow international society, Vincent leans towards defining
world society in terms of those who oppose international society because they are excluded from it. He offers one definition of world society
as: 'the individual and certain actors and institutions in world politics
whose concerns have been regarded conventionally as falling outside
the domain of "diplomacy and international relations"' (Vincent 1978:
20). He is keen to make the point that non-state actors are excluded by
a state-based international society from having their justice claims considered. 'I use the term "world society" to describe the framework of
morality that encompasses groups of this kind whose claims, not being
accommodated by the society of states, are voiced in a tone which is hostile to it' (Vincent 1978: 28). World society in this sense could also be a
society of ideologically similar states out of step with mainstream international society (he mentions republican states during the monarchical
age, and dictatorships of the proletariat amidst a liberal democratic majority). He suggests that these excluded entities can include individuals
claiming human rights, tribes and cultural groups, multinational corporations, and exploited classes and shows how each of these has some audience for the legitimacy of its claims to rights against the state (Vincent
1978: 29). Vincent's theme of world society as oppositional to international society can also be found in Reus-Smit (1997: 566–8) and Barkin

(1998: 235). Elsewhere, Vincent hints at both more cosmopolitan and more 'Stalinist' views. Echoing Bull and James, he sees 'world society in the sense of some great society of mankind' (Vincent 1978: 28–9), or more specifically, as some kind of merging of states, transnational actors and individuals where all have rights in relation to each other (Vincent 1978: 37; 1992: 253–61). Elsewhere he links world society specifically to TNAs (Vincent 1992: 262). Sometimes, echoing Wight, he sees 'a world society properly so-called might be one in which all human beings owed allegiance to one sovereign, or one in which a universal cultural pattern prevailed such that no part of the society could mount a defence against it' (Vincent 1978: 28–9).

If one had to extract a dominant thread from all of this, it would probably be that Vincent's view of international and world society was more historical and moral than analytical. Vincent was much less concerned with abstracting a theory of international relations out of English school concepts than he was with identifying, and trying to promote, an evolution in human political affairs. He did not so much see international society and world society as separate analytical constructs, but rather understood them as two historical forces needing to grope towards a reconciliation of their contradictions. Vincent's problematique, narrowly taken, is the disjuncture represented by human rights problems between the 'establishment' of a pluralist international society of states on the one hand, and repressed individuals and groups on the other. Taken more broadly, it is about the general exclusion from international society of a periphery composed of individuals, groups, some TNAs and possibly some types of state. His looked-for solution is to merge the two. At times, the form of this merger seems to lean towards a solidarist international society of liberal states. In his view, a fully solidarist international society would be virtually a world society because all units would be alike in their domestic laws and values on humanitarian intervention (Vincent 1986: 104). But his dominant image merges international society into world society, possibly growing out of Bull's idea of a 'world political system' as mixing state and non-state actors. The difference is that Vincent elevates this mixture from system to society. Thus: 'international society might admit institutions other than states as bearers of rights and duties in it, recognizing to that extent their equality and welcoming them into what would then have become a world society' (Vincent 1978: 37). Vincent's preferred future is one in which a Westphalian-type international society, defining itself as an exclusive club of states, gives way to a world society that is no longer defined by opposition to international society. Instead, the new world society is defined by an inclusive, somewhat neomedieval, mixture of states, groups, transnational entities and individuals, all sharing some key values, and having legal standing in relation to each other (Vincent 1986: 92–104). Since many international non-governmental organisations (INGOs) have already achieved limited official standing within many IGOs (Clark 1995), it might be argued that Vincent's vision has moved some way towards practical realisation.

The normative and predictive force of this vision of merger may be considerable, but from a theory-building point of view the consequences are huge, and not necessarily good. Going down Vincent's route requires merging two of the pillars of English school theory into one, thereby losing all of the analytical purchase gained by keeping the ontologies of state and individuals distinct. Those English school thinkers with primarily normative concerns do not seem to care much about this cost. Vincent's approach is still alive and well in the mind of Dunne (2001a: 7): 'Bull is arguably mistaken in interpreting international society as a "society *of states*" since many of the rules and institutions of international society predated the emergence of the modern state. It is time that the English School jettisoned the ontological primacy it attaches to the state (Almeida 2000). International society existed before sovereign states and it will outlive sovereign states.' He goes further (2001b: 37–8) to argue that world society should be folded back into international society. On the other hand, Hill (1996: 122) keeps the ontologies separate by distinguishing between *international* and *world* public opinion along the lines of states versus non-state actors (leading individuals, firms, NGOs, religions and media). Buzan and Little (2000) also operate by keeping the state and individual ontologies distinct. There is a rift opening up here between those primarily concerned with normative argument, and those interested in analytical leverage.

Thus from a theory-building perspective, Vincent is more interesting for what he has to say about human rights than for what he contributes to the development of English school theory. He does not really advance the conceptualisations of international and world society beyond the positions developed by Wight and Bull, and in some ways his conceptual landscape is less clear than Bull's. Whether intentionally or not, his focus on human rights blocked off any other considerations of what might constitute either solidarist international society or cosmopolitan world society – most obviously shared economic norms rules and institutions. Vincent's human rights focus also reinforced Bull's mistake of looking only at global developments. Because, for Vincent (1986: 117), the principle of human rights had to be universal, so also was his vision of world society. The strong linkage between universal principles and global scale is nowhere more obvious than in Vincent's thinking. Consequently, Vincent (1986: 101, 105) shared Bull's (1977a: 279–81) rejection of regional-level developments, like Bull seeing them as threats to potential global ones.

One can sum up key points from this intellectual history of world society in classical English school thinking as follows.

- The concept of world society generally has a marginal position in the literature. It is mostly discussed in the context of other things and not systematically developed in itself. It remains distinctly secondary to the development of international society, and is somewhat blighted by its association with revolutionism, which many rationalists found distasteful.
- Despite its marginality, world society occupies a central position in English school thinking. It is crucial to the persistent moral sense animating the search for order that the society of states was only a second-order phenomenon, underneath which lay the morally prior, but as yet unrealised, society of all humankind. The later Bull, and much more so Vincent, saw it as the ideal to strive for.
- There nevertheless remains a strong division of political positions on world society, with Wight and Bull more or less defending the necessity of international society to the provision of world order, and Vincent seeking ways to reduce the bad human rights consequences of the sovereignty/non-intervention principles of international society.
- World society remains something of an analytical dustbin, uncomfortably containing revolutionism, cosmopolitanism and transnationalism. There is a fairly strong agreement that international society and world society, at least for the present, rest on an ontological distinction between the state level on the one hand, and a rather complicated matrix of individuals and non-state groups and TNAs, on the other. Vincent (and Dunne) wants to break down this distinction, but Vincent, like Bull and Wight, starts by accepting its reality. A second thread also exists in which world society is partly seen in terms of shared culture (*Gemeinschaft*), and partly in terms of more rational, bargained social structures (*Gesellschaft*). How, or if, these two elements of world society fit together is not really addressed. Wight (1966: 92)

perhaps provided the lead for this neglect with his view that since 'Sociologists have not agreed on a satisfactory distinction in usage between the words "society" and "community"' he would use them interchangeably. Failure to address this distinction led to the curious situation of having one view of world society as a precondition for international society, another view of it as the enemy and a third one as the prospective partner in marriage.

• There has been no follow-up to Wight's idea that commerce was part of the rationalist agenda.

• There is a strong presumption that international and world society have to be thought about in global terms, and that regionalist or subsystemic developments of them must subtract from the whole by creating competing centres.

More recent works in the English school tradition have not really moved things forward. Except as a normative goal, world society remains at the margins and has not been developed conceptually. Wæver (1992: 104) offers the definition that world society is 'the cultural homogeneity and interlinkage of societies', but it is not clear what this contributes, and it could also serve as a definition of liberal solidarism in an international society. Dunne, Wheeler and others whose principal concern is the human rights issue (e.g. Knudsen), have more or less stuck with Vincent's position of wanting to merge international and world society on normative grounds.

Whether one wants to keep the ontologies of states and individuals separate, or merge them, the question of what constitutes world society still has to be answered. As I have shown above, it does not get a very clear answer in such direct discussions of it as exist. But another way of approaching the question in the English school literature is through discussion of the boundary between international and world society: where does international society stop and world society begin? This discussion occurs within the debate about pluralism and solidarism.

The pluralist–solidarist debate

The pluralist–solidarist debate is about the nature and potentiality of international society, and particularly about the actual and potential extent of shared norms, rules and institutions within systems of states. Within the English school, this debate hinges mainly on questions of international law as the foundation of international society, and especially on whether the international law in question should be (or include) natural law (as it was for Grotius), or positive law. The main issue at stake in this debate has been human rights, and the closely related questions of humanitarian intervention and the responsibility of the West towards the third world (Bull 1966a; 1984; Vincent 1986; Dunne and Wheeler 1996; Linklater 1998; Wheeler and Dunne 1998; Knudsen 1999; Wheeler 2000; Mayall 2000; Jackson 2000). Without this focus there would have been much less theoretical development than has in fact taken place. The new generation of solidarists in particular deserve credit for picking up the pluralist–solidarist distinction staked out by Bull and carrying it forward. Nevertheless, the somewhat relentless focus on human rights by both pluralists and solidarists has kept the whole theory discussion in a much narrower frame than the general logic of the topic would allow. The debate has sometimes been unhelpfully emotive (Jackson 2000), with pluralism and solidarism cast against each other in almost zero-sum terms. This section aims both to sketch the English school debate as it has unfolded, and to start looking at the pluralism–solidarism question in a wider perspective by divorcing the terms of the debate from the human rights issue (a process that will be completed in chapter 5).

The basic positions can be summarised as follows. Pluralist conceptions lean towards the realist side of rationalism (see figure 1). They are strongly state-centric, and empirical, and consequently assume that international law is positive law (i.e. only made by states). They presuppose that states are *de facto* the dominant unit of human society, and that state sovereignty means practical legal and political primacy. More discreetly, pluralism, like realism, is about the preservation and/or cultivation of the political and cultural difference and distinctness that are the legacy of human history. All of this makes the scope for international society pretty minimal, restricted to shared concerns about the degree of international order under anarchy necessary for coexistence, and thus largely confined to agreements about mutual recognition of sovereignty, rules for diplomacy and promotion of the non-intervention principle (Jackson 2000; Mayall 2000). As Mayall (2000: 14) puts it, pluralism is:

> the view that states, like individuals, can and do have differing interests and values, and consequently that international society is limited to the creation of a framework that will allow them to coexist in relative harmony . . . For pluralists, one of the features that distinguishes international society from any other form of social organisation is its procedural and hence non-developmental character.

The assumption of major differences among the states and peoples in a system is supported by thinking of international society on a global scale. If international society must cover the whole system, then the historical evidence is overwhelming that states are culturally and ideologically unlike. Since this debate arose during the Cold War, the evidence for the depth of cultural and ideological differences among states was all too palpable (Bull 1977a: 257–60). Pluralism stresses the instrumental side of international society as a functional counterweight to the threat of excessive disorder, whether that disorder comes from the absence of states (a Hobbesian anarchy), or from excesses of conflict between states, whether driven by simple concerns about survival, or by rival universalist ideological visions.

By contrast, solidarist conceptions lean towards the Kantian side of rationalism. As Mayall (2000: 14) notes, solidarists root their thinking in cosmopolitan values: 'the view that humanity is one, and that the task of diplomacy is to translate this latent or immanent solidarity of interests and values into reality'. It is probably fair to say that many solidarists believe that some cosmopolitanism, and concern for the rights of individuals, is <u>necessary</u> for international society. As Linklater (1998: 24) puts it: 'An elementary universalism underpins the society of states and contributes to the survival of international order.' On this, if on not much else, the pluralists and solidarists agree, Jackson (2000: 175) taking the view that world society is the domain 'in which responsibility is defined by one's membership in the human race'. Solidarists presuppose that the potential scope for international society is much wider than the 'non-developmental character' that limits the pluralist vision, possibly embracing shared norms, rules and institutions about functional cooperation over such things as limitations on the use of force, and acceptable 'standards of civilisation' with regard to the relationship between states and citizens (i.e. human rights). In this view, sovereignty can in principle embrace many more degrees of political convergence than are conceivable under pluralism (as it does, for example, within the EU). Solidarism focuses on the possiblity of shared moral norms underpinning a more expansive, and almost inevitably more interventionist, understanding of international order. The solidarist position is driven both normatively (what states should do, and what norms should be part of international society) and empirically (what states do do, and what norms are becoming part of international society).

Because the pluralist position is entirely state-based, it is relatively straightforward and coherent. The solidarist position is more problematic. Because it ties together state and non-state actors, and draws on cosmopolitan notions of individual rights and a community of humankind, it cannot help but blur the boundary between international and world society. There is also room for confusion about whether solidarism requires specific types of ethical commitment, such as human rights, or whether it is simply about the degree and depth of shared normative agreement in general. Consequently, although the pluralist–solidarist debate is mostly constructed as one about how states should and do behave within international society, world society questions are constantly dancing around its edges. Two questions about the structure of this debate arise:

(1) Are pluralism and solidarism positions on a spectrum between which movement is possible, or mutually exclusive opposites about which a choice has to be made?

(2) Is solidarism something that can be discussed within the confines of international society, or does it necessarily spill over into the domain of world society?

On question 1, it has been a matter of debate as to whether pluralism and solidarism are separated by fundamental differences, or whether they simply represent different degrees of a fundamentally similar condition. As far as I can see, the view that pluralism and solidarism are mutually exclusive rests on an argument over whether primacy of right is to be allocated to individuals or to states. If one takes the reductionist view that individual human beings are the prime referent for rights, and that they must be subjects of international law, carrying rights of their own, then this necessarily falls into conflict with the view that the claim of states to sovereignty (the right to self-government) trumps all other claims to rights. Either individual human beings possess rights of their own (subjects of international law), or they can only claim and exercise rights through the state (objects of international law). If pluralism is essentially underpinned by realist views of state primacy, and solidarism is essentially a cosmopolitan position, then they do look mutually exclusive. This rift can be reinforced by different views of sovereignty. If sovereignty is given an essentialist interpretation, seeing it mostly in what Jackson (1990) calls 'empirical' terms (in which sovereignty derives from the power of states to assert the claim to exclusive right to self-government), then states cannot surrender very much to shared norms, rules and institutions without endangering the very quality that defines them as states. The existential threat to sovereignty in this sense is especially acute in relation to questions about human rights, which is one reason why this issue has featured so much in English school debates. Human rights, as Wheeler (1992: 486) observes, opens up fundamental issues about the relationship between states and their citizens, and 'poses the conflict between order and justice in its starkest form for the society of states'. There have been advantages in pursuing the 'starkest form' hard case, but one cost has been to force the pluralist–solidarist debate into an excessive polarisation in which non-intervention and human rights become mutually exclusive positions.

The alternative case is that the two concepts comprise the ends of a spectrum, and represent degrees of difference rather than contradictory positions. This view rests on a more 'juridical' view of sovereignty, in which the right to self-government derives from international society. Seen in this perspective, sovereignty is more of a social contract than an essentialist condition, and the terms in which it is understood are always open to negotiation. A softer view of sovereignty along these lines poses no real contradiction to solidarist developments, though these may well be cast in terms of individuals as the objects of international law rather than as independent subjects carrying their own rights. In this case, pluralism simply defines international societies with a relatively low, or narrow, degree of shared norms, rules and institutions amongst the states, where the focus of international society is on creating a framework for orderly coexistence and competition, or possibly also the management of collective problems of common fate (e.g. arms control, environment). Solidarism defines international societies with a relatively high, or wide, degree of shared norms, rules and institutions among states, where the focus is not only on ordering coexistence and competition, but also on cooperation over a wider range of issues, whether in pursuit of joint gains (e.g. trade), or realisation of shared values (e.g. human rights). At the pluralist end of the spectrum, where international society is thin, collective enforcement of rules will be difficult and rare. Towards the solidarist end, where international society is thicker, a degree of collective enforcement in some areas might well become generally accepted, as has happened already for aspects of trade, and somewhat less clearly in relation to arms control. In this view, so long as one does not insist that individuals have rights apart from, and above, the state, there is no contradiction between development of human rights and sovereignty. If they wish, states can agree among themselves on extensive guarantees for human rights, and doing so is an exercise of their sovereignty, not a questioning of it. This was Vincent's position, and along with other solidarists he saw cosmopolitan forces and TNAs as crucial in pushing states towards understanding themselves and their commitments in that way.

This difference of view matters because if pluralism and solidarism are mutually exclusive, then they simply reproduce within the rationalist, international society, *via media* a version of the polarisation between realism and liberalism that splits IR theory more generally. Placing this polarisation within the linking framework of international society and world society concepts lowers the ideological heat of the debate, and opens the possibility of conducting it in a shared institutional and evolutionary context. But it fails to escape the essential tension, which would weaken the potential of the English school to offer its methodological pluralism as a foundation for grand theory. If they are not mutually exclusive, but more ends of a spectrum, then they reinforce the position of international society as the *via media* between state-centric realism and cosmopolitan world society.

This line of thinking leads automatically to question 2, and the nature of the boundary between international and world society. There are two issues here. What is the difference between a solidarist international society on the one hand, and a Kantian world society of homogenous states on the other? And do increasing degrees of solidarism necessarily bring transnational units and individuals into the picture, as in the thinking of the Vincentians, so marrying international and world society? On the first issue, Bull clearly wants to draw a line. He rejects the idea that an ideologically homogenous states-system equates with solidarism (Bull 1977a: 245). He does so partly on the weak ground that it is unlikely to happen, and the process of arriving at it would be highly conflictual (because of inability to agree on universal values), and partly on the basis of a distinction between genuinely harmonious Kantian world societies (an idea he rejects as utopian) and international societies that have learned to regulate conflict and competition, but have not eliminated it. In effect, Bull tries to eliminate the idea of a Kantian model of ideologically harmonious states altogether. Like Carr (1946), he rejects the possibility of ideological homogeneity leading to harmony. And because he maintains a strong global-scale assumption about international and world society, he can plausibly argue against the probability of ideological harmony ever occurring. Because he rejects the Kantian model, Bull is able to avoid the boundary question by keeping solidarism firmly within the cast of international society. Yet if international society is defined in terms of a society of states, and world society as the non-state sector, one begins to wonder what 'Kantianism' is doing in the world society pillar of the English school triad in the first place. If Kantianism means a society of states marked by a high degree of homogeneity in domestic structures, values and laws, then it is a type of international society, not an element of world society.

This issue of homogeneity in the domestic structures of states was perhaps Vincent's key point of departure from Bull. For Vincent (1986: 104, 150–2) a fully solidarist international society would be virtually a world society because all units would be alike in their domestic laws and values on humanitarian intervention. Homogeneity would make it more likely that they would find common ground in agreeing about when the right of humanitarian intervention overrides the principle of non-intervention. This line of thinking has more recently been explored by Armstrong (1999) in the context of developments in international law. Armstrong talks in terms of world society, seeing a shift from international law for a society of states to 'world law' for a world society of people. His argument hinges on changes in the nature and interests of the leading states as they have become more democratic and interdependent, and he acknowledges a certain imperial quality to this development as the leading states seek to impose their own standards of governance and commerce on to others. Armstrong avoids the term solidarism, yet his argument is exactly for a Vincent-style solidarist international society based on homogeneity in the domestic values of states. Neither Bull's rejection, nor Vincent's advocacy, answers the question of just how solidarist a states-system can become before it can no longer be thought of as an international society. The narrow way in which the pluralist–solidarist debate has been conducted within the English school, largely focused on the single question of human rights, has discouraged investigation of this question.

The second issue, whether increasing degrees of solidarism necessarily bring transnational units and individuals into the picture, also raises questions that have not really been fully explored in English school writing. Vincent and his followers assume that it does, and want to merge international and world society. Arguing from a different starting point, I have elsewhere (Buzan 1993) made the case that solidarism can only develop up to a point without there being accompanying developments in world society. I did not argue for merging the two concepts, but did take the position that a solidarism confined to international society can only go so far before further development has to bring in world society elements. These questions quickly link back to whether pluralism and solidarism are opposed choices or positions on a spectrum.

Bull set out the pluralist–solidarist framework, and so his conception of society is a good place to tap into this debate. Bull's (1977a: 53–7) conception of society comes out of a kind of sociological functionalism in which all human societies must be founded on understandings about security against violence, observance of agreements, and rules about property rights. He sees rules as the key to sharpening up mere common interests into a clear sense of appropriate behaviour (1977a: 67–71). The making of rules ranges from the customary to the positive, but whatever type they are, they fall into three levels.

(1) Constitutional normative principles are the foundation, setting out the basic ordering principle (e.g. society of states, universal empire, state of nature, cosmopolitan community, etc.). In Bull's view what is essential for order is that one of these principles dominates: because the principles are usually zero-sum, contestation equals disorder. Contestation at this level is what defines Wight's revolutionists. For an international society, the key principle is sovereignty. This level is comparable to Waltz's first tier of structure (organising principle of the system), though Bull's range of possibilities is wider than Waltz's.

(2) Rules of coexistence are those which set out the minimum behavioural conditions for society, and therefore hinge on the basic elements of society: limits to violence, establishment of property rights and sanctity of agreements. Here we find Bull's 'institutions' of classical European international society: diplomacy, international law, the balance of power, war and the role of great powers.

(3) Rules to regulate cooperation in politics, strategy, society and economy (1977a: 70). About these Bull says (1977a: 70) 'Rules of this kind prescribe behaviour that is appropriate not to the elementary or primary goals of international life, but rather to those more advanced or secondary goals that are a feature of an international society in which a consensus has been reached about a wider range of objectives than mere coexistence.' Here one would find everything from the UN system, through arms control treaties, to the regimes and institutions for managing trade, finance, environment, and a host of technical issues from postage to allocation of orbital slots and broadcast frequencies.

Note first that this is a highly rational, contractual, rule-based conception of society. It has nothing at all to do with shared culture or the 'we-feeling' of community, and is by definition completely distinct from the shared culture, civilisational precursors of international society that feature in Wight's and Watson's work. Note, second, that Bull's first and second levels mainly define the pluralist position on international society, with sovereign states representing the choice of constitutional principle, and the rules of coexistence reflecting a mainly Westphalian scheme. Solidarism finds its scope mainly in the third tier of 'more advanced' but 'secondary' rules about cooperation, though international law under rules of coexistence is sufficiently vague to allow in quite a bit of solidarism. It is worth keeping this third tier in mind when considering Bull's position in the pluralist–solidarist debate. Rules about cooperation seem to offer an open-ended scope for the development of solidarism. Yet in his defence of pluralism, and his fear of solidarism, Bull seems to forget about this third tier. Since this is where the big growth has been in contemporary international society, especially in the economic sector, the placing of this as a kind of shallow third tier comes into question, and the odd juxtaposition of the classifications 'more advanced' but 'secondary' begins to look contradictory. Develop enough down these 'secondary' lines, and the 'more advanced' elements begin to bring the constitutive principles themselves into question. The development of the EU illustrates this potential, and shows that the two are not necessarily contradictory in the disordering way that Bull seemed to think inevitable. Why did Bull's underlying concern with order, and his pessimism about its prospects, drive him to box himself in like this when the underlying logic of his concepts does not seem to require doing so?

Bull sets out the terms for solidarism and pluralism (Bull 1966a, see also 1990; and Keene 2002) by exploring the positions represented respectively by Grotius and Lassa Oppenheim. The core of the argument is about whether the international law on which international society rests is to be understood as natural law (Grotius, solidarist), or positive law (Oppenheim, pluralist). According to Bull (1966a: 64) it was Grotius's view, deriving from natural law, that 'individual human beings are subjects of international law and members of international society in their own right'. Because Grotian solidarism comes out of natural law, it is inherently universalist in the sense of having to be applied to all of humankind. While Bull accepts the universalism, he rejects natural law as a basis for international society, and particularly dismisses the idea that individuals have standing as subjects of international law and members of international society in their own right. He argues (1966a: 68) that Grotius's attachment of solidarism to natural law was rooted in the needs of Grotius's own times 'to fill the vacuum left by the declining force of divine or ecclesiastical law and the rudimentary character of existing voluntary or positive law', and that 'Grotius stands at the birth of international society and is rightly regarded as one if its midwives' (66). Seeing the Grotian position as relevant to a long-past set of historical conditions, and fearing that Grotius's blending of individual rights and state sovereignty was a recipe for conflict, Bull plumps for Oppenheim's view (1966a: 73): 'it may still be held that the method he [Oppenheim] employed, of gauging the role of law in international society in relation to the actual area of agreement between states is superior to one which sets up the law over and against the facts'. This view seemed to strengthen over time: 'there are no rules that are valid independent of human will, that are part of "nature". Natural law cannot accommodate the fact of moral disagreement, so prominent in the domain of international relations' (Bull 1979: 181). For Bull, international society is, and should be, based on positive law.

Bull's primary concern here is to restrict the idea of international society to states, and in that sense he is helping to draw a clear boundary between international society (states) and world society (individuals). Adopting the positive law position accomplishes this by putting international law wholly into the hands of states. But while identifying pluralism with positive international law (Bull 1966a: 64–8) does exclude individuals as subjects of international law, the distinction between positive and natural law does not provide an adequate basis for distinguishing between pluralism and solidarism *per se* in terms of degree of shared norms, rules and institutions. It is true that natural law provides one possible foundation for solidarism, particularly where the concern is to establish a basis for human rights, but as argued above, this puts pluralism and solidarism necessarily at odds. Remembering Bull's third tier of rules to regulate cooperation, it seems clear that adherence to positive law does nothing to prevent states from developing such an extensive range of shared values, including in the area of human rights, that their relationship would have to be called solidarist. This important loophole seems to have escaped Bull's notice, not least because his disinterest in both economic and regional developments blinded him to the very significant empirical developments of solidarism going on there. Adherence to positive law not only opens the way for as much cooperation among states as they wish to have, but since positive law is an expression of sovereignty, does so in a way that does not necessarily, or even probably, bring sovereignty into question. As Cutler notes, it also undercuts the assumption of universalism on a global scale that is strong in Bull's thinking about international society (Cutler 1991: 46–9). Within a positive law framework, states can by definition do what they like, including forming solidarist regional or subsystemic international societies. Acceptance of positive law draws a straight line between the pluralist and solidarist positions, and eliminates the logic of their being opposed. Pluralism simply becomes a lower degree of shared norms, rules and institutions (or a thinner body of positive law), solidarism a higher one (or a thicker body of positive law).

Bull never seemed to grasp this implication of his acceptance of positive law. Instead, he goes on to develop what seem like rather arbitrary criteria for solidarism, namely that it is defined 'with respect to the enforcement of the law' by states – pluralism sees states as 'capable of agreeing only for certain minimum purposes which fall short of that of the enforcement of the law' (1966a: 52). By the device of discussing it only in relation to 'high politics' issues such as collective security and human rights, this enforcement criterion is made to seem more demanding than it often is. In this perspective solidarism opposes alliances as sectional, and favours collective security on a universalist basis. Pluralists argue for the centrality of sovereignty and non-intervention as the key principles of international society 'and the only purposes for which they could be overridden were that of self-preservation and that of the maintenance of the balance of power' (Bull 1966a: 63). It is this very demanding concept of solidarism, attached to collective security (Bull 1977a: 238–40), that goes forward into *The Anarchical Society*, where Bull (148–9) sees solidarism as expressed by the development of consensual international law, where norms and rules can achieve the status of international law not only if unanimously supported, but also if supported by consensus.

Bull also (1977a: 152) continued to identify solidarism with Grotius's natural law position, and this led him to the view that:

> Carried to its logical extreme, the doctrine of human rights and duties under international law is subversive of the whole principle that mankind should be organised as a society of sovereign states. For, if the rights of each man can be asserted on the world political stage over and against the claims of his state, and his duties proclaimed irrespective of his position as a servant or a citizen of that state, then the position of the state as a body sovereign over its citizens, and entitled to command their obedience, has been subject to challenge, and the structure of the society of sovereign states has been placed in jeopardy.

This position does not change much in his later, allegedly more solidarist, work (Bull 1984: 13): 'The promotion of human rights on a world scale, in a context in which there is no consensus as to their meaning and the priorities among them, carries the danger that it will be subversive of coexistence among states, on which the whole fabric of world order in our times depends . . .'.

The fierceness of Bull's defence of pluralism is understandable when seen as a response to a normatively driven solidarism, based in natural law, pitting a universalist principle of individual rights against the state, and so compromising the principle of sovereignty. But it does not make sense against the logic of Bull's own positive law position, in which like-minded states are perfectly at liberty to agree human rights regimes amongst themselves without compromising the principle of sovereignty. Interestingly, Manning (1962: 167–8) was crystal clear on this point: 'What is essentially a system of law *for* sovereigns, being premised on their very sovereignty, does not, by the fact of being strengthened, put in jeopardy the sovereignties which are the dogmatic basis for its very existence. Not, at any rate, in logic.' Bull's global-scale universalist assumptions make the best the enemy of the good by cutting off acknowledgement of sub-global human rights developments. In principle, Bull should have no difficulty with individuals as objects of international human rights law, so long as that law is made by states.

If Bull's strong defence of pluralism was a response to the normative cosmopolitanism of human rights solidarists, it has reaped its reward in spirited counterattacks. The ongoing debate has made some progress, but partly because it remains focused on the human rights question, it has also carried forward many of the analytical weaknesses and distortions from the earlier rounds. Indeed, since interest in collective security has fallen away, the more recent pluralist–solidarist debate is almost exclusively focused on human rights. The assumption of universalism (and therefore global scale) still dominates on both sides, as does the blindness or indifference towards all the real-world solidarist developments at the regional level and in the economic sector.

Some of the solidarists such as Knudsen (1999) remain committed to the natural law approach, and so take Bull as a particular target. Knudsen argues strongly against the polarisation between pluralism and solidarism which he sees as stemming from Bull's work. He uses a Grotian position on human rights and international society to argue that human rights can be (and in his view already is) an institution of international society. He brings individuals into international society through natural law, but still holds solidarism to be an empirical feature of state-based international society. Wheeler (2000: 41) is distinctive for not appealing to natural law, and makes it a priority to avoid clashes between international law and human rights. Instead, he builds his case on empirical grounds, and seeks ways to strengthen the moves towards a human rights regime that he sees as already present in positive international law. Vincent, as sketched above, does not explicitly enter into the pluralist–solidarist debate. But the logic of his argument implicitly equates international society with a pluralist model, and solidarism with a move to a world society in which states, other groups and individuals, all have legal standing in relation to each other (Vincent 1986: 92–102). By threatening to merge world society into solidarism, Vincent and his followers both lose the extremely central distinction between state-based (international) and non-state-based (world) societies, and divert attention from the necessary task of thinking through world society more carefully, and relating it to international society as a distinct factor.

Perhaps the most prominent current exponents of solidarism are Tim Dunne and Nicholas Wheeler. They correctly place Bull as rejecting the 'foundationalist universalisms' aspect of revolutionism, and also natural law (Dunne and Wheeler 1998). They recognise that Bull's idea of moral foundations in international society rested on positive law, and they also see that this was in principle open ended as regards potential development between pluralism and solidarism. Rather than setting Bull up as a target, they try to reinterpret him as a kind of proto-solidarist, perhaps hoping to enlist his status in order to help legitimate those concerned to build up the normative elements in English school theory. They themselves seem to be in Vincent's tradition, seeing solidarism not as a feature (or not) of international societies, but as intimately bound up in the transition from international to world society. They try (1996) both to push Bull into a more solidarist position, and to extend the Grotian line that solidarism crosses the boundary between international and world society. They draw attention, rightly, to the later Bull's concerns for justice as a component of order, and to his awareness of the limits of pluralism exposed by the Cold War ideological polarisation of the great powers. They even (1996: 92) want to pull out of Bull 'three paradigms of world politics: realism, pluralism and solidarism . . . centred upon the themes of, respectively, power, order and justice'. In terms of a structural interpretation of English school theory, this is a potentially huge move, though one not yet worked out. It would follow Wight in locating on normative ground the entire theoretical foundation of the English school triad, taking out of the equation the whole question of units (states, transnational, individual) and the state/individual ontology, on which the existing structural distinctions are built. As I have argued above, Bull's commitment to positive law did provide an opening towards solidarism. But it was an opening that Bull himself did not go through. Bull's awareness of the pitfalls of pluralism, and his sensitivity to justice claims, were not sufficient to override his clear commitment to state-centric pluralism. In particular, they did not override his commitment to an ontology based on keeping states and individuals analytically distinct, which is what makes his work a major contribution to developing a more social structural approach to English school theory. Trying to co-opt Bull into solidarism risks confusing the pluralist–solidarist question with that about the boundary between international and world society, on which Bull was clear. As I will argue in chapter 5, there are good analytical reasons for keeping the ideas of pluralism and solidarism distinct from the definitions of international and world society.

What this discussion reveals is that a great deal hinges on the question of what solidarism is understood to be. If it is simply cosmopolitanism dressed up in English school jargon, then pluralism and solidarism must be mutually exclusive, and world society can only be achieved by merging international society into a wider cosmopolitan frame. Something of this sort is hinted at in Linklater's (1996: 78) idea of extending citizenship both up and down from the state, and having the state 'mediating between the different loyalties and identities present within modern societies'. If, as might be inferred from Bull's discussion of rules, and from some of Dunne's and Wheeler's writing about positive international law, solidarism is better understood as being about the thickness of norms, rules and institutions that states choose to create to manage their relations, then pluralism and solidarism simply link positions on a spectrum and have no necessary contradiction.

Given its many costs, the only reason to hold the cosmopolitan position is either a dyed-in-the-wool methodological individualism, or the hope that doing so gives some political leverage against the many states that have so far proved unwilling to embrace a human rights agenda. Against it is the argument made by Williams (2001) that world society, contrary to the hopes of some solidarists, is more thoroughly and deeply fragmented and diverse, and therefore more embeddedly pluralist, than international society. Whereas states, because they are like units, and relatively few in number, do have the potential for solidarism underlined by Kant, the diversity and un-likeness of the entities comprising the non-state world make it a much more problematic site for the development of solidarism. The case for taking the less dogmatic line is not just the expedience of avoiding difficulties. Sticking with the cosmopolitan view of solidarism confines one to a perilously narrow liberal view in which the issue of human rights dominates what solidarism is understood to be. It leaves one unable to describe, as solidarist, international societies that make no concession to individuals as subjects of international law, but which nevertheless display a rich and deep array of shared norms, rules and institutions, some of which may give individuals extensive rights as objects of international law. On the face of it, the inability to label such international societies as solidarist makes a nonsense of much of what the pluralist–solidarist debate is about in terms of whether international society is about mere rules of coexistence, or is, as Mayall (2000: 21) puts it, about turning international society 'into an enterprise association – that exists to pursue substantive goals of its own'.

In substantive terms, pluralism describes 'thin' international societies where the shared values are few, and the prime focus is on devising rules for coexistence within a framework of sovereignty and non-intervention. Solidarism is about 'thick' international societies in which a wider range of values is shared, and where the rules will be not only about coexistence, but also about the pursuit of joint gains and the management of collective problems in a range of issue-areas. Thinking about pluralism and solidarism in terms of thin and thick sets of shared values runs usefully in parallel with Ruggie's (1998: 33) constructivist understanding of international systems:

> the building blocks of international reality are ideational as well as material . . . At the level of the international polity, the concept of structure in social constructivism is suffused with ideational factors. There can be no mutually comprehensible conduct of international relations, constructivists hold, without mutually recognised constitutive rules, resting on collective intentionality. These rules may be more or less "thick" or "thin" . . . Similarly they may be constitutive of conflict or competition.

If one takes this view, then pluralism and solidarism become ends of a spectrum. They represent degrees of difference rather than contradictory positions. This position also allows one to keep solidarism as a feature of international society (i.e. a society of states) and therefore to keep distinct the idea of international society as being about states, and world society as about non-state actors. World society encompasses the individual and transnational domains, and it remains a question to be investigated as to whether and how these tie into the development of solidarism. Contrary to the Vincentians, world society becomes not the necessary absorption of international society into a wider universe of individual and transnational rights, but a distinct domain of actors whose relationship with the state domain needs to be understood. Among other things, this perspective requires closer attention to the question of what the shared norms, rules and institutions that define solidarism and pluralism are about, and what values they represent. Answers to that may well condition the type of relationship between international and world society that develops, and whether and how individuals and transnationals become players in solidarism; more on this in chapter 5.

For those in the solidarist tradition there is an interesting, and as yet not well explored area of linkage to other elements of IR theory, to be found in the question of homogeneity of units. Bull's pluralism is again a useful foil. As noted above, Bull rejected as Kantian (and therefore world society) the idea that solidarism could be produced by states becoming more internally alike. Vincent, Armstrong and Dunne and Wheeler seem in many ways to hinge their ideas of solidarism precisely on the possibility of such homogenising developments. If homogenisation is a route to solidarist international societies, then IR theory offers grounds for optimism. Several powerful trends in IR theory note the existence of homogenising forces, and this would seem to work in favour of the normative approach to international society – at least so long as liberal states are in the ascendent in the international system as the model around which homogenisation occurs. Halliday (1992) focuses on the issue of homogenisation of domestic structures among states as one of the keys to international (and by implication world) society. He implicitly picks up on themes from Wight, and carries the same blurring of categories: pluralist/realist, transnational/non-state links and homogenisation among states in their internal character and structure. Halliday notes the normative case for homogenisation (Burke and democratic peace), the Marxian idea of capitalism as the great homogenising force, and the Kantian/Fukuyama idea of science and technology and democracy as homogenising forces. Halliday ignores entirely Waltz's (1979) argument about the operation of socialisation and competition as homogenising forces, an idea picked up by me and adapted to thinking about international society (Buzan 1993). Interestingly, the

Stanford school (Meyer *et al.* 1997: 144–8) also ignore the powerful homogenising argument in Waltz. Unlike Halliday, they acknowledge Waltz, but they dismiss him as a 'microrealist' even though they also take the striking isomorphism of the 'like units' of the international system as their key phenomenon for explanation. Their explanation for isomorphism could be seen as complementary to that in Waltz (more on this in chapter 3). If homogeneity is overdetermined in the international system, then the implications of this for solidarism need to be more closely investigated.

One can sum up key points from the pluralist–solidarist debate as follows.

- That the debate about solidarism in <u>not</u> primarily (or even at all) about shared identity or common culture. In one sense, it is about whether one starts from a cosmopolitan position driven by ethical commitments, or from a state-centric position driven by positive law. In another, simpler and less politically charged, sense, it is about the extent and degree of institutionalisation of shared interests and values in systems of agreed rules of conduct. Arguably, it is also about collective enforcement of rules, though whether this is a necessary condition for all rules is unclear.
- That there is confusion about the relationship between homogeneity of states on the one hand, and solidarism on the other. Does homogeneity point towards Kantian world society or solidarist international society?
- That it remains a contested question as to whether solidarism is (or should be) a quality of interstate international societies, or whether it is (or should be) a quality that necessarily bridges between, and merges, international and world society. Is solidarism the quality that merges international and world society, or is it a concept that can be applied to international society (states) and world society separately? If the former, then the distinction between international and world society as distinct pillars within English school theory collapses. If the latter, then the question is how the two relate, particularly when, and to what extent, the development of solidarism in an interstate international society requires corresponding developments in world society.
- That there does not seem to be any necessary contradiction between acceptance of positive law as the foundation for international society and the development of solidarism.

- That acceptance of positive law as the foundation for international society would seem to require, or at least enable, abandoning both the universalist-global-scale assumption inherited from natural law, and the blindness to solidarist developments in areas other than human rights and collective security. In practice, neither has yet happened.

The pluralist–solidarist debate dances on the border between international and world society. But while it opens up some interesting and useful perspectives both on the border and on what lies on either side of it, it still does not generate a clear understanding of world society.

Conclusions

On the evidence in this chapter, it does not overstate the case to say that, as things stand, the English school's understanding of world society is both incoherent and underdeveloped. Yet this observation is not the basis for a contemptuous dismissal. The reasons for it are perfectly understandable in the context of what the various writers discussed above were trying to do. And the main point is that although the concept is neither well worked out nor clearly defined, it is located in an extremely interesting and central position within an overall framework of IR theory. World society bears heavily on the most important debates within the English school, so much so that even the relatively well-developed concept of international society cannot be properly understood without taking world society into close account. For all of its shortcomings, the English school approach to world society does show exactly why the concept is important, and also shows where (if not yet how) it fits into a theoretically pluralist approach to IR theory. My conclusion, then, is not that the English school's thinking on world society should be set aside, but that it should be taken as the definition of a challenge. There is interesting and important thinking to be done in working out just what world society does mean, how it fits into the larger frame of English school theory, and what the consequences of a clearer view of it are for that larger frame. In order to advance that project, it helps now to look at the several bodies of thought outside the English school that also use the concept. What other understandings of world society are there, and do they offer insights which can be brought to bear on the difficulties that world society raises in the English school?

3 Concepts of world society outside English school thinking

The English school has successfully made the concept of international society its own. Because the meaning of international society (as the society that states form among themselves) is quite specific, there are not many attempts to impart other meanings to the term. The same cannot be said of world society. As shown in chapter 2, the English school's usage of this term is confused, diverse and on the margins of its discourse. In addition, many others have taken up the term, or synonyms for it, as a way of questioning the narrowness inherent in the state-centric quality of international society. World society is used widely to bring non-state actors into the social structure of the international system. This chapter surveys these alternative conceptions with a view to the lessons they offer for thinking about the meaning of world society, and how it should be staged in English school thinking.

There are in practice two broad ways of using the concept of world society. The first, typified by Bull, is to see it as a specialised idea aimed at capturing the non-state dimension of humankind's social order. Buzan and Little (2000), for example, use it as an expression meant to capture either or both of the society (*Gesellschaft*) or community (*Gemeinschaft*) aspects of the non-state and individual levels of world politics. In this form, world society is distinct from, and counterpointed to, international society. The second way, exemplified by Vincent and his followers, and prevalent in most sociological approaches, is to use the concept in an attempt to capture the macro-dimension of human social organisation as a whole. In this usage, world society ultimately incorporates and supersedes international society. Yet along the way it is often opposed to international society as a way of conceptualising the world social order.

In the English school's discussions of international society, and also more generally in the discussion about the structure of states-systems, the distinction between the system element (understood as interaction) and the society element (understood as socially constructed norms, rules and institutions) is in general explicit. The terms 'international system' and 'international society' are employed specifically in the structural side of English school theory to represent this distinction. It also features strongly in the debates between neorealists, whose theory hangs on the material aspects of system, and constructivists, who want to develop more social views of international structure.

Curiously (and regardless of whether or not one thinks the system–society distinction tenable or not, on which more in chapter 4) no similar separation attends the discussions about world society. As noted above, Bull (1977: 276–81) did distinguish between world society and the 'world political system', but this concern to differentiate the mechanical and the social in relation to the non-state world has not become part of English school practice. Outside the English school, and indeed outside the mainstream of IR, this issue has been addressed not by attempting to distinguish between the mechanical, or physical, and the social, but by setting up different understandings of what constitutes 'society'. Much of the non-English school discussion about world society can be understood as the taking of positions ranging from relatively light to relatively heavy in what definitional benchmarks are set for 'society'. On the lighter end, world society becomes not much more than a synonym for Bull's 'world political system', or what was referred to in chapter 2 as 'world system' (not Wallerstein's meaning). This view stresses global patterns of interaction and communication, and, in sympathy with much of the literature on globalisation, uses the term society mainly to distance itself from state-centric models of IR. On the heavier end, world society approximates Vincent's holistic conception, and is aimed at capturing the total interplay amongst states, non-state actors and individuals, while carrying the sense that all the actors in the system are conscious of their interconnectedness and share some important values. This can come in fairly non-specific forms, where the emphasis is on the fact that a great deal of socially structured interaction is going on amongst many different types of actor on a planetary scale. It can also come in more focused versions where the whole assemblage is characterised according to some dominant ordering principle, such as capitalism or modernity.

Bull's understanding of world society has the attraction of resting on clear assumptions about both 'world' and 'society'. In relation to 'world' Bull's position is that it is about the non-state aspects of international systems and therefore distinct from international society. In relation to 'society' Bull's position is in parallel with that on international society, that 'society' is about shared values. The shared values idea comes in different forms in that it can be arrived at by various routes: coercive universalism (imposition of shared values by force), cosmopolitanism (development of shared values at the level of individuals) or Kantian (development of shared values at the level of states). The transnational element in English school world society thinking is not so obviously about shared values, though a degree of necessity of shared values can be assumed to underlie it. Transnational organisations, whether firms or INGOs, are by definition functionally differentiated, and it can be argued that functionally differentiated organisations presuppose a system of shared values in order to allow for their creation and operation within a division of labour. In highly liberalised international systems, like that amongst the contemporary Western states, transnational organisations exist and function because of a framework of agreed rules and institutions. Similarly, the transnational system of medieval Europe was structured by the shared values and institutions of Christendom and feudalism. Using world society to refer to non-state elements means that while Bull's concept of world society is generally pitched at the global scale (humankind as a whole), it is not holistic in the sense of being about everything. It represents a particular line of distinction within the frame of the international system overall. The idea of shared values means that Bull's concept of society is a relatively strong one, with quite demanding criteria, a view shared by Krasner (1999: 48). The Vincentians share Bull's strong understanding of society as meaning shared values, but not his narrow conception of world society as confined to the non-state world.

Compared to Bull, and at some risk of oversimplification, it can be said that most non-English-school users of the concept want to define world society more loosely along either or both of these lines. That is to say, like the Vincentians they want 'world' to be used as a holistic umbrella term to include everything in the international system, state, non-state and individual. Rengger (1992: 366–9) also argues for incorporating the narrow idea of international society into a cosmopolitan frame. But in contrast to almost everyone within the English school, the other users of world society want 'society' to mean something less demanding than shared values, and closer to what in English school (and IR) parlance would be thought of as 'system'. The most obvious motive behind these moves is consciousness of the shrinkage of time and space in the contemporary global political economy, and the consequent need to take into account the multitudinous patterns of interaction and interdependence that knit the world together more tightly and more deeply than ever before. Some of these concepts of world society are thus precursors of, or analogues for, globalisation. A second motive probably springs from the direction and character of debates in different disciplines. In IR, the system–society distinction is well embedded. In sociology, the tradition of debate is more focused around how 'society' is to be defined.

The rest of this chapter comprises a survey of world society and analogous concepts as they have been developed outside the English school. The aim is to relate their ways of understanding world society to the problem of conceptualising world society within the English school's theoretical framework. The first section looks at three writers located mainly within the IR debate but with a stronger sociological orientation than the IR mainstream: John Burton, Evan Luard and Martin Shaw. The second section examines a range of debates and traditions located mainly in Sociology: Luhmann, the Stanford school, the World Society Research Group and macro-sociology. The third section turns to a debate that stems mainly from a mixture of political theory and political activism: global civil society.

IR writers with a sociological turn: Burton, Luard and Shaw

Two IR writers outside the English school who can be read in the same way as the Vincentians and Rengger (i.e. as favouring an all-inclusive interpretation of 'world') are Burton and Luard. Both men ploughed somewhat lonely furrows in IR, and might best be thought of as forerunners of globalisation. In that sense neither was responding to the same impulses that inspired the British Committee, in particular, and the English school, more broadly, even though they used similar concepts.

Burton (1972: 19–22) wanted to differentiate 'interstate' relations, which he saw as the dominant IR approach, from a holistic approach that focused on the entire network, or system or 'cobweb' of human interactions. In part, he argues that the behaviour of states cannot be understood without taking into account the wider context of human interactions. In part, his ambition was to shift the focus of analysis away from the particularities of states to the dynamics of the interhuman system as a whole. His idea of world society meant covering all the levels of analysis at once. He wanted maps of human behaviour, and the key to his perception of world society is perhaps found in the statement (Burton 1972: 45) that: 'Communications, and not power, are the main organising influence in world society.' Like the English school, Burton was reacting against the excesses of mechanistic, state-centric realism in IR theory. Unlike them, he wanted to move much further away from the states-system as the central frame for thinking about international relations.

Luard (1976, 1990) was much more animated by the task of constructing a specifically sociological approach to the study of international relations. In his earlier work (1976: 110, 364) he insisted that his subject was the society of states, but later (1990) he took the whole nexus of states, transnational actors and individual networks as the unit of analysis. Like Burton, he did not differentiate between international and world society, and he used the terms interchangeably (1990: 2). His concern with 'consciousness of interrelatedness' (1990: 3) came close to Burton's focus on communications, but he wanted to consider a whole set of variables (structure, motives, means, norms, institutions, elites and, most of all, ideology), and the interplay amongst them, as the basis for differentiating types of international society. Luard's approach was consciously sociological and comparative. His 1976 book can be grouped with Wight's and Watson's as comparative historical sociology approaches to international society. His key theme, which would resonate with most contemporary contstructivists, was that in any given era there exists 'a common pattern of belief about the nature of international society and the behaviour within it seen as normal' (1976: 110). This pattern of belief is a social structure that strongly conditions the behaviour of the units in the system no matter what their internal differences. He wanted to establish international/world society as a type of society with its own distinctive features (larger, looser, with stronger subunits) than others, but still recognisably similar in structure to some of the larger states. He wanted to open the study of society away from the tight, small-scale, community models of anthropology, while keeping the holistic focus allowed by the concept of society.

This type of thinking developed mostly in reaction to the state-centric models of international relations promoted by realism, but also in some ways by liberalism, which has its own version of state-centrism. The English school can be attacked also for state-centrism, <u>but only</u> if it is interpreted as being about international society <u>and nothing else</u>. Some do see it in this way (Brown 1999: 6–7; Keane 2001: 25–6), and would be happy to think of it as 'the international society school'. With that interpretation, the English school can easily be accused of sharing the state-centric ontology of realism, and therefore as missing, or worse, excluding from consideration, the rising salience of non-state elements in the international system. As has been shown above, this is not a tenable interpretation of the English school. Although the bulk of the school's work has indeed been in the area of international society, its foundation is the theoretical pluralism embedded in the three traditions. The three pillars of English school theory do encompass the holistic agenda. Its big advantage over other holistic approaches is that it does not surrender ontological and epistemological distinctions, and therefore retains a much greater degree of analytical leverage. Most other holistic approaches dump everything into a single category, often labelled world society, so presenting an impossibly complicated subject for analysis. While the English school can certainly be accused both of neglecting world society, and of not making its meaning and content clear enough, it cannot fairly be accused of realism's ontological (or, indeed, epistemological) narrowness.

Shaw also leans towards equating the English school with international society, but this is not his main point. Like Luard, Shaw is rightly concerned to raise the sociological consciousness of the IR community. But rather than ignoring the English school, as Luard largely did, Shaw takes it as a target, particularly the English school's strong conception of society as shared values. Shaw wants a wide definition of 'world' and a weak one of 'society'. In terms of 'world', Shaw, like Luard, and perhaps Burton, wants to reintegrate the study of the states-system, the global economy and global culture (1996: 56). At some points he seems to take up an anti-state position, similar to that which Brown (1999: 10–14) attributes to Burton, almost bringing him into line with Bull's view that international society and world society are in important ways opposed concepts. He argues that 'The global society perspective, therefore, has an ideological significance which is ultimately opposed to that of international society' (Shaw 1996: 60). Yet elsewhere (1996: 55), he seems almost close to a 'three traditions' position when he suggests, but does not follow up, that the key question is how global society and international society relate to each other.

Shaw is on clearer ground when he argues that the definition of society used by Bull, and through him the English school, is too demanding. In Shaw's view, the requirement for a substantial degree of social consensus works, up to a point, to identify international society, but is the reason why Bull cannot bring world society into practical focus. Shaw sees this strong definition of society as discredited. He wants a weaker definition that rejects the distinction between system and society in order to bring the growing reality of a global society more clearly into focus (Shaw 1996: 54). Here Shaw's critique comes close to the holistic line present in Burton and Luard: 'World society exists through the social relations involved in global commodity production and exchange, through global culture and mass media, and through the increasing development of world politics' (1996: 55). Although this definition is open to interpretation in different ways, its thrust suggests a watering down of 'society' to a meaning not much different from Bull's 'world political system'.

Shaw's apparent motive for wanting a weaker definition of society is to enable him to make a stronger empirical claim that a significant world society already exists, and needs to be taken into account. This is the position of some globalists, and reflects promotional as much as analytical goals. In this sense, Shaw and others are quite right to draw attention to the difficulty that the strong definition of society poses for the English school. It is pretty clear in Bull's writing that the demanding requirement for 'society' leads directly to the conclusion that not much is to be found by way of really existing world society. This in turn forces him to defend pluralist international society in the name of international order. The gap between Bull's position and Shaw's call for a weaker definition of world society draws attention back to the 'missing' element of 'world system' (or in Bull's term 'world political system') in the English school triad noted earlier. Recall that in the English school's triad, international system represents the physical interaction element at the level of states, and international society the socially constructed one based on shared norms, rules and institutions. Recall also that world society is defined in parallel terms to international society, but that there is no place in the triad scheme for a physical interaction analogue ('world system') to international system. The position of Shaw and the globalisationists might thus be understood in English school terms as a call to recognise the standing and significance of the 'world system' element, which is currently absent from the English school's theoretical scheme. Its absence in English school thinking is probably explained by the tension between the Wightian mode of thinking, from which the three traditions derive, and more structural modes. In Wightian mode, 'world system' does not register because unlike the other three pillars it has not been part of the conversation about international relations. The demand for it comes from structural logic. Whether it is a good idea to address this problem, as Shaw would have us do, by conflating world system and world society, so weakening what is meant by 'society', is much more open to argument (more on this in chapter 4).

It is not clear what would be gained analytically from adopting Shaw's approach other than a stronger basis for a claim that world society already exists. In the end, his expanded and weakened formulation contains many of the same ambiguities as are found in the English school, and his weaker concept of society pushes towards a mere system view, and drains away the distinctiveness of a social as opposed to a merely mechanical/physical approach.

Sociological conceptions of world society

Sociology is of course the home discipline of 'society' even though some of its leading lights (Mann 1986: 2; Wallerstein 1984: 2) would like to abolish the concept on the grounds that no unit of analysis can be found that corresponds to it. Most of Sociology has been concerned with societies composed of individual human beings, and thus confined itself to entities that are subglobal in scale. Some sociologists, most notably in the subfield of historical sociology, have become concerned with the state and power, and developed a perspective on the global level not dissimilar to that of realism (Mann 1986; Tilly 1990). Sociologists have not generally been attracted by the idea of second-order societies, such as the society of states, with the consequence that this topic was left largely to IR, and an intellectual community trained more in politics than sociology. But quite a few sociologists have been attracted to macro-conceptions of society, and it is not surprising that several species of world society are to be found within the debates of sociology.

Luhmann's concept of world society represents a far more radical departure from both standard IR and sociological theory than anything else discussed in this chapter. Most IR theory has its roots in classical sociological theories which are in one way or another based on the idea that society is about various types of normative cohesion (shared norms, rules, institutions, values; common identities and/or cultures). Most inside/outside understandings of the state share this approach, as does the

English school's understanding of international and world society. Luhmann's concept is opposed to all of this, seeking to replace a normative understanding of society with one based on processes and structures of communication (Albert 1999). According to the World Society Research Group (WSRG) (1995: 8–9) Luhmann wants to move away from the 'old European concept of society' based on normative expectations, and towards 'cognitive expectations' within networks of social relations based not on universal norms and their enforcement but on functional issues within science, and the economy and other areas of organised human life. Within these networks, individuals have a willingness to learn, and to 'reconsider their own claims'. As Diez (2000: 3–4) puts it:

> society for Luhmann is the agglomeration of a number of diversified functional systems, such as law or the economy. Each of these systems comes into being through communication (and not through some grand normative foundations) and operates according to its own codes, with one basic code such as legal/illegal in the case of law at its heart . . . these systems (or most of them) are functionally and not territorially differentiated. In fact, politics (and law) are the only systems still territorially differentiated. But if society exists only as (and through) a conglomerate of systems, and if these systems because of their functional definition operate transnationally, society is only possible on a world scale – it is world society.

Luhmann's conception is basically hostile to distinctions between state and non-state, or amongst international system, international society and world society. Its communication perspective does not privilege any particular form of organisation (though it does have a place for organisations as a social form), and it pushes norms, identities and shared values well away from the centre of what forms society. The only concession in this direction is that the process of communication itself requires 'the production of secure frameworks of expectation' within the functional systems (Albert 1999: 258). In other words, there have to be accepted rules of communication around basic codes such as legal/illegal, true/false in order for functional subsystems to exist.

In one sense (and probably only one) Luhmann's view is similar to Shaw's in that it is a weaker (and therefore more really existing) conception of world society than that in the English school. Bull might well have understood Luhmann as a rather convoluted statement about the 'world political system'. Moving away from the highly demanding criteria for a society of shared values/identities means that more 'world society' can be said to exist already, which in turn supports claims that the states-system is not as dominant as its supporters assert, and that the rising replacement system therefore deserves more attention than it is getting. This is the standard stuff of academic politics. Luhmann, however, is about much more than that agenda, and it is probably a zero-sum choice between following the Luhmannian scheme and developing most of the other ideas about world society, including English school ones, surveyed here. Luhmann's emphasis on communication echoes Burton's, and in that sense does fit into the general picture that globalists are trying to sketch. But in reconceptualising society in terms of communication Luhmann is going down a path that diverges from the one that the English school has carved out for itself. Neither his notion of 'world' nor his understanding of 'society' lines up with English school usage. From a Luhmannian position, the English school is too similar to the classical sociological conceptions from which Luhmann is trying to depart. From an English school perspective, Luhmann's scheme rips away the entire framework within which international society has been understood. Consequently, there is probably not much scope for complementarity between these two modes of thought.

It is tempting, though probably wrong, to link Luhmann's ideas to IR thinking about epistemic communities (Haas 1992). In Luhmann's terms, epistemic communities are too much about networks of individuals rather than systems of communication. But there is a link in the idea of recognising, learning and participating in a structured system of knowledge, language and/or practice. Nevertheless, Luhmann's concept of world society is too alien to help much in thinking about world society in an English school context. If there is a lesson it is perhaps the rather oblique one that there is analytical advantage in adopting a normatively neutral view of world society. The significance of this will become clear in the discussion of global civil society below.

Desite Shaw's sociological critique of the English school's strong concept of society, there are other sociologists who want to tie the idea of world society to shared norms, rules and institutions. The *Stanford School* (Thomas *et al.* 1987; Meyer *et al.* 1997; Boli and Thomas 1999) styling themselves 'macrophenomenological sociological institutionalists', put global culture at the centre of their concept of world society. They seem to be unaware of the work of Wight, Bull and others in the English school who have focused on a society of states, and like most other users of 'world society' construct it as a holistic, all-embracing concept. Their disinterest in the English school is unfortunate, because a great deal of what they have to say focuses on states, and how to explain the striking isomorphism of 'like units' in the international system. In many ways, their concerns are close to those of international society, and run alongside the English school's debates on solidarism. The core idea in the Stanford school (or sometimes 'world polity') approach is that there are powerful worldwide models about how humans should organise themselves. These models are carried by academic and professional associations, and by the network of intergovernmental organisations, and are deeply embedded in all the levels of the international system (IGOs, states, TNAs, individuals). Rather in line with Vincent's vision of world society, the Stanford school thinks it is already the case that 'legitimated actorhood operates at several levels' (Meyer *et al.* 1997: 168), and that these levels mutually reinforce and legitimate each other in terms of the shared values embodied in the worldwide models.

> Individuals and states mutually legitimate each other via principles of citizenship, while individuals and international organisations do the same via principles of human rights. Between individuals and nation-states lie any number of interest and functional groups that have standing as legitimated actors due to their connections with individuals and states. These include religious, ethnic, occupational, industrial, class, racial and gender-based groups and organisations, all of which both depend on and conflict with actors at other levels. For example, individual actors are entitled to demand equality, while collective actors are entitled to promote functionally justified differentiation.
>
> (Meyer *et al.* 1997: 171)

Conflict is intrinsic to this view of society, imparting to it 'the dynamism that is generated by the rampant inconsistencies and conflicts within world culture itself' (Meyer *et al.* 1997: 172).

The Stanford school's approach to world society hangs on the argument that this strong world culture has an independent existence, and that it is the main cause of isomorphism among states. They insist that world culture is a significant causal factor, and that it is a systemic phenomenon, not just located in the units. What is interesting about this effort from an English school perspective is how much it focuses on the centrality of the state, which is acknowledged in world culture as the central institution, even though accompanied by other legitimate actors (Meyer *et al.* 1997: 169–71). The Stanford school concede that much of what they identify as world culture is Western, and that a good deal of the story is about how 'the poor and weak and peripheral copy the rich and strong and central' (Meyer *et al.* 1997: 164–8). But sadly for the literature, they do not explore the obvious link that this line of argument creates both to neorealism and the English school. They cite Waltz without having registered that one of the most central features of his theory parallels their concern with the phenomenon of isomorphism: that under anarchy, socialisation and competition imperatives generated by the structural pressures of balance of power result in like units.

In many ways, the Stanford school's ideas are of greater relevance to English school thinking about international society than world society. Their idea that the legitimising ideas even for the states-system are largely carried by non-state actors (Boli and Thomas 1999) gives an interesting twist to thinking about international society, but is somewhat betrayed by the Western origins of most of both the ideas and the carriers. It does, however, set down a marker about the importance of TNAs in world society. One key insight is that the values of world society are often inconsistent and conflictual, a theme perhaps underdeveloped in English school thinking (except in relation to human rights and sovereignty), but wholly apparent to anyone who has investigated nationalism and sovereignty, or the market and sovereignty. It is well to be reminded that 'society' is not necessarily either nice or harmonious (more on this in chapters 5 and 6).

The *World Society Research Group* (WSRG) (1995, 2000) also stress a holistic, multilevel approach to 'world', and put some emphasis on shared culture and values as the essence of 'society'. They focus particularly on the Weberian differentiation between *Gesellschaft* (society) and *Gemeinschaft* (community), departing from the original Tönnies (1887) idea that society was a degraded development from community (WSRG 2000: 6–7). In this approach, society is about rational agreements over mutual adjustments of interest. It is based on the sorts of shared values that allow actors to make contracts governing their behaviour and interaction. Community is about feelings of belonging together, constituting a 'We' that differentiates itself from 'Other(s)'. Community is rooted in tradition and/or affection. Society is rooted in calculation of self-interest. This is an analytical distinction based on ideal types, and the expectation is that all real social relations will be a mixture of the two forms (WSRG 2000: 7, 12). It is almost impossible to imagine communities without contracts, and difficult, though perhaps not quite impossible, to imagine contracts in the complete absence of any sense of community (e.g. as fellow human beings, or at the ultimate stretch, as fellow sentient life forms).

The WSRG approach bears some strong and explicit resemblance to the English school's triad, except, like Vincent, they see international system, international society and world society, as cumulative stages, with world society incorporating the other two as the most developed social form (WSRG 2000: 11–13). They think (WSRG 1995: 14–17) that the English school (represented, curiously, by Bull – fair enough – and Brown and Buzan – both decidedly on the margins) mistakenly locate society in international society and community in world society. They disagree, wanting to allow society formation processes amongst non-state actors, and community formation ones among states. Their interpretation of the English school on this point is, I think, mistaken, though Brown (1995) could be read as they suggest. Bull hardly discusses identity at all. In my earlier work (Buzan 1993: 333–40) I simply build the idea of identity into society, both international and world, while failing to recognise, as the WSRG rightly does, that the society and community conceptions are fundamentally different (see also Wæver 1998: 108). Nevertheless, the WSRG approach raises a lot of interesting and stimulating questions that the English school has so far not confronted squarely.

The society–community distinction has big implications for solidarism and international society, as well as for how world society is to be understood. The WSRG raise the idea that there is interplay between society formation and community formation, with the latter sometimes opposed to the former, sometimes supportive of it (1995: 24–5). They also take the view (WSRG 2000: 12–13), along with Brown (1995: 100–6), that the idea of a universal sense of community (i.e. a universal sense of identity) is at the very least seriously problematic, and at worst an oxymoron (because a sense of being 'We' requires an 'Other' against which to define itself). If true, this poses major difficulties for some aspects of the world society concept. The WSRG are keen to avoid any sense of inevitability about progress up the stages from system to society to community. Reverse movement is possible. Weller (2000) also builds on the society–community distinction, establishing society and community as different, but interacting types of social relations. He too takes the view that the relationship between them is complicated, and not subject to simple generalisations about development from one to the other in either direction.

These questions about society and community are implicit in English school discussions of culture, but the approaches taken by the WSRG and Weller point the way towards a much clearer formulation. The society–community question starts from the assumption that the two are distinct types of social relationship that are almost always co-located and strongly interactive, but with no clear pattern of determination running in either direction about what causes what. In this form, the question is structured similarly to the English school's triad which also features different social forms existing simultaneously with a strong but indeterminate relationship.

The last of the sociological approaches to world society might be labelled *macro-sociology*. As various writers have noted, it is possible to locate a substantial amount of Marxian thinking in a world society frame (Vincent 1978: 29–30, 44; WSRG 2000: 3–4), and others fit into this group as well. The key linking this group together is the idea of a dominant organising principle for a macro-level world society. The notion of a central organising principle as the key to structure is familiar in IR through the work of Waltz particularly, but also realists generally, and the English school, and more recently Wendt (1999). But whereas in IR the focus is almost always on the political order, macro-sociologists take a wider, more multisectoral, view. Marxians have their own version of an already existing world society defined by a capitalist mode of production and the hierarchy of classes structured in the centre–periphery formation made famous by the world system theory of Wallerstein. In its cruder forms, the idea of a capitalist world society pits the forces of capital against the state, creating a structure of dominance, dependency and conflict. With the movement to 'bring the state back in' by recognising its relative autonomy, Marxian thinking, and also much mainstream IPE, took on the appearance of a holistic world society view. This was consciously offered as an alternative to, and 'critical' view of, the state-centric mainstream of IR theory. Cox (1986, 1994), Strange (1988) and Underhill (2000) all talk about the close interlinkage of states and markets, and try to unfold a conceptualisation that expresses the simultaneous interplay of political, economic and social forces.

Perhaps the work of this type that makes the most explicit use of world society is Jung (2001). Jung is amongst the holists who want to use world society to capture the whole human system. His key organising principle, reminiscent of Gellner (1988), is the distinction between tradition and modernity as a fundamental watershed in the organisation of human society. This distinction bears some relationship to that between community (tradition) and society (modernity). For Jung, the tension between traditional social forms and rational social action is not only a historical divide, but an ongoing dynamic in a world which is not yet modern, but still an uneasy mix of modern and traditional social structures. Like Shaw, Jung rejects the English school's normative integration criteria for society as too demanding, wanting instead to understand society as 'the totality of social reproduction' (Jung 2001: 452).

The macro-sociological way of thinking is undeniably powerful and attractive. Reducing the entirety of the interhuman system to a single organising principle offers not only a seductive simplification, but also the possibility of designing deductive theory stemming from the single idea. The danger is oversimplification, with the consequent need, as the Marxians discovered, to bring things back in. More specialised approaches to world society, like that of the English school, cannot compete with the sweep of the single encompassing idea. But by embedding some key differentiations early on, they avoid the danger of oversimplification, and retain a more detailed analytical toolkit.

Global civil society

Even though it does not deploy the term 'world society', one other school of thought requires close consideration here: the discourse about *global civil society*. Both world society and global civil society (GCS) highlight the political dimension of the non-state universe, and both also carry a liberal programme aimed at constraining and/or reforming state power. Both therefore share two problems: how to define the content of the non-state universe; and how to handle the tensions between the needs of activists pursuing a normative agenda on the one hand, and those of analysts needing a concept with which to capture the non-state, deterritorialised elements in world politics on the other. These problems are linked, and examining the better-developed GCS debate throws useful light on how to develop the world society concept. Activists are constrained not only by their campaigning needs, but also by a dual meaning inherent in 'civil', to define GCS in ways that construct it as nice. Doing so raises two questions: (1) how to handle the dark side of the non-state world represented by various kinds of organised extremists and criminals; and (2) how to handle the global economy and its non-state actors (whether as part of GCS or as one of its targets). Analysts need a concept that captures the non-state political universe, whether nice or nasty. The argument is that the needs of activists and analysts may well be irreconcilable. The debates around these concepts have roots in classical ideological divisions. Until recently, they opened a divide between economic and social liberals, but with the rise of concern about terrorism, they may return to a much older and deeper clash between liberal and conservative views of the relationship between state and society.

The two concepts share a common foundation in the tradition of liberal thinking about civil society, which stretches back to the eighteenth century. The English school's concept of world society can be understood as perhaps the first systematic attempt to lift the liberal conceptualisation of civil society based on individualism and the right of association out of the state, and place it alongside international society as part of a toolkit for understanding the international system. It was in this sense more ambitious than the Kantian idea of an eventual convergence amongst republican states, from which it mistakenly took its label. It was also distinct from both early liberal versions of civil society, and Marxian reactions to them, that linked civil society closely to the social structures of capitalism, the liberals positively, the Marxians negatively (Alexander 1998). If world society shared anything with the Marxians, it was the attempt to question, and possibly transcend, the dominant framework of states and nations as the defining entities at the international level.

The liberal idea of civil society always carried some cosmopolitan assumptions about civilised communities separate from, and transcending, the framework of states, and having distinct social and/or legal codes (Lipschutz 1996: 106–9). But the main thrust of civil society was at the domestic level, counterpointing the state, though at the same time being deeply entangled with it. Depending on one's view of human nature, the state might be seen in Hobbesian terms, as a necessary condition for civil society (because civil society is dependent for its own functioning on the defended civil space created by the state), or as irrelevant, or even obstructive, to civil society (because human beings are perfectly capable of forming societies without an oppressive Leviathan).

Hobbes was pretty radical for his day, and is claimed as a founder both by conservatives (for the necessity of the state) and liberals (for his emphasis on individualism and a disarmed civil society). For him, the Leviathan state was necessary to contain the anarchic and violent qualities of an ungoverned (and uncivil) society (the war of each against all). The assumption was that unless constrained by a superior power, human society lacks the ability to regulate itself and falls into thuggery and warlordism. Later (eighteenth-century and onward) liberal thinking starts both from a more positive view of human nature, giving better prospects for uncoerced cooperation, and from a sharp historical consciousness that Leviathan has often been a profoundly flawed saviour, itself generating unacceptable amounts of violence and repression. In this view, if humans were properly educated, and left more to themselves, both a more efficient political economy, and a more 'civil' society, would be the probable outcome. The civil society tradition reflects not only an analytical distinction between state and non-state modes of social organisation, but a deep and longstanding ideological battle between conservative and liberal understandings of the human condition, and views about how best to achieve the good life.

Civil society thus has descriptive functions (that which is not the state, where 'civil' takes its meaning from 'civilian'), and normative ones (still non-state, but where 'civil' takes its meaning more from 'civilised', representing a particular preferred form of social order). In descriptive mode, civil society is neutral about whether what composes it is good, or bad, or some mixture. Those with a conservative view of human nature will tend to see civil society as the problem (because the power-seeking, ruthless and self-interested nature of human beings generates conflict, criminality, injustice, inequality) and the state as the solution (by imposing disarmament and enforced laws). Those with a more liberal view of human nature see the state as the problem (because nothing constrains its monopoly of force, which is therefore too frequently abused), and civil society as the solution because of the natural sociability of humans and their rational tendency to seek joint gains (in the less radical version as an organised democratic counterweight that can constrain the state and keep it minimal; in the more radical version as an alternative to the state).

This normative side of civil society is both a great strength and a main weakness. It is a strength, because it opens up powerful opportunities for political mobilisations both within the state (aimed at redefining the relationship between citizens and government) and outside it (possibly with the same aim of reforming the state, possibly aimed at bypassing and superseding the state). In this mode, civil society had its most recent airing in the last decades of the Cold War, when both state and non-state actors in the West cultivated the emergence of civil society within the Soviet bloc as a way of undermining the totalitarian control and social atomisation that was the key to the power of communist parties (Lipschutz 1996: 103). Both state and non-state actors in the West, and non-state actors in the East, aimed at reforming the communist states by changing the balance within them between civil society and government. Some of the non-state actors in the West also aimed at reforming the Western states, which they saw as at least equally responsible for generating the Cold War and the threat of nuclear obliteration of humankind (Burke forthcoming).

The problem with defining civil society in this normative, politically activist, way is that it almost inevitably opens up a gap between what is incorporated in the wider descriptive meaning, and what is incorporated in the narrower normative one. In descriptive mode, civil society equates with 'non-state', and therefore includes mafias, pornography merchants and a host of other dark-side entities as well as the nicer side of civil society. There is of course plenty of room for disagreement about what counts as nice, and what nasty: religious organisations, or terrorists, or drug dealers might be placed in either camp according to individual taste. There is a substantial grey zone occupied, for example, by those prepared to use nasty means (violence against the property and staff of abortion clinics and research facilities that use live animals) for 'good' ends. But regardless of either disagreements or grey zones, it remains the case that a normative understanding of civil society will almost inevitably represent only a partial selection of what exists in the non-state world. Therefore, if the term civil society is used in this narrower way, it cannot avoid both casting civil society as nice, and leaving a vacuum about what term is to be used analytically to label the whole of the non-state social world.

The shift to global civil society as a primary focus occurred during the 1990s, and in one sense can be seen as a result of the stunning intellectual and political victory of liberalism represented by the end of the Cold War and the ideological collapse of communism (Fukuyama 1992). With the communist Leviathan routed, and democracy spreading, two changes became apparent. First, and demonstrated in part by the role played by transnational civil society forces in the victory against communism, it was clear that both the power of GCS and its scope for operation had increased. A more liberal-democratic system of states wound down the significance of national borders as barriers to many (not all) types of interaction, and in doing so opened up substantial transnational economic, societal, legal and political space in which non-state actors could operate. This development was already under way during the Cold War, with many firms and some INGOs moving into transnational space. But the ending of the Cold War gave neoliberal ideology more scope to blow away geopolitical barriers, both opening up new areas for non-state actors and giving them more leeway in areas already open.

The second change resulting from the ending of the Cold War was that with the spread of democratic states, the domestic agenda of civil society versus Leviathan became less relevant, at least within core areas of Western civilisation. It remained relevant in parts of the third world, but there the problem was as much the failure of states as it was the impositions of overbearing Leviathans. Failed states provided a new arena for the transnational vanguard of GCS in the form of aid and development INGOs. Where there were still repressive Leviathans posing political and/or cultural barriers to civil society, the issue was no longer largely one between particular states and their citizens, but between such states and coalitions of transnational and domestic civil society forces.

The ending of the Cold War thus strengthened both the descriptive and the normative aspects of what was now referred to as 'global civil society'. In the descriptive sense, GCS was a kind of synonym for globalisation. It captured the general understanding that non-state actors, entities and structures of all sorts were a more influential part of international relations than they had been during the Cold War. TNAs of all stripes were now out there, some of them enabled by the liberal character of the leading states, some of them enabled by the political vacuums opening up where failed states were tearing holes in the fabric of international society. Not everyone agreed that this added up to global civil society: Peterson (1992: 388), for example, seeing instead 'strongly connected national civil societies living in a system of many states'. But most analysts, whether or not they advocated the continued primacy of the state, were happy to concede that the transnational domain was uncommonly lively, and there was little doubt that GCS in this sense was making a difference to international norms and rules through successful campaigns on issues ranging from landmines and famine relief, through debt and terms of trade, to human rights and the environment.

But, in the normative sense, and in an ironic twist, a substantial part of the newly confident political forces of GCS constructed 'globalisation', mainly seen as the operation of neoliberal global capitalism, as their principal target. The most prominent public manifestation of GCS in the decade after the implosion of the Soviet Union was an anti-globalisation movement that bundled together a diverse transnational coalition ranging from environmentalists and humanitarians, through various kinds of cultural nationalists and socialists, to outright anarchists. Rather than pitching liberals against conservatives, this move opened up the split always present in liberalism between economic liberals (who put the market first, and see it as the key to delivering the other goods on the liberal agenda) and social ones (who start from individualism and human rights, and are much less tolerant of the inequalities generated by un-constrained operation of markets) (McKinlay and Little 1986).

The development of an anti-globalisation global civil society is rich with contradictions, and highly instructive for any attempt to understand the English school's concept of world society. Among other things, many of the transnational actors that compose GCS are in alliance with, employed by, funded by, and sometimes even created by, states and/or state dominated IGOs (Risse 2002). If globalisation is understood superficially to be a neoliberal alliance of state and corporate elites, then the opposition to it of GCS makes sense. Globalisation is posed either as a conspiracy, or as a set of impersonal structural forces. In the hope of maintaining the engine of growth, state elites rejig legal and political frameworks to facilitate the operation of capital. Corporate elites promise economic efficiency and growth, and fatten themselves at the expense of workers, the environment and civil society at large. In this reading, GCS is an activist manifesto picking up the Marxian tradition. As Anheier, Glasius and Kaldor (2001: 15) note, GCS 'has increasingly occupied the emancipatory space left by the demise of socialism and national liberation'. This means that it often comes in the clothes of an aspirational left oppositional project aimed at creating a third force to resist both the states-system and global capitalism.

Partly because it is a carrier of this ideological energy, the definition of GCS remains hotly contested, and not just in the details, but in the basic conceptualisation. The narrower, more political, understanding is rooted in the Gramscian understanding of civil society as a social force standing between state and market, and attempting to call their power to account. Anheier, Glasius and Kaldor (2001: 17) define it as 'the sphere of ideas, values, institutions, organisations, networks and individuals located between the family, the state and the market and operating beyond the confines of national societies, polities and economies'. Tacked onto this is the idea that GCS is nice, because it rests on ideas of trust and non-violence, and carries a commitment to 'common human values that go beyond ethnic, religious or national boundaries' (Anheier, Glasius and Kaldor 2001: 15). This definition feels close to what must have been in the minds of Bull (1977), and up to a point, Vincent (1986) and his followers, when they talked of world society. It rests on the same idea of individuals and non-state organisations as carriers of values in opposition to the impositions of a state-created Westphalian international society. This view of GCS, however, is more clearly formulated than the English school's concept of world society, particularly so in relation to the economic sector. English school thinkers have been largely silent about the economic sector, and it could be inferred from that silence that they agree with the political proponents of GCS in differentiating the two in order to exclude the economic from the civil.

But on a deeper reading of globalisation, GCS is itself part of the process. Capitalism is a principal mover in the process of globalisation, but not the only one, and not necessarily the principal definition of what globalisation is about. In this reading, interestingly prefigured by Rosenau (1990), the key is the development of 'powerful people' and a consequent across-the-board shift in the nature of authority structures and political relationships. Starting from the industrial revolution, it has served the interests of both state and capital to have better-educated, healthier and wealthier citizens and workers. Only by improving the capacities of their citizens/workers could the state increase its power and capital increase its returns. But as more and more individuals have become more capable, they have become less subservient to authority, more willing to define their own agendas, and more able to create their own nodes and networks in pursuit of those agendas. This development underpinned the flowering of Western democracy during the twentieth century, and has a certain teleological force. The question is not only the happy liberal one of what happens if democratising and decentralising forces begin seriously to transcend the state, but also, post 11 September, the darker Hobbesian one of what happens if 'powerful people' express themselves by organising crime and pursuing extremist agendas?

Rosenau's scheme (1990: 40) generates an international system divided between 'sovereignty-bound' and 'sovereignty-free' actors whose fate depends on both the balance of power between the two worlds, and, with echoes of the Stanford school's approach, on whether or not they agree or differ on what the prevailing norms of the system should be. This comes very close to the English school's division between international and world society, and reflects the same dilemma about whether the two are in tension or in harmony. It reflects a complex interplay among political, economic and social structures in which a strong historical line of development is changing the capabilities and requirements of all kinds of actors simultaneously. Since capitalism is immensely effective at stimulating and spreading technological innovation, this whole package is pushed and pulled by opportunities and dangers arising from new technological capabilities. Powers of destruction become so great that total war becomes absurd, and the planetary environment moves from being a background constant to a foreground variable. Powers of communication become so widespread, and so cheap, that geography no longer determines the shape of community, and the world becomes a single information space. Powers of transportation become so efficient and so dense that the world becomes a single market, and interdependence effects ripple easily from one end of the planet to the other. In this wider view of globalisation, GCS cannot be separated from capitalism and can only be understood as part of it. GCS exists through, between and around states rather than just within them. Rather than being counterpointed against a global state, as civil society sometimes was against the territorial state, it is itself part of and entangled with a loose and rather hazy structure of global governance. This structure has been generated mostly by the leading capitalist states, but now has a quasi-autonomous standing.

A recent reflection on this wider, more analytical, understanding of global civil society is offered by John Keane (2001). He rejects the Gramscian separation of civil society from the economic sector on the grounds that this generates a major misunderstanding of what GCS is and how it works. Like Rosenau, he sees the global economy as part of GCS, with 'turbo-capitalism' as one of the driving forces underpinning it:

> the contemporary thickening and stretching of networks of socio-economic institutions across borders to all four corners of the earth, such that peaceful or 'civil' effects of these non-governmental networks are felt everywhere . . . It comprises . . . organisations, civic and business initiatives, coalitions, social movement, linguistic communities and cultural identities. All of them . . . deliberately organise themselves and conduct their cross-border social activities, business, and politics outside the boundaries of governmental structures, with a minimum of violence and a maximum of respect for the principle of civilised power-sharing among different ways of life.
>
> (Keane 2001: 23–4)

Keane's more comprehensive definition fleshes out an understanding of GCS that goes much further towards filling the non-state side of a state/non-state distinction. He correctly points out that there is no sharp line between state and non-state (Keane 2001: 35). Within democratic states there are numerous quasi-autonomous non-governmental organisations (QUANGOs) that blur the boundary, and during the Cold War communist states were notorious for constructing short-leash versions of QUANGOs such as the various official peace councils. Similarly, at the global level many INGOs receive support and funding from governments, whether they be humanitarian aid organisations or various forms of ideological fifth column. The Red Cross, for example, is closely integrated into the states-system as a key supporter for some aspects of international law. Keane seems absolutely right in insisting that the non-state dimension cannot be understood without incorporating the economic sector, even though doing so necessarily wrecks some of the emancipatory political agenda that the activists want to pin on to the concept.

But although Keane's definition is more analytical, he does not wholly abandon the political project. Keane is also committed to the idea that GCS is nice, in the sense of committed to non-violence, civility and tolerance. His incorporation of the economic sector, however, makes it difficult for him to maintain coherence on this issue. Although he rightly points out that the corporate world by and large supports the value of non-violence in the interests of business efficiency, he also concedes that 'Inequalities of power, bullying, and fanatical, violent attempts to de-globalise are chronic features of global civil society' (Keane 2001: 33, 39). This hints strongly, though it does not explore, that there is a dark side to global civil society. Keane (2001: 40) is also rightly aware that GCS does not stand above the grimy issues of force and coercion. Because it is vulnerable to ruthless uncivil elements, whether state-based or not, GCS needs protection, and can most easily acquire it from states. On the grounds that 'civil' carries two meanings (non-state, and civilised) both Keane (although he comes closer to acknowledging it), and Anheier, Glasius and Kaldor, marginalise the dark side of the non-state world from their definitions of GCS. If the narrower and/or nicer view of GCS is accepted, then for analytical purposes one would need a parallel concept of global uncivil society to cover what has been left out of the non-state picture. This would be true whether or not one's purpose was primarily analytical or primarily political. The existence of such uncivil society, and the need to contain it, is of course the prime (Hobbesian) justification for the existence of the state, and by extension also for the existence of an international society created and maintained by states. Nothing could illustrate this more clearly than the terrorist attacks on the US on 11 September 2001.

The dark side of the non-state world is a problem for the advocates of both global civil society and world society. The GCS school, especially its activist wing, is stuck with the nice meaning of 'civil', which pushes it towards regarding the non-state as inherently a good thing. It does not take a vast amount of empirical research to demonstrate that both the benign and the malign views of civil society are incorrect as characterisations of the whole non-state world. In reality, there is always a mixture of the two. The 'nice', non-violent side of civil society both domestic and global is to be found everywhere in voluntary associations, NGOs, INGOs and firms. But the nasty side is everywhere too, in the form of crime, hoodlum anarchism and self-righteous extremists of all stripes. The anti-globalisation movement has run up against this in the form of its anarchist wing, which is useful at generating media attention, but destructive to its political image. The neoliberal-driven globalisation of the last decade also has to come to terms with the consequence that opening borders for commerce is a boon to organised criminals and extremists. Indeed, after the events of 11 September, there is firm ground for expecting that the politics of global civil society/world society will shift away from economic versus social liberal, and back more into the frame of liberal versus conservative. Al-Qaeda has highlighted the dark side of global (un)civil society, and in doing so has strengthened the Hobbesian case for the state, and/or international society, as a necessary defence against the disorders of an underregulated human condition.

Because GCS rests on the same distinction between state and non-state as does world society, there are many useful lessons here for English school thinking. The GCS literature has a better developed view of the economic sector than can be found in English school thinking. Its normative commitments run in parallel to the solidarist wing of the English school, but in principle the English school is better placed to take into account the dark side of the non-state world. First, its concept of world society is not restricted to 'civil' and therefore has an easier time in incorporating the whole of the non-state world. Second, it is less focused on transnational actors, and therefore better placed to deal with the non-state identity components of world politics such as Islam. Islam is an excellent example of a world society element that is not in itself a transnational actor. It is a non-state identity that does not have actor quality itself, but which carries a mobilising power that enables a range of non-state (and state) actors. When it mobilises terrorism, it is a much stronger challenge to international society than human rights, because it privatises the use of force, thus undermining the foundations of the Westphalian political order. Third, world society is better adapted to thinking about the global level, having originally been designed for that purpose. GCS is still hung about with many of the political trappings carried over from its roots in the debates about civil society. These make it an effective idea for activists, but a problematic one for analysts. Whatever their flaws, concepts such as GCS and world society are an essential part of the toolkit that we need to develop if we are to equip ourselves to think meaningfully about globalisation. If this discussion highlights anything, it is the necessity to encompass the whole of the non-state political universe when trying to conceptualise the politics of globalisation.

Conclusions

Setting this review of concepts of world society from outside the English school against the English school's discussion of world society reviewed in chapter 2, the lessons for any attempt to rethink world society can be summed up as follows.

- There is a need to take a position on whether 'world' means all types of social relations or just the non-state universe, and whether it has to mean global in extent, or can apply to sub-global levels. There are two contrary pressures on this decision: first, the advantages of coining a single concept to encompass a whole sphere of activity, and second, the dangers of creating an overburdened idea into which too many things get thrown, and which loses the analytical power of drawing distinctions.
- There is a need to take a position on how 'society' is understood, whether in a weaker sense, close to what is generally meant by 'system' in IR, or whether in the stronger sense of shared values and identities from classical sociology.
- In conjunction with the previous point, there is a need to take seriously the distinction between society and community and the interrelation-ship(s) between them, and to investigate the implication of thinking in this way for international and world society, both separately, and in how they relate to each other. In this context, there is also a need to think about whether there can be a global community given the need for an 'Other' against which to define a 'We'.
- There is a need to be aware of the tensions between the analytical and activist uses of concepts, both in terms of the inevitable normative implications of any analytical construct of 'society' or 'world', and the inevitable costs to descriptive accuracy of any activist application of these concepts.
- There is a need to take into account the dark side as well as the nice aspects of the non-state world, and to understand that society is just as easily a site for conflict as it is a site for peace and harmony.

My own response to these points is two-fold. First, I take the message that we need to look closely at all of the key terms in English school theory with a view to clarifying meanings. This is especially so for the three concepts that make up the English school's triad, and for pluralism and solidarism. Second, I want to move away from any attempt to lump too much together under a single heading. The rather sorry condition of the globalisation debate stands as a warning against creating undifferentiated concepts, and in my view the English school's rendition of world society is running the same risk. I have no problem with holism, but I want the 'whole' to be composed of analytically distinct parts whose operation and interaction become the subject of study. Wholes that subsume everything within them have the same attractions and the same drawbacks as the idea of god – they explain everything and nothing. Even if one rejects the move of the Vincentians (and Luard, Burton, Shaw, many Marxians, and the WSRG) of aggregating states into world society, there is probably still too much in the world society box. As currently constructed in both English school and some other formulations, it contains both the physical interaction and socially constructed sides without these being clearly distinguished along international system/international society lines. Within the socially constructed side it contains both the *Gesellschaft* (society) and *Gemeinschaft* (community) elements, which seem deserving of analytical distinction, though also tied together in complicated ways. And it also contains the individual-cosmopolitan-communitarian element of identities on one side, and the world of transnational actors on the other.

My inclinations lean towards the strategy of Rosenau and Bull, which is to find the point of interest in the balance between the state and the non-state worlds. In the distant future, the state may well have become obsolete, and humankind may find itself organised in some deterritorialised neomedieval form. In the meantime, we seem to be in the presence of a shift away from a pure Westphalian mode of international relations, in which the key tension is among rival states. For now, and for some decades to come, the interesting question is about how the state and the non-state worlds do and will interact with each other. What makes this question interesting is more than just shifts in the distribution of power, or immediate relevance to real world events. On top of these is the deep and excruciating tension between the state and non-state worlds. In some ways, they are deeply antagonistic, both in concept and in practice. In other ways, they are deeply interdependent, again both in concept and in practice. This tension, it seems to me, is the big political question of our time, and in order to get at it analytically, it is vital to keep the two worlds conceptually distinct.

The next stage of this enquiry is to take the lessons learned in this chapter, and use them to unpack and remake the contents not just of world society, but also of international society, and indeed the English school's whole classical triad as set out in figure 1.

4   Reimagining the English school's triad

The survey in chapter 3 exposed four underlying conceptual dyads on which much of the discussion (and the confusion) about international and world society hang:

- state and non-state levels, and whether or not the distinction between them is what defines the difference between international and world society;
- physical (or mechanical) and social concepts of system, and whether the distinction along these lines between 'international system' and 'international society' should be retained, and/or carried over into one between 'world system' and 'world society';
- society and community, and whether or not these two conceptions of social relations need to play a larger role in thinking about both international and world society, and what the implications of their doing so are for understanding pluralism and solidarism;
- individuals and transnational actors as the units of analysis that define world society, and whether or not they can comfortably be considered together, or whether more analytical leverage is acquired by keeping them distinct.

The choices posed by these dyads need to be made explicit, and to be resolved in some way, before any clear sense can be made of English school theory as a social structural project. For the reasons given above, my starting position will be to reject the inclinations of the Vincentians and many of the non-English school users of world society, to construct world society in holistic terms that combine the state and non-state into a kind of higher, or better developed, social form. Instead, I will proceed from the position that state and non-state represent distinct social domains that are simultaneously mutually supporting and in tension with each other. This is the chapter in which I begin to redefine some established terms and to introduce new vocabulary.

State and non-state

I have already committed myself to defending this distinction, so what has to be done here is to deepen the explanation for this move, and to support it against alternative interpretations.

English school theory is based on the idea that there is something special and unique about the state (or more generally about any sort of 'independent political community') that justifies giving it a prominent and distinctive role in the conceptualisation of international relations. In English school theory, both international system and international society are concepts built around the state as the defining unit. So the first, and in some ways most important, step in bringing the concept of world society into focus, is to establish the desirability, and in terms of a structural presentation of English school theory, the necessity, of making a sharp separation between state and international society on the one hand, and non-state and world society on the other. On this point, I intend to defend a position close to that of Bull, and up to a point, James and Jackson. Any conflation of state and non-state will effectively destroy the analytical leverage of the English school's triad, and create an unmanageable object of analysis in the name of holism. There is nothing unusual in privileging the state in this way. It remains special because of its central role in the processes of law, organised violence, taxation, political legitimacy, territoriality and in some ways social identity. This view is of course central to all forms of political realism. There are many other routes, including the English school, to the same conclusion. Marxians, historical sociologists and IPE have all 'brought the state back in', the Stanford school reaches the same conclusion from a more legal and normative perspective, as does Brown (1995: 105–6) discussing world community from the perspective of political theory.

Controversy rightly attends this privileging of the state if it is taken, as some realists do, to the extreme of excluding all other types of actors from the definition of the international system (or world politics, or world system or globality . . .). That is not my intention. Rather, I want to preserve the distinctive idea of a society of states in order to acknowledge the special role of the state in the overall picture of human social relations, while at the same time acknowledging the significance of other elements (cosmopolitanism, TNAs) in that picture. In the

English school triad, international system and international society capture the distinctiveness of the state, while world society is the vehicle for bringing the non-state elements into the picture. In other words, while there is no doubt that significant deterritorialisation has taken place in human affairs, territory remains a crucial factor for many key aspects of humankind's social, economic and especially political structures. If I am right in accepting Rosenau's (1990) argument that the central political question of our time is the working out of a new balance between the territorial and the non-territorial modes of human organisation, then it is vital to keep the territorial element in clear focus.

Differentiating between state and non-state places an immediate burden on definitions. What counts as a state? On this issue I intend to stick with the traditions in most realism, historical sociology, and the English school – note the latter's phrase 'states (or . . . independent political communities)' – of taking a broad view. Realists understand the state through the idea that 'conflict groups' are 'the building blocks and ultimate units of social and political life' (Gilpin 1986: 305), and that interpretation enables them to see 'states' of one sort or another stretching back at least 5,000 years. The definition used in Buzan and Little (2000: 442) puts less emphasis on conflict, and will serve as my benchmark here: 'any form of post-kinship, territorially-based, politically centralized, self-governing entity capable of generating an inside-outside structure'. This notion of state takes in city-states and empires, kingdoms, republics, various forms of national state, and the late modern (or in some view postmodern) states emerging in the twenty-first century. Its emphasis is on the political and the territorial, though it does not require either sovereignty (Paul 1999) or hard boundaries, both of which are quite recent inventions. Using a broad definition like this means that one should expect to find much variation in the character and institutions of international society, depending on what sort of 'state' is dominant (more on this in chapter 6).

One tricky part in this approach comes in setting values for 'independent' and 'politically centralised' and 'inside/outside'. On a generous reading, the EU or the later Holy Roman Empire might count as 'states' under this definition, raising the awkward problem of having two sorts of entity in the same territory, and therefore at least two layers of inside/outside. In the case of the EU, its political centralisation is weak, but it is definitely independent, territorial and capable of generating an inside-outside structure. Similar problems arise for various types of dominion or commonwealth or protectorate, where independence is not total, but sufficient. Other sorts of mixed entities, combining political with other elements, such as the chartered companies of the seventeenth century, or the Roman church in some periods, also pose boundary problems, raising another tricky question about how to draw the line between what counts as part of the state, and what counts as non-state. In most postmodern states there are substantial numbers of QUANGOs sitting on the boundary between the two. There are also IGOs, on which I take the position set out in Buzan and Little (2000: 266–7) that these are creations of the states-system, and for the most part best seen as part of social interaction capacity. Different analysts might well want to reach different conclusions about exactly where to draw the line in such cases. But these are familiar problems of classification in the social sciences. With this definition the general location of the line is clear enough, and the contents of the inevitable grey zone between state and non-state relatively tightly constrained.

A firm analytical separation between state and non-state, however drawn, has some substantial consequences for the English school triad. In terms of Bull and Wight, it means two things. First, Kantianism almost certainly has to move out of the world society section and into the solidarist end of international society. Bull's case against doing this (reviewed in chapter 2) is unconvincing. As Jackson (2000: 180) notes, Kantianism is based on increasing homogeneity in the domestic structures of states with a liberal international society becoming the supporting framework for cosmopolitan values. Its key idea, important also to the Vincentians, is that a convergence in the dominant domestic social values of states will generate a solidarist international society amongst them. Since this is about a form of solidarist (as opposed to Westphalian, pluralist) states-system, it has to count as a species of thick international society, and not a type of world society. Second, a pretty strong case emerges for moving the coercive universalism element of revolutionism (i.e. unifying the world by force) into the imperial end of the realist spectrum. Unipolarity is, after all, the extreme position on the realist spectrum (Hansen 2000). State-based seekers after imperial power or world domination will, if they are efficient, almost always carry a universalist ideology to justify their claims, and in social structural terms, this seems to belong in the realist domain more than to world society.

These moves mark a sharp departure from the Wightian understanding of world society. Moving Kantianism and coercive universalism out of the world society pillar might be thought to do violence to the Wightian conception of revolutionism as historically operating ideas that work to challenge the states-system. In one sense, such a move does reflect the priorities of a structural approach as opposed to a political theory one, and the normative drive of Wight's scheme is sacrificed. But, on second look, the contradiction is perhaps more apparent than real. The baseline for Wight's discussion was not the states-system *per se*, but the particular pluralist, Westphalian, form of it that dominated modern history. Because his view of a states-system was quite narrowly cast, the scope for revolutionism was large. A less realist view of the state makes more room for evolutions of states-systems into different types. Wight's ideas remain in play, but they are located and understood differently.

At this stage of the argument, the separation between state and non-state has two consequences for those working in Vincent's tradition. First, for now, it requires rejecting their move to use world society as a term to cover the merger of state and non-state. This rejection is not done on descriptive or normative grounds, and it does not mean that the human rights issues they want to examine cannot or should not be a prominent feature of English school work. The rejection is done on analytical grounds, and simply means that their agenda needs to be looked at in terms of the interplay between international and world society on human rights (more on this below). Second, a more analytical approach to the concept of the state creates a tension with those in the solidarist tradition who want to insert into the definition of states that they 'only exist to promote the welfare and security of their citizens' (Dunne 2001b: 7). With the quite broad definition of state given above, most states in history would not comply with this highly liberal view, yet would be perfectly capable of being members of international society. As discussed in chapter 3, society is not necessarily nice in a moral sense, and neither is the state. Dunne's move is part of a normative argument aimed at shifting the contemporary foundations on which the juridical side of sovereignty is based. It is an aspirational 'ought' seeking to become an actual 'is', and aimed at promoting the development of a particular type of state (liberal democratic) within a particular type of liberal solidarist international society. But states can and do have many other purposes, and they can be members of some types of international society even when their concerns for the welfare and security of their citizens are low. I do not want to lose sight of all of these other possibilities in international society by taking on an excessively liberal, or even modern, view of what gets defined as a state.

If the state sector is to be treated as distinctive, and as embodied in the concepts of international system and international society, then it

follows that English school theory has to take a keen interest in the evolving character of both the state, and sovereignty as the defining concept
of the state. In this sense, Dunne and the Vincentians are quite right to
focus on these issues. Unlike neorealism, which largely confines itself to
the international system pillar, takes an essentialist view of sovereignty
and makes system structure dominant over the units, English school
theory is much more inside-out, than outside-in. International society
is constructed by the units, and particularly by the dominant units, in
the system, and consequently reflects their domestic character (Hollis
and Smith 1991: 95). In this sense, Wendt's (1992) view that 'anarchy is
what states make of it' is a restatement of the English school's general
position. English school theory, especially in the pluralist versions of
Bull and Jackson, accepts as true for international society the neorealist
injunction that international systems are largely defined by the dominant units within them, but it does not follow neorealism in presetting
the character of states. This being so, the English school needs to be particularly interested in the evolution of the leading modern states from
absolutist to nationalist to democratic to postmodern, charting the impact on international society of these domestic transformations (Buzan
and Little 2000: 243–75). It must also be interested in the question of
sovereignty, not as a static concept but as an evolving institution of modern international society. Any solidarist/progressive view of international society requires sharp moves away from essentialist conceptions
of what sovereignty is and how it works. As the case of the EU illustrates,
thick international societies have to unpack and redistribute elements
of sovereignty. English school theory needs to understand all of this
better than it now does. Bull saw solidarism as problematic because of
its incompatibility with the Westphalian state. A more flexible approach
sees it as part and parcel of how the postmodern state is itself evolving.
It does not go too far to say that both postmodern states and premodern, weak, ones may only be sustainable within strong international
societies.

In defending a state/non-state approach to international and world
society I have claimed to be building on Bull's thinking. But it is possible to read Bull to support a different, and more Vincentian, interpretation than mine of the international/world society distinction.[1] In this
argument, Bull derives the international versus world society distinction from his inquiry into world order. Bull saw the state as the main

---

[1] I am grateful to Stefano Guzzini and Ole Wæver for this insight.

present and future supplier of such world order as was obtainable, and world society as a potential threat to this through its questioning of sovereignty in pursuit of human rights objectives. Vincent's jumble of ideas about world society also contained a formulation that set world society as the excluded and oppositional voices to the Westphalian order, and this view links back to Wight's understanding of revolutionism as ideas opposed to the existing interstate order. Staying within Bull's focus on international order, but adding to it some of the globalist views about the roles of non-state actors, it is possible to construct a Bullian, and in some ways a Vincentian, argument that the providers of world order are now not just states, but states plus the whole array of IGOs and INGOs that provide and support global governance (Boli and Thomas 1999: 1–48; Keck and Sikkink 1998: 199–217; Risse-Kappen 1995b; Held *et al.* 1999). In this view, the Red Cross and Amnesty International, and the WHO, the WTO and the IAEA, are as much providers of world order as are states. This way of thinking supposes (rightly) that history has moved on, and that the sources of international order have evolved substantially since Bull was observing the international system (Hurrell 2002: xv–xxii). It also supposes (perhaps more arguably) that Bull's commitment to the order problematique would have opened his eyes to this if he were looking at the twenty-first-century world. In this perspective, international society is represented not just by states, but by 'Davos culture' comprising both the dominant structure of ordering ideas, and all of the providers of order within that framework, whether states, IGOs or INGOs. World society then becomes more Wightian, comprising the set of political ideas that can be used to mobilise opposition to this hegemonic consensus, and the set of actors, whether states, IGOs or INGOs that promote such opposition.

The nub of the tension between this interpretation and mine is whether the focus of the differentiation between international and world society rests on the type of actor (state *vs.* non-state) or on attitude towards the dominant ideas and institutions of international/world order (supportive or opposed). Wight would almost certainly opt for the latter view, though as shown in chapter 2, his three traditions thinking never led him to any very clear conceptualisation of international and world society. Bull clearly leaned towards the distinction based on type of actor, being driven to do so by his rather narrow, Westphalian, interpretation of sovereignty. Whether he would change his mind now is a moot point, but a defensible hypothesis. Vincent was torn, leaning sometimes towards Wight, sometimes towards Bull. But in the end both

Vincent and his followers have opted for a solidarist vision in which they hope, via a kind of extended Kantian homogenisation based on liberal values, to reduce or eliminate the differences in attitude, so creating a world society in which states and non-state actors share a set of norms, rules and institutions.

It seems to me that trying to define the difference between international and world society on the basis of support for or opposition to the dominant order, while certainly viable, is a less interesting and less useful approach than the focus on types of unit. On technical grounds, the difficulties of trying to draw a line between state and non-state pale into insignificance compared to those posed by finding the boundary between opposition and support. On which side does one put reformers, and those who question and pressure from within? How does one deal with the large mass of indifference that is nearly always the third position in any political polarisation? Opposition to a dominant order is no doubt a deep and durable feature of human society, though its particular forms and intensities vary hugely across times and places. On analytical grounds I would argue that the distinction between territorial and non-territorial modes of organisation is just as deep and durable. Non-state actors represent an enduring feature of human social organisation that would exist even in a solidarist world. And as I hope to show below, keeping the state and the non-state distinct opens up analytical opportunities not available through the alternative approach for thinking about non-liberal types of international society. As I argued in chapter 1, this is not a zero-sum game. English school theory can support a number of different interpretations, and my hope is that setting out a structural interpretation will not only generate interesting insights in itself, but also stimulate and challenge the other interpretations to improve their act.

The consequences for the 'standard view' of English school theory set out in figure 1 of defining international and world society in terms of type of actor, are sketched in figure 2. This first step towards an explicitly structural interpretation of English school theory more or less leaves in place the international system and international society pillars of the triad. It moves Kantianism out of the world society pillar and into the international society one, and coercive universalism out of the world society pillar and into the international system one. Those two moves leave unclear what then defines the boundary zones between what remains in the world society pillar (non-state actors), and the other two pillars. That problem is confronted in the next section.

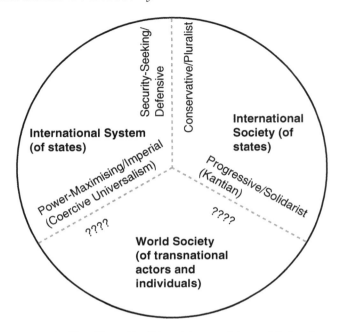

Figure 2. The 'Three Traditions' first revision: with the three pillars seen in structural terms and reserving world society to non-state units

Physical/mechanical and social concepts of system

Underpinning the idea of system in English school theory, and clearly evident in Bull and Watson's (1984b: 1) definition of international society, are two different modes of interaction: physical and social. I have already made some play with this distinction, pointing out the inconsistency of having it for the domain of states, but not for the domain of world society. Bull and Watson's definition is widely cited within the English school, and as far as I am aware has not been contested. Its distinction between international system and international society seems to rest on a separation of the physical system from the social one:

> a group of states (or, more generally, a group of independent politi-
> cal communities) which not merely form a system, in the sense that
> the behaviour of each is a necessary factor in the calculations of the
> others, but also have established by dialogue and consent common
> rules and institutions for the conduct of their relations, and recognise
> their common interest in maintaining these arrangements.

System here represents the physical mode of interaction typical of the mechanistic, realist-style analyses of the balance of power as an automatic process rooted in the relative material capabilities of states. The social side is minimally present through the element of 'calculation', though as will become clear further on in this chapter calculation could also underpin the common rules and institutions. The main social element is represented by the establishment and maintenance of common rules and institutions for the conduct of interstate relations. This distinction is deeply embedded in quite a bit of IR theory other than the English school, drawing the lines, for example, between the materialist theories of neorealism, and various institutionalist and constructivist approaches to understanding international order.

Despite its embeddedness in IR theory, it might nevertheless be argued that the distinction between physical and social is not nearly as interesting as it first appears. There is no doubt that taking a physical/mechanical view of international systems is one way of theorising about them, as the endless debates about polarity amongst both IR theorists and the policy community attest. As some readers will know, I have been and remain a participant in those debates myself. The point to be made here is that one can cover much of the ground claimed by physical theories such as neorealism from within a social structural theory, whereas the reverse move is not possible. The key to such an interpretation is the high degree of overlap between physical and social systems. All human social interaction presupposes the existence of physical interaction of some sort, and physical interaction without social content is, if not quite impossible, at least rather rare and marginal in human affairs (Almeida 2001). Alan James (1993) demonstrates in some detail that Bull's distinction between the two is shot through with ambiguities and difficulties, leading him to the conclusion that international system is a meaningless idea, and international society is the key concept. Taking a different tack, Jackson (2000: 113–16) interprets Bull's 'system' as not representing a physical, but a social (i.e. Hobbesian) interpretation to cover the domain of realism. Adam Watson (1987, 1990), though accepting Bull's distinction, is one of the few within the English school to have thought hard, and empirically, about the boundary between international system and international society that the distinction necessitates. His detailed agonisings over the difficulties of drawing it reinforce the idea that few physical interactions in international relations are without significant social content. He concludes definitively that: 'no international [i.e. in the terms used here 'physical'] system as defined by Bull has operated without some regulatory rules and institutions' (Watson 1987: 151–2).

Beyond the English school, most of the physical interactions which excite globalists and those promoting holistic conceptions of world society require significant social content. Everything from the internet to epistemic communities depends on some shared social background in order for communication to occur. The most primitive physical interactions such as trading practices (which go back a very long way in human history) require some basic social understanding about both the nature of the act and the relative values of different goods. Even war often reflects social agreements about honour, terms of surrender, treatment of the dead and suchlike. If all human interaction is in some sense social and rule-bound, then what results is not a distinction between international systems and international societies, but a spectrum of international societies ranging from weak, or thin or poorly developed, or conflictual, to strong, or thick or well developed or cooperative.

The one obvious direct exception to this rule, where asocial, purely physical, systems of interaction, can occur, is wars of extermination. Humans by and large do not negotiate with ants and termites, they simply try to destroy them, just as ants and termites sometimes try to destroy each other. Such asocial systems of interaction are mostly of interest to historians and/or science fiction fans. Looking backwards, the initial thirteenth-century encounters between the Mongols and the agrarian civilisations in China and the Middle East come about as close to being asocial as one can get. Instances of exterminism, where invaders treated the local inhabitants as vermin, can also be found in the records of European imperial expansion. Asocial systems and battles of extermination are much more common in the Manichaean structure of much popular science fiction, from H. G. Wells' *War of the Worlds*, to *Alien*, *Independence Day*, *Starship Troopers* and the 'Borg' episodes of *Star Trek*. The Borg greeting of 'Resistance is futile – you will be assimilated', hardly counts as social interaction. Where contact is direct, the assumption that asocial systems will necessarily be conflictual seems sound. War is the only interaction that can be carried on without any social development, and complete indifference seems unlikely in the presence of sustained contact. Direct asocial systems will therefore almost certainly be built around 'conflict groups'. Although rare, they do represent a possible form of physical international system. What is seen through some neorealist eyes as the mechanistic operation of the balance of power can also be interpreted as the behavioural characteristics of a particular type of social structure. If states understand themselves and their relations in what Wendt (1999) calls Hobbesian (enemy) or Lockean (rival) terms, then that type of social structure will broadly conform to realist expectations. Treating international systems as social does not rule out the options of materialist theory. It then becomes a hypothesis to explore whether material factors such as polarity shape the social world so strongly that they can act as reliable predictors for behaviour.

There is one other case where asocial systems are possible, but here the lack of sociality rests not on unwillingness to allow the existence of the other, but on limited interaction capacity. The defining case here is the Eurasian trading system that connected Han China and classical Rome. Significant quantities of goods moved between Rome and China, enough to make a noticeable impact on their economies (notably the drainage of specie from Rome). But this was relay trade. There was no direct contact between Rome and China. The goods moved along a series of trading stages, each one of which represented a social structure, but which did not provide any social connection between Rome and China. In this sense, Rome and China were part of a physical economic system even though each link in the chain was social (Buzan and Little 2000: 91–6).

If one treats these cases of pure wars of extermination and relay trading systems as marginal to the general pattern of modern international relations, then the argument for dissolving the distinction between physical and social systems as a major distinction within English school theory, and adopting James's reading of Bull, runs as follows: social interaction cannot occur without physical interaction, so for most practical purposes the two are bundled together. The key question is therefore not about the distinction between physical and social systems, but about how any physical–social system is structured. What is the dominant type of interaction? What are the dominant units? What is the distribution of capability? What is the interaction capacity of the system? What type of social structure is it, and how is it maintained?

Dissolving the distinction between physical and social systems, or at least downgrading it to what Wendt (1999: 109–38) calls 'rump materialism', helpfully removes the question discussed in earlier chapters about why there is no 'world system' as a counterpart to world society. Instead, it turns the spotlight on to whether English school theory needs to retain the distinction between international system and international society. It is important to reiterate that this move does not take the physical out of the analysis altogether. Physical elements such as the distribution of power, and the nature of interaction capacity remain central to the analysis of all social systems. What changes is that the physical aspect ceases to provide the principal basis for distinguishing one type of international system from another. Instead of thinking in a frame of two basic forms (international systems and international societies), this move pushes one inexorably down the path of seeking a classification scheme for a spectrum of types of international society, an idea already inherent in Wendt's (1992) famous proposition that 'anarchy is what states make of it'. English school theory contains some elements for such a scheme, but no systematic attempt. Wight (1977) explored the difference between states-systems and suzerain systems, and Watson (1990, 1992; Wæver 1996) continued that line with his pendulum theory about the spectrum from anarchy to empire, of centred to decentred international societies. In addition, the whole debate about pluralism and solidarism can be seen largely as a debate about types of international society, with the Westphalian model at the pluralist end, and something else, not very clearly specified, at the solidarist one (more on this in chapter 5). There is a sustained, but not all that systematic, attempt at a typology in Luard (1976), which runs parallel to English school thinking at many points.

Wendt (1999) has taken up his own challenge with a scheme for classifying what kind of socialisation a system has and how it is maintained. Usefully, Wendt's scheme runs in quite close parallel to the structural interpretation of English school theory that I am presenting here (see Suganami, 2001). Indeed, some of Wendt's conceptualisation, most notably his classification of three types of international social structure as 'Hobbesian', 'Lockean' and 'Kantian', are derived from the English school's three traditions, though Wendt's scheme is limited by being wholly state-based (no world society component). His social structures rest on the nature of the dominant roles in the system (or subsystem), respectively: enemy, rival and friend. However, from an English school perspective, it may well be the case that Wendt's most interesting contribution is his taking up of the issue of how norms and values – the building blocks of any sort of society – are internalised by the actors involved. In other words, Wendt shifts the focus from what the shared norms, rules and institutions are, and who shares them, to the means by which these norms are held in place as a form of social practice. As far as I am aware, this core issue of theory has not been raised specifically either in the English school or any other of the debates about world society, though it is often present implicitly. Wendt himself does not develop the idea very far. There is perhaps the beginning of an approach to it in Bull's concerns about what it is that creates compliance to international law, whether mere utilitarian calculus, or some more constitutive sense of legimacy about rules, or shared identity as part of a moral community (Alderson and Hurrell 2000: 31). But this lead has not been systematically followed up.

Wendt (1999: 247–50) offers three possibilities which he sees as both degrees, and modes, of internalisation: coercion, calculation and belief. Something close to this formulation is also present in Kratochwil's (1989: 97) much more complicated account, which talks of 'institutional sanctions' (Hobbes), 'rule-utilitarianism' (Hume), and 'emotional attachment' (Durkheim); in Hurd's (1999) set of coercion, self-interest and legitimacy as the determinants of social behaviour; and, with coercion excluded, in March and Olsen's (1998: 948–54) discussion of the bases of social action in terms of either a logic of expected consequences (= calculation) or a logic of appropriateness (= belief). In all of these schemes, the shallowest, and least stable, is coercion, when the social structure is essentially imposed by an outside power. A social structure built on this foundation is hardly internalised at all, and is unlikely to survive the removal of its outside supporter. The underlying fragility of a social system of coercively imposed norms is amply illustrated by the rapid collapse of the Soviet empire, and then the Soviet Union itself, and many similar cases can be found in the history of empires. In the middle is calculation, when the social structure rests on rational assessments of self-interest. Such a structure is only superficially internalised, and remains stable only so long as the ratios of costs and benefits remain favourable to it. A concert of powers, for example, will collapse if one power comes to believe that it can and should seek hegemony, and a liberal trading system will collapse if enough of its members begin to think that the costs of exposing their societies and economies to global trade and finance outweigh the benefits. As Hurd (1999: 387) puts it: 'a social system that relies primarily on self-interest will necessarily be thin and tenuously held together and subject to drastic changes in response to shifts in the structure of payoffs'. The deepest and most stable mode is belief, where actors support the social structure because they accept it as legitimate, and in so doing incorporate it into their own conception of their identity. Deep internalisation of this sort can survive quite major changes of circumstance, as shown by many cases of the persistence of religion long after its sponsoring imperial power has faded away (Christianity after Rome, Islam after the Abbasid dynasty, Buddhism after the Mauryan Empire). Wendt offers the penetrating twist that, in principle, each of these modes of socialisation can apply to any of his three social structures. Thus a seemingly Kantian social structure of friendship might be based on coercion and thus unstable (the Soviet Union and its 'socialist' fraternity), while a Hobbesian social structure might well be based on the deeply internalised values of a warrior culture, and thus held as legitimate (e.g. Klingons, for *Star Trek* fans, or a long history of nomadic, 'barbarian' warrior cultures for others, most visible these days in places like Somalia and Afghanistan). A Lockean social structure mixing limited rivalry and limited cooperation might be supported only by instrumental calculation (as some fear about the current global economy) or it might be quite deeply internalised (on the basis of Enlightenment beliefs about human nature, or about the best way to achieve economic progress).

Wendt's scheme is attractively neat and simple, and at first glance seems to cover the main possibilities. On reflection, however, one could question it in several ways. For one thing, it is based on an analogy with individual behaviour that misses out some important differences that affect the way states or other collective actors internalise shared values. Hurrell (2002: 145–6), for example, points out the incorporation of norms into bureaucratic structures and procedures, and into legal codes (domestic and international) as forms of internalisation that would be distinctive to collective entities. Perhaps more troubling is that Wendt's three categories all require conscious awareness of the mechanism on the part of the actor(s) concerned. Is there a case for considering a fourth category to cover behaviour that is driven by unconscious internalisation of norms, whether as traditions or as 'doxa', the unquestioned norms embedded in the social background of any society (Guzzini 1993: 466)? There is also room for debate about whether a value is 'held' if what holds it in place is coercion. If contracts signed under duress are not legal, do values 'held' under duress actually count as values? Some might think not. Wendt's and Hurd's schemes force one to rely on sustained behaviour as the indicator that a value is held. This rather behavioural view of values will not convince everyone, and will be particularly problematic for those normative theorists for whom the holding of a value equates with belief in it (more on this below). These issues deserve more thought than I have space to indulge in here. In what follows, I am simply going to try to apply Wendt's scheme as given, on the grounds that it opens up vital and inadequately explored ground within English school theory. I leave open the possibility that others might want to refine

104

the ideas if this first rough cut turns out to be interesting. It seems to me that the issue of how norms are held in place is a crucial one in any understanding of how international or world societies develop, and how stable or unstable they might be. I will make extensive use of Wendt's formulation in both the later sections of this chapter and in subsequent chapters of this book.

Inter alia, Wendt's scheme offers insight into Watson's (1990; 1992) pendulum theory (that international societies swing back and forth on a spectrum from extreme independence (anarchy), through hegemony, suzerainty and dominion, to empire). Empire is too crude a term for the hierarchical end of the spectrum. The social structure of empire is held together by a mixture of coercion, calculation and belief in which coercion is generally the largest element and belief the smallest. Rome was created and maintained by its army, but it had enough legitimacy to fuel a millennium of nostalgia after its fall. More purely brutal empires such as the Mongol and the Assyrian, left much less nostalgia amongst their former subjects. An alternative form of hierarchy is (con)federation, where belief is generally the largest element, and coercion the smallest. These two types of construction are different enough so that using the label empire for both misleads more than it clarifies. Wendt's separation of mode/depth of socialisation is helpful here. It allows one to think of a single form of social structure (e.g. hierarchy at the extreme end of Watson's spectrum), while leaving open the question of whether this is achieved and maintained more by coercion (Wight's 'Stalinism'), more by calculation (as some fear, and some hope, about the EU) or more by belief (a deeply rooted federation such as the US).

Thinking along these Wendtian lines poses some probing questions for how the history of international society is told. The question of what holds norms in place is implicit in the English school's accounts of the spread of Western international society, which involved a good deal of coercive imposition of a 'standard of civilisation', as well as some calculated, and some principled, acceptance (Gong 1984; Bull and Watson 1984). This still-expanding literature could usefully incorporate Wendt's ideas. Similar, though less militarised, coercive practices continue today (Armstrong 1999: 558–61), and can most clearly be seen in action in the operation of 'conditionality' imposed on periphery states by the core whether in relation to applications for NATO, EU or WTO membership or bids for loans from the IMF and World Bank. But perhaps the real challenge opened up here is to those following in Vincent's tradition of promoting human rights objectives in pursuit of a more solidarist international society. It is perfectly clear that Western, individualist, versions of human rights are held as legitimate, and deeply internalised, by a substantial community of states and people. It is just as clear that any attempt to impose these values on a universalist, global basis will require the use of coercive and calculative modes of socialisation against those who do not share them. Is this a desirable and durable way to pursue the creation of a more solidarist international society? (More on this in chapters 5 and 8.)

Abandoning the physical–social distinction as a primary organising device for theory effectively collapses one pillar of the English school triad, reducing the scheme to a dyad between international and world society. In so doing, it heightens the need to think systematically about the range of structural possibilities within international and world societies. This task has so far only been picked away at and not addressed systematically by the English school, and not much addressed by other versions of world society either, many of which tend towards even more homogenous interpretations.

Going down this route means following Wendt and other constructivists in privileging the social over the physical. According to this way of thinking it will matter both what the shared norms, rules and institutions are, and how they are held in place. Wendt's scheme adds a new dimension to the solidarism–pluralism debate. It asks not only how many, and what type of, values are shared, and whether they are about just survival, or about more ambitious pursuit of joint gains, but also about the mode of socialisation in play. Privileging the social also raises questions about what happens to the neorealist types of structural analysis that would previously have fitted into the international system pillar of the English school's triad. The first thing to note is that Waltz's (1979) first two tiers are social rather than material anyway: organising principle, and structural and functional differentiation are about the social structures created by political ideas, not material capabilities. These two ideas can stay in play without contradiction in the scheme set out in figure 2. Distribution of capabilities is more obviously physical, and, like interaction capacity, has to be treated as an essential question that one asks of any social system. Neorealists assume that the international system is composed of enemies and rivals, and that polarity therefore matters primarily in relation to military and political security. But as thinking about hegemonic stability in IPE suggests, polarity can also matter, and in a very different way, in a system or a sub-system composed of rivals and friends. In a social structural perspective polarity does not determine the nature of the game or the players, but it does affect how the game will be played, whether it be a Hobbesian, Grotian or Kantian one.

The consequences of the argument in this section for the 'first revision' view of English school theory set out in figure 2, are sketched in the second revision in figure 3 and are quite radical. Dropping 'system' as representing a distinctive physical, asocial form of interstate relations, means eliminating (or rather relocating in a redefined form) one of the three main pillars in the classic English school triad of concepts. In return for this, the problem of the missing 'system' side complementing world society also disappears. This revision, when combined with the one in figure 2, solves the boundary problem created there by changing the nature of the boundary between international and world society. Instead of being a frontier where one classification blends into another, it becomes a clear separation based on type of actor. In addition, and following from the incorporation of Wendt's ideas, one can begin to see the spectrum of types of international society set out in the plan view. Pluralism and solidarism no longer, as in the classical English school triad of figure 1, define the outer boundaries of international society. Instead, they occupy the middle part of the spectrum. Cronin (1999: 8–17) conducts a similar exercise in defining types of international community. His spectrum has international state of nature at the asocial end of the spectrum and universal collective security at my (con)federative end. In between are balance of power, great power concert, pluralist security community, common security system and amalgamated security community. He accompanies this with a second spectrum of degrees of identity, starting from hostility (Other as anti-self), and proceeding through rivalry, indifference, cohesion (some sense of common good and group identity), altruism (willingness to sacrifice for others) to symbiosis (shared core identity dissolves self–Other distinction). Beyond solidarism one finds the Kantian model (where the states composing international society become very alike domestically), and (con)federalism (where the degree of political integration is on the border of transforming a system of states into a single hierarchical political entity). Beyond pluralism (which more or less stands for Wendt's Lockean social structure) one finds more Hobbesian social structures based on enemy relationships. At the extreme end of this side of the spectrum, one finds the asocial scenario sketched above where enemies are locked into a permanent war of extermination. In this view, international society incorporates the whole spectrum of social structures possible between states, from virtually nothing (therefore absolutely conflictual) to the brink of complete political integration.

If one stays true to Wendt's scheme, then it is necessary to add a dimension of thickness to the plan view, set out in the elevation view, to take into account not just the type of social structure, but also its mode/depth of internalisation. For every position on this spectrum one has to ask on what mixture of coercion, calculation and belief the observed social structure rests. On the pluralist/Hobbesian side, the observed social structure could be deeply internalised as an expression of a warrior culture; or it could be a shallower instrumental calculation based on the existence of some bad apples in the basket, and fear of them amongst the other states; or it could be coerced by the existence of one very powerful warrior state that threatens all the others. Similarly, on the solidarist/Kantian side, the observed social structure could be deeply internalised as a result of shared belief in liberal principles; or it could be the result of more instrumental calculations of advantage; or it could be a result of a coercive hegemonic or imperial power able and willing to impose its values on others. The English school has implicitly rested its understanding of society on belief, and has therefore not asked this question with anything like the necessary clarity and consistency. But as its accounts of the expansion of European international society to global scale show, coercion and calculation matter. Much of the non-European world was simply forced into international society through the process of colonisation and decolonisation. The few that escaped, such as the Ottoman Empire, China and Japan were much motivated by the prospect of coercion, and calculated the need to adapt in order to survive. Society, even when defined in strong terms as shared values, can rest on other foundations than belief. Following Wendt, figure 3 requires this question to be asked of all types of international (and world) society.

Society and community

If one is going to deploy the concept of society, then the question of definition and meaning cannot be avoided. Both humility and caution are called for here. Sociologists have been debating the meaning of society for generations without coming to any very clear resolution (Mayhew 1968). It is unlikely that IR theorists are going to solve this problem, but

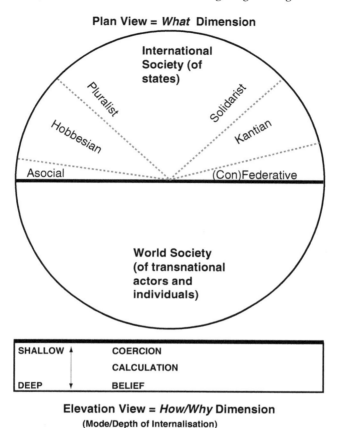

Plan View = *What* Dimension

Figure 3. The 'Three Traditions' second revision: dropping the physical element of international system, extending the spectrum of types of international society, and adding Wendt's mode/depth of internalisation

if they are going to deploy the concept then they must at least take a position, especially so if like the English school they want to defend the strong version of society based on shared values highlighted in chapter 3. In general, the concept of society aims to identify what it is that constitutes individuals into durable groups in such a way as to give the group ontological status: societies can reproduce themselves and outlive the particular individuals that compose them at any given point. Defining societies as bounded units has proved particularly difficult. So has deciding what kind of binding forces constitute the essential ingredient that makes a collection of individuals into a society; must it be deep internalisation in the form of shared belief about identity, or can society be calculated, or even in some sense coerced, in which case shared behaviour is sufficient to identify it? The literature about society is almost totally based on the idea that however they might be structured, societies are composed of individual human beings. The English school's core idea that the units of international society are states – second-order societies composed of collective units rather than individuals – is a striking departure, recently picked up by some constructivists. This departure deserves more attention than it has received.

Societies can and have been defined in political, economic, historical, identity, cultural and communication terms. These can, perhaps with the exception of Luhmann and his followers, be simplified down to two main lines of approach. One focuses on patterns of interaction structured by shared norms and rules, while the other focuses on identity and 'we-feeling' as the key to society. These two lines are captured by the distinction first drawn by Tönnies (1887) between 'society' (*Gesellschaft*) and 'community' (*Gemeinschaft*). There is a long history of debate around these terms, much of it bound up in the distinction between the traditional and the modern, and analysis of the process of modernisation. Much of this debate is freighted with German historical baggage not relevant to the IR debate about second-order societies. To oversimplify this history, *Gemeinschaft* community broadly represents the organic, premodern, small-scale way exemplified by clans and tribes that humans grouped themselves together in before the onset of modernity. In this sense, community is a deep concept, implying not only membership of an identity group, but also a degree of responsibility towards the other members of the group. It would be almost impossible to apply the concept in this form to a loose second-order construct such as international society, and difficult, if not quite impossible, to imagine applying it to world society. As Luard (1976: vii) observes: 'there is reason to doubt whether the aggregation of states possesses the common values and assumptions, which are, by definition the essential conditions of community'. *Gesellschaft*/society broadly represents the rational, contractual, large-scale way of organising humankind that has become dominant since the onset of modernity. In principle and in practice *Gesellschaft* fits comfortably with the international domain. Luard (1976: viii) sees international society as 'possessing some common customs and traditions, common expectations concerning the relationships and behaviour to be expected among its members, even, in many cases, common institutions for discussing common problems'.

There is plenty of room in this longstanding sociological formulation for casting the two as opposed forces, and for mounting polemics in support of, or opposition to, one or the other (progressive versus conservative views). As shown in chapter 3, the world society approach of Dietrich Jung seeks to build a macro-historical sociology understanding of the contemporary international system directly on the basis of the interplay between tradition and modernity set up in the *Gemeinschaft/ Gesellschaft* formulation of the German debate. But as pointed out by the WSRG, there is another way of building on this tradition. Instead of taking it as a macro-historical sociological approach, one can instead extract the essential distinction embedded in *Gemeinschaft/Gesellschaft*, and use it to identify different types of social relations in any historical context. This second, more abstract, approach is the one I intend to pursue. Jung's approach is more or less an alternative to the existing IR traditions, and is interesting for that reason. The approach of distinguishing between society and community as types of social relationships is powerful because it offers insight into the existing IR debates about international and world society. From here on in I will signal this move away from the traditional *Gemeinschaft/Gesellschaft* conception, and all of the political and intellectual battles associated with it, by abandoning the German terminology and sticking to the English terms 'community' and 'society'. The principal cost of the abstraction away from history is that one dilutes the traditional, organic, deep sense of community by adding in the idea that communities can also be consciously constructed. In the formulation proposed here, society becomes essentially about agreed arrangements concerning expected behaviour (norms, rules, institutions), and community becomes essentially about shared identity (we-feeling). In this sense, community can be quite shallow, as for example amongst the worldwide fandom of Manchester United or Elvis Presley. The main advantage of the move is that it divorces society and community from a particular interpretation of history, and makes them available as concepts for analysing the rather different world of second-order societies, whether 'international' or 'world', at the levels above the state.

The distinction between society and community features quite strongly in some of the schools of thought about world society surveyed in chapter 3. It is not unknown in English school thinking, but neither is it much explored, and what is said leans in contradictory directions.[2] Wight's (1977: 33) much-cited idea that 'We must assume that a states-system [i.e. an international society] will not come into being without a degree of cultural unity among its members' seems to lean towards community as a key element in international society, though 'culture' can be read in both society and community senses (Adam Watson [personal conversation] says that community was what the British Committee had in mind when it talked about common culture). Bull, by contrast, seems to lean firmly towards a 'society' interpretation. His idea of society (1977: 4–5), as noted in chapter 2, rests on the presence of rules of coexistence regarding limits on the use of force, provisions for the sanctity of contracts, and arrangements for the assignment of property rights. The key question is whether society and community represent fundamentally different forms of social relationship, or are just different elements within what can be considered a single phenomenon. If they are fundamentally different forms, then the question has to be put as to whether they can be conflated within concepts such as international and world society. If they are aspects of a single phenomenon (a wider sense of *society*), then such bundling together is both more easily justified and less analytically suspect. In some of my earlier writing (Buzan 1993: 333–40) I simply added the element of identity into the concept of society, without adequately recognising the need to ask this question.

In trying to formulate a position on whether society and community are fundamentally different, or aspects of a single phenomenon, Chris Brown's (1995a) attempt to draw a distinction among system, society and community is instructive, not least because it addresses the problem more or less in the terms of the English school's classical three pillars. He defines a *system* as existing when: 'whatever rules and regularities exist in the world are the product solely of an interplay of forces and devoid of any kind of normative content' (Brown 1995a: 185). That definition would also satisfy most neorealists, and some readings of Bull. *Community* he places as the 'polar opposite' of system, seeing it as a 'heavily contested' concept at the centre of which:

> is the idea that whatever order exists in a community is normatively grounded, based on relationships which constitute a network of mutual claims, rights, duties and obligations that pull people together in ways that are qualitatively different from the impersonal forces which create

[2] I am grateful to Ana Gonzalez-Pelaez for pointing out to me the potential significance of community in English school thinking.

a system. Community implies the idea of common interests and at least
an emerging, common identity. The notion of community on a world
scale implies a cosmopolitan belief in the oneness of humanity . . . What
is central is the idea of unity based on notions of fellow feeling.

(1995a: 185)

This understanding of community is echoed by Cronin (1999: 4): 'communities require some degree of group cohesion and a shared sense of self'. Between these two, Brown positions *society*, which 'lacks the affective unity' of community:

> Society is a norm-governed form of association, but the norms in question emerge out of the requirements for social co-operation and do not *necessarily* require commitment to any common projects, common interest or common identity beyond what is required for social coexistence . . . the norms that constitute *society* are different from those that would constitute a world *community*. They are essentially the norms that are required for successful pursuit of peaceful coexistence by states, whereas the norms involved in world community are neither limited to those of coexistence, nor restricted in their application to inter-*state* relations.   (Brown 1995a: 186, italics in the original)

Although Brown ignores the link, his formulation runs in close parallel with the distinction between pluralism (as about the rules of coexistence) and solidarism (as about common projects, collective responsibility and shared identity) in English school thinking.

Brown's formulation provides a useful path into the society–community question, not least because it is troubling in a number of ways. Most obviously, the complexity and vagueness of his definition of community squeezes the space left for defining society. This is perhaps explained by his concerns, as a political theorist, to put norms, or the absence of them, at the centre of his definitions. One consequence of his squeezed definition is his attempt to limit society to states (and therefore in my understanding to international society), whereas community is by implication allowed to apply to states and other entities, including individuals. This raises, but does not really answer, the question of just what sorts of units the concepts of society and community can or cannot be applied to, a crucial issue if one is to develop the idea of second-order societies. Brown's approach to community runs close to Vincent's idea of world society as states plus transnational actors plus individuals, and again his position is echoed by Cronin (2002a: 66), who defines international communities as:

> historically-situated collectivities of regional political actors who maintain formal, ongoing relations with each other in international affairs on the basis of an integrated set of procedural and political norms. Such actors include government officials, diplomats and representatives from international and transnational organisations and social movements.

These definitions contain elements of the society–community distinction, particularly in allocating affective and shared identity elements to community. But the main drift is to see community as a thicker form, incorporating the thinner form of mere society, and adding to it elements of shared values and identities. Brown denies (1995a: 186) that he is posing system, society and community as a spectrum. But he doesn't develop the reasons for his denial, and his overall presentation strongly suggests exactly such a developmental sequence, with system being the simplest and most basic construction, where interaction generates some mechanical rules; society adding a layer of conscious rule-making among states onto that; and community being the most fully developed form, bringing in elements of identity, and more elaborate forms of normative kinship. This developmental spectrum model is also strong in the thinking of Vincent and the WSRG.

This question of development is vital, because, as noted in the discussion of the WSRG in chapter 3, determining what the relationship is between society and community remains one of the unresolved controversies at the core of the sociological debate. That there is a strong relationship of some sort is not in doubt for the two are frequently co-located and nearly always interactive. But what that relationship might be is hotly contested, with no clear pattern of determination running in either direction about what causes what. In the sociological tradition of Tönnies (WSRG 2000: 6) community is an organic, historical idea that comes before, and is in some ways superior to, the rational but hollow society relationships typical of modernity. Gellner (1988: 61) is also in this tradition, arguing for 'a rough law of the intellectual history of mankind: logical and social coherence are inversely related'. In other words, Gellner thinks that primitive human societies perform better in terms of community and identity, and more advanced ones perform better in terms of society and rationality, and that the two characteristics, being contradictory, are inversely related to each other. This same opposition can also be seen in debates that pose religion (a strong form of community) against science (the ultimate in modernist rationality). Wight (1977) seems to think that community, in the sense of shared culture, precedes the development of international society, though his view of the relationship is more positive than Gellner's. Yet if one recalls the work of Vincent, and probably most of those in the solidarist tradition of the English school, the view is, like that of Chris Brown, the other way around. Their hope seems to be that a sense of community, a normative kinship, will grow out of the thinner practice of society. Bull seems to fear that society and community will prove to be contradictory, with community undermining society. Whatever else might be true, it seems clear that an inadequate distinction between society and community lies at the heart of some of the central confusions in English school theory. Is it that the world society pillar in English school theory is actually about community, so representing a semantic wrong turn? Or is the problem more serious than that, with the society and community elements simply not having been given adequate recognition in the whole theoretical construction of both international and world society?

Resolving this question in some way becomes even more important if one accepts the argument made in the previous section for privileging the social over the physical in conceptualising international system structure. If the 'social' is in fact made up of two distinct, intertwined types of relationship, the connections between which are complex and indeterminate, then making the 'social' central carries an obligation to be clear about what is understood to compose it. In this regard, it is of more than passing interest that Wendt's understanding of social structure is strongly linked to identity, and therefore in the terms set out here, to community. 'When states engage in egoistic foreign policies . . . more is going on than simply an attempt to realize given selfish ends. They are also instantiating and reproducing a particular conception of who they are' (Wendt 1999: 340–1). 'Structural change [is] a problem of collective identity formation', it 'occurs when actors redefine who they are and what they want' . . . 'We are – or become – what we do' (Wendt 1999: 338, 336, 342). Wendt links his constructivist approach to the idea that social interaction is not just about 'the adjustment of behaviour to price', as the rationalist would see it, but also about the reproduction of the agents involved, of their identities and interests (Wendt 1999: 316). The strong implication of these remarks is that, for Wendt, the types of social structure represented by Hobbes, Locke and Kant are all rooted in identity, and are therefore species of community.

In Wendt's scheme, the distinction between society and community seems to emerge most clearly in his discussion about modes and depths of socialisation outlined in the previous section. The rational, contractual, calculated, instrumental definition of society fits closely with Wendt's middle mode of internalisation (calculation of self-interest), whereas the internalisation of identity that defines community seems close to the internalisation of belief that forms Wendt's third and deepest mode of internalisation. But, as explained above, Wendt specifically does not tie together the mode/depth of internalisation and the type of social structure, and keeping this relationship open is one of the powerful and innovative elements in his scheme. How to fit Wendt's thinking with the society–community discussion is something of a puzzle. In Wendt's scheme it is not immediately obvious whether society–community is a distinction between two different types of social relations, or a statement about how any 'society' (in the general sense) is internalised. His Kantian structure of 'friendship' is indeterminate as regards society or community, and could be read either way (Wendt 1999: 297–308).

The simplest way through this minefield, and also the one best suited to dealing with the second-order societies of interest to IR, is to accept the arguments offered by Weller (2000) and the WSRG (2000). Their formulation treats as distinct forms of social relationship, on the one hand, contractual social relations based on agreements about rational self-interest (i.e. society), and, on the other hand, social relations of shared identity based on affection or tradition (i.e. community). This Weberian formulation is open about the units to which the concepts might apply (individuals, non-state actors, nations, states, civilisations) and takes 'society' and 'community' as ideal types, seldom if ever found in pure form. It postulates the near certainty that the two will always come entangled with each other in some way, but argues that the relationship is both complex, and indeterminate as to which precedes or causes which, and whether they will be harmonious or conflictual. Indirect support for this move can be found in the work of the anthropologist Mary Douglas (2001), whose use of two variables, *integration* and *regulation*, to characterise any human collectivity, runs in quite close parallel to the community/society scheme proposed here.

From an English school perspective this move has the attraction of providing some leverage on the strong version of society (as shared values) that Shaw and others criticise it for. Perhaps the main cost (other, of course, than the inconvenience of having to think again about things previously taken for granted) is that one more or less has to abandon hopes for both predictive theory (not a great loss to most English school types), and linear developmental models (perhaps of concern to some solidarists). Given the apparent absence of any clear lines of general causality between society and community in either direction students of the subject will largely be confined to situational and comparative analysis. This loss is balanced by the gain that the indeterminacy of the society–community relationship takes the heat out of the worry that world society and international society must in some way be necessarily at odds with each other. They can be, but they can also be mutually supportive. Some epistemic communities, for example, might well be opposed to the state-based international society (some human rights and environmentalist groups), but others may well be deeply entwined with it (international law, for example, or 'big science' research projects in astronomy, space exploration and physics).

Another benefit is to enable the English school to take up Weller's (2000: 64–8) idea that one key variable affecting what the relationship between society and community will be is whether their geographical boundaries are the same or different. Bringing the geography of society and community into line has of course been one driving rationale behind the nation-state, which if nothing else underlines the political salience of Weller's question. Weller's question is a neat way of formulating the many agonisings of the English school about the expansion of European international society into areas not sharing the history of European civilisation. It is also a way of addressing the English school's reluctance to talk about regional international societies as anything other than a threat to global international society (more on this in chapter 7).

It is also worth noting that there is an opportunity here for the English school (and indeed others of like mind in IR) to make a distinctive contribution to the wider debate about society. The relationship between society and community has not yet been sorted out in any definitive manner by either political theorists or sociologists. Common to their endeavours has been the assumption that both society and community are composed of individual human beings. There is scope for IR theorists to play here, in that the consequences of social structure are almost certainly quite different when the units concerned are not individuals, but collectivities with ontological status of their own. If such second-order societies are indeed fundamentally different from societies composed of individual human beings, then there will be limits to both the lessons and the problems that can be carried over to the international level from discussions about primary human societies.

Some, even within IR, reject the idea of second-order societies altogether (Jones 1981: 5) on the grounds, presumably deriving from a strongly held methodological individualism, that societies can only be composed of individual human beings. Anyone taking that view has to reject any concept of international society altogether, and confine themselves at most to a reductionist idea of world society. Doing so, it seems to me, throws away a hugely important concept for understanding international relations. The main insights so far developed in IR on second-order societies come in reflections about international anarchy, and suggest that such societies do differ significantly from primary ones. The question has been to what extent, if any, the Hobbesian 'war of each against all' image of primary anarchy carries over to international (i.e. secondary) anarchies (Bull 1977: 46–51; Buzan 1991: 21, 37–8, 148ff.). The lesson from those discussions is that the second-order structures are indeed different from the primary ones because the nature of the constituent social units (individual human beings versus states) is profoundly different on issues ranging from physical vulnerability through processes of reproduction, to death. If what is true for international anarchy is true for international society, as seems likely, then IR theorists have a responsibility to develop distinctive models of society to cover this second-order domain. If second-order societies are different from primary ones, then study of them may open up new perspectives on how society and community interrelate. Such a question is compatible with the central project of the English school, and could also be taken up by constructivists such as Cronin (1999) and Wendt (1999), who are already working with the idea of second-order societies.

If one takes the bold step of treating society and community as distinct forms of social relationship between which lines of causality are indeterminate, what are the consequences for thinking about international and world society? How, in other words, is the distinction between society and community to be worked into a revision of figure 4? Before turning to that task it helps first to deal with the last of the dyads defining this chapter: individuals and transnational actors (TNAs).

Individual and transnational

I suggested in chapter 1 that world society had become something of an intellectual dustbin in English school theory, and this could still be a problem even if one confined its content to non-state entities. If world society is about a mixture of non-governmental organisations and individuals, then the question is whether or not the logic of transnationalism and the logic of cosmopolitanism can comfortably be composed as a single coherent phenomenon, or whether more analytical leverage is acquired by keeping them distinct. In order to get to grips with this issue it helps to go back to basics. The exegesis of English school and other world society theories conducted in chapters 2 and 3 revealed considerable consistency in the analytical construction of what the relevant units are. Three types of unit are in constant play: states, transnational actors and individuals. Taxonomic logic suggests that this trilogy could and should be abstracted into two general types: individuals on the one hand, and various kinds of collective units (i.e. substantially autonomous social collectivities sufficiently well structured both to reproduce themselves and to have decision-making processes which enable them to behave in a self-conscious fashion), on the other. Collective units in this sense would be problematic, or even nonsensical, for methodological individualists. Because such units are understood to have sufficient actor quality to constitute them as distinctive agents in a social world, they have to be understood in methodologically collective terms.

In practice, however, taxonomic neatness surrenders to the primacy of the state, and the collective units category remains divided into state and non-state. The English school (and realism, International Law, Historical Sociology and much neoliberalism) privilege the state as still central to international order, providing the essential political framework for much else. On this basis a strong distinction is made between states and TNAs (e.g. firms, INGOs, mafias, etc.). Alan James (1993: 288), for example, argues that non-state actors are not members of international society because they do not possess the attributes that would give them the right of admission. But they can be seen as 'participants' in the international society that is created and maintained by sovereign states. This view is widely reflected in the literature on TNAs (Vincent 1992: 261; Keck and Sikkink 1998: 217; Risse-Kappen 1995b: 280–300; Krasner 1995: 258). Noortmann, Arts and Reinalda (2001: 299–301), for example, argue that while non-state actors 'have become part of the institutional structure of international politics and policy-making' their influence in comparison with states 'should not be exaggerated'. The position in international law is complicated. Noortmann (2001: 59–76) argues that the positivist tradition in international law automatically privileges the state as the sole subject of international law, while other traditions make more room for non-state actors. He argues (2001: 64, 69–74) that 'no intrinsic rule of international law that excludes non-state actors from acquiring a degree of legal personality exists', and that *de facto*, transnational corporations (TNCs) are so heavily bound up in international legal rights and duties, and can make and be held to legal claims to such an extent, that they must have standing as effective subjects of international law. INGOs have a much less clear position, but even though they are usually denied standing as subjects of international law, they often have formal standing with IGOs.

So at this point I run into the argument made and accepted in the previous section for setting the state apart as a distinct focus for analysis using the concept of international society. Acknowledging the risk of perpetuating a historical privileging of the state that justifies itself mainly by looking backwards, I nevertheless have to accept the division of collective units into state and non-state. The grounds for doing this are that the state remains central to the political structuring of humankind, with no obvious successor in sight (and no obvious way of doing without political structure of some sort). I exclude IGOs as actors on the grounds set out in Buzan and Little (2000: 266–7) that because of their generally low actor quality, IGOs are more generally part of social interaction capacity than units in their own right. So while it would make more strictly taxonomical sense to bundle states and TNAs together, TNAs nevertheless get pushed down into world society along with their unnatural partner, individuals. Can this pairing be sustained? To answer this question it helps to conduct a thought experiment around the three basic types of unit in play, and the sorts of systems they might form. Given that we are looking at three types of autonomous actor, what kinds of social systems can they form?

If one accepts the trilogy of unit types, then it follows that there can be three types of pure basic 'international' social systems: interstate (state-to-state interaction), transnational (TNA-to-TNA interaction) and interhuman (individual-to-individual interaction). Nothing forbids these from coexisting, and indeed overlapping (e.g. state-to-TNA, etc.). In theory and in practice all sorts of mixtures are possible. Such mixing (often without thinking too hard about it) has been part of English school thinking, e.g. Vincent's idea of world society as states + TNAs + individuals. The same tendency can be found in Cronin's (1999: 33–8; 2002b) idea of 'transnational political community' among elites, both state and non-state, as a kind of Davos-culture counterweight to the realist logic of anarchy, and his understanding of the UN (Cronin, 2002a: 54) as 'an institutional embodiment of an "international community"' that integrates both state and transnational actors. But it is nevertheless a useful foundational exercise to start by thinking through each of these types of social system in pure form. In doing this, and with a view to the goal of revising figure 3 in the light of the discussion in this section and the previous one, it is helpful to try to bring the society–community distinction into play in relation to the three pure forms.

In the case of states, the ideas of international society, and with somewhat less coherence international community, are pretty well established in IR theory. International society has been the primary focus of English school writing, and is about the instrumental norms, rules and institutions created and maintained by states (or independent political communities), whether consciously or not, to bring a degree of order into their system of relationships. As shown in figure 3, such societies can range from being quite thin, or minimalist, to quite thick, covering a wide range of issues in considerable depth. Warrior societies might generate a Hobbesian international society where the main rules are about conflict and honour. Pluralist international societies might well take Westphalian form, with the states wishing to preserve maximum autonomy and distinctiveness, and therefore agreeing mainly on the principles necessary for coexistence: sovereignty, non-intervention and rules for diplomacy. More solidarist international societies will want to do more than that, moving beyond coexistence to pursuit of common interests defined in terms of joint gains. The will to move towards solidarist arrangements arises most easily if states become more internally alike, and therefore share a wider array of ideas and values (about human rights, or market economies or property rights, for example). In principle, solidarist international societies could generate a very wide array of shared norms, rules and institutions covering economy, law, politics, environment, education and so on. The EU is a living example of this potentiality.

International community has not been systematically discussed by the English school, but in the meaning of community set out in the previous section would hinge on shared identity and we-feeling among states. Shared identity, like instrumental cooperation, can range from low to high intensity, and can come in either exclusive (one overriding identity) or multiple forms. The identity that many individuals feel as members of the human race, for example, is generally of fairly low intensity, and is seldom if ever exclusive. By contrast, many individuals have high intensity, and sometimes exclusive, identity with family, clan, religion, nation or some ideologically motivated party or movement. This is the basis of the realists' emphasis on 'conflict groups' noted above. How does this work with states? In the contemporary international society, the bottom line of shared identity that could define international community is mutual recognition of sovereignty. All states that share such mutual recognition acknowledge each other as being the same type of entity, and this is nearly universal. But that is a fairly low intensity we-feeling, and certainly does not stand in the way of stronger, generally subglobal, forms of interstate community such as the late communist community, the club of Western liberal democracies, the community of Islamic states, or, going back a bit in Western history, Christendom. Other types of more instrumental identity groupings can arise, such as landlocked states, great powers and the third world. Most of the more intense forms of international community are not universal, and none of them is very intense in an absolute sense. International community might well thus exist to some degree on a global scale, but is unlikely to be as strong there as on sub-global scales.

How is one to read this depiction of international community in relation to the question, much agonised about in political theory, about whether the very nature of shared identity requires an 'Other', therefore ruling out the possibility of a universal identity? Can there be an 'Us' without a 'Them'? Both the WSRG (2000: 13, 17) and Brown (1995b: 100–6) note that this question raises contradictions in the idea of universal community that could make it impossible to achieve in practice. Brown's solution is to pose international society, seen as a second-order society (of collective units) each of which comprises a primary community (of individuals), as the via media between the reality of particularist communitarianism and the (probably hopeless) aspiration to universalist cosmopolitanism. In his scheme, second-order society is called in to rescue primary society from the impossibility of achieving unity in the absence of an 'Other'. If these arguments are taken seriously, they rule out the possibility of universal international and/or world communities. One possibility is that what may be true for primary communities of individuals, may not necessarily hold for second order communities of states. Perhaps states do not require an 'Other' in order to create a universal community. In support of that would be the weak, but still extant, global community of states based on mutual acceptance as like units on the basis of sovereignty. This community pretty much incorporates all the members of the class of states. Another possibility is that states do require an 'Other', but they find it in the form of individuals organised in forms other than itself (e.g. primary anarchy, or transnational neomedievalism). Ole Wæver also raises the possibility, exemplified in the history of the EU, that states could find their collective 'Other' in a fear of returning to their own violence-ridden past (Buzan and Wæver

2003: ch. 11). There will of course be attempts to finesse this problem by linking a sub-global identity to the good of the whole (Carr 1946: 80–1). The practice of the Western states of representing themselves as 'the international community' generally hinges on an appeal to Western values that are understood to be universal even if they are contested by some outside the West.

Trying to visualise pure transnational and interhuman societies and communities set apart from an accompanying states-system takes one away from much of history and onto unfamiliar ground. It raises questions about whether the concept of world society can be thought of independently from states-systems (therefore having the same ontological standing), or whether it is somehow dependent on an accompanying international society (therefore only an epiphenomenon).

Starting with individuals as the unit underlines the case for taking a social view of international systems made in the previous section. It is scarcely possible to imagine purely asocial interhuman systems in any realistic sense. Hobbes's image of the war of each against all captures one possibility, but has no basis in what we know about human social life before the coming of Leviathan (Buzan and Little 2000: part II). Humans acting as individuals in a system very quickly find powerful reasons to form cooperative groups, especially if fighting is in prospect. It is almost impossible to imagine a large-scale interhuman society or community coming into being without first going through many stages of development focused on collective units of one sort or another. Without going through the intermediary stages of collective units, how would the whole population of humans ever establish communication with each other, or learn how to align their identities or coordinate their actions, on a large scale? Given a numerous and geographically dispersed population, the processes by which humans interact seem inevitably fated to form collective entities each of which encompasses only a small part of the total human population. These entities might be collective units of some kind (possessing actor quality), and/or they might be patterns of shared identity (religious, ethnic, etc.), with network types of association amongst individuals poised somewhere in between.

If the entities are clearly units with actor quality, then we move straight into the realm of transnational or state units. This makes it difficult to imagine world society in terms of individuals because a second-order transnational or interstate society would form before any full-scale interhuman system could arise. An interhuman world society unmediated by collective units can just about be imagined in a world vastly more technologically and socially developed than our own, when evolutions of the internet have become both universal, and deeply embedded in human society (and probably physiology as well). But such a development would only come about as a result of long evolution through inter-unit societies of some sort. It is thus difficult to think about world societies of individuals without immediately conjuring up collective units of one sort or another and thus departing from the individual-as-unit scenario.

It is much easier to see individuals in the community terms of shared identity without encountering this problem. The idea of shared identity among individuals is well covered in the extensive literature on communitarianism and cosmopolitanism, which is one of the major stocks in trade of political theory. Humans seem to fall naturally into identity groups based on such things as kinship, ethnicity, language, religion and/or political allegiance. The entities thus formed do not necessarily, or even usually, have actor quality. The problem in relation to any idea of world community is, as noted above, that such associations form more easily on small scales than on larger ones, and that universal community amongst individuals is on some readings impossible because of the lack of an 'Other' against which to define shared identity. Community certainly operates, but when does it become justified to use the term 'world'? In a strict usage, 'world' would have to mean global, and in that case world community in terms of individuals would only occur after a very long period of development and aggregation of shared identities on a smaller scale. With this meaning it could just about be argued that humankind is beginning to develop a world community (because of the widespread acceptance of the principle that all humans are equal, and possessed of some basic shared human rights). But a looser meaning of 'world', along the lines of Wallerstein's world systems and world empires, can also be justified, and offers more scope. Here 'world' means occurring on a large scale relative to other aspects of human organisation, and having substantially self-contained qualities. With this usage, a variety of religious and civilisational foundations for claims about 'world' communities can come into play. In either case, the necessity of development through successive aggregations from smaller to more encompassing groups means that the idea of world community amongst individuals would have to be part of a set of multiple identities, something that moderated the effects of more sectional, parochial types of we-feeling, rather than replacing them. It is hard to imagine an overriding identity of humankind without a large range of less-than-universal identities being embedded in it.

Turning to TNAs as the unit reinforces the case for taking a social view of international systems. Imagining a purely physical transnational system is almost as problematic as for the interhuman case. TNAs represent a division of labour and a differentiation of function, and such developments can hardly be contemplated outside the context of some sort of society–community.

Amongst transnational actors society is easier to imagine, and community more difficult. Pure transnational world societies are easier to imagine because they are analogous to that other system of collective units formed by states. But envisaging pure transnational societies requires that one eliminate states (or, more generally, types of collective unit claiming exclusive powers of government and rights to use force over defined territories and peoples). Eliminating states leaves behind an almost infinite array of functionally specific entities that ranges from hobbyist clubs and sporting associations through mafias and religious institutions to firms and interest lobbies and professional associations (Risse-Kappen 1995a; Boli and Thomas 1999; Noortmann, Arts and Reinalda 2001: 303; Risse 2002). Only one historical example comes even close to this model: in medieval Europe, both property rights and political rights (or more to the point, duties) were divided up across a range of entities from guilds, crusading orders and monasteries; through bishops, barons and princes; to cities, Holy Roman emperors, and popes (Ruggie 1983, 1993; Fischer 1992; Buzan and Little 1996). This medieval model is not purely transnational since some of its components (city-states, some kings) would count as states under the definition given above, and the same is true of Hedley Bull's much-cited idea of neo-medievalism, which captured the possibility that the future might develop a similar mix. The Westphalian states-system eventually replaced the medieval one, and gave it a bad press as 'the dark ages'. But medieval Europe nonetheless stands as an exemplar of the possibility of a predominantly transnational world society.

It is perfectly possible to imagine firms, and indeed clubs, mafias and various other types of association agreeing pluralist type rules of recognition and conventions of communication amongst others of a similar type, and working out practical measures of coexistence. Cartel agreements amongst firms or mafias not to compete with one another in certain markets or territories are parallel to rules of non-intervention among states. It is harder to imagine why different types of transnational organisation would behave in this way. Because states (or firms) are the same type of entity, they may well fall into zero-sum rivalry and therefore have need of rules of coexistence. But chess clubs and steel manufacturers hardly compete for the same social terrain, and can as well remain indifferent to each other as seek structured social relations. Similarly, it is not difficult to imagine elements of solidarism in transnational societies. Chess or sports clubs may want to cooperate in setting up system-wide standards and tournaments. Firms may want to agree on common standards for everything from screws to software systems. Stock exchanges might want to make their buying and selling practices interoperable. As with states, therefore, other types of collective units have choices about how they relate to each other, and these choices can range from zero-sum rivalry, through pluralist modes of coexistence, to more solidarist modes of cooperation in pursuit of joint gains and interoperability. There is perhaps some echo in this image of Luhmann's idea of world society as consisting of distinct functional systems of communication, each structured by its own basic code into self-referential communities.

It is more difficult to think about a purely transnational world community, the problem being that unlike states and individuals, the units of the transnational world are similar only in the sense that they are not states. Little else about them is similar, and therefore the foundations for shared identity are hard to imagine. Partly for this reason, Williams (2001) rightly points out that world society, contrary to the hopes of some solidarists, is perhaps more embeddedly pluralist, and more problematic as a site for the development of solidarism, than international society. World communities of transnational actors might develop <u>among</u> similar types (all chess clubs, all mining companies, all terrorist groups), but this would be so narrow as to make the term 'world' seem inappropriate. Perhaps the only plausible route to a widely based transnational world community would be if the shared identity as non-state became strong. For that to happen, not only would a core political rivalry between the state and non-state worlds have to develop, but also a sophisticated consciousness of division of labour among the different types of non-state units, such that they could construct a shared identity as part of a grand idea about the human social world. Such a scenario probably exists only in the minds of the more extreme proponents of globalisation, global civil society and/or classical anarchism.

In principle, a transnational world society could exist in the absence of states (notwithstanding the nonsense that would make of the term transnational itself), and is therefore a possible alternative to international society. It can also exist in conjunction with states, as now, when transnational and international society overlap and interweave.

Taking all this into account, the answer to the opening question of this section – 'Can the logic of transnationalism and the logic of cos-mopolitanism be composed as a single coherent phenomenon labelled world society/community?' – would seem to be <u>no</u>. The ontological dif-ference between individuals and transnational actors is profound, and it leads to quite different logics and potentialities in the way in which each of these types of units can or cannot form societies and communities. Thinking about the individual level is very largely focused on ques-tions of identity and community. This is reflected in the debates within political theory about cosmopolitanism versus communitarianism. As demonstrated, it is actually quite difficult to think about a pure interhu-man society because the dynamics of society almost immediately jump to the transnational and/or state levels. By contrast, thinking about the transnational level is mostly focused on questions of society. While it is not impossible to think about community at the transnational level, the huge diversity of actor types among TNAs tends to impose pretty strict limits on how far shared identity can go.

Following the argument (made on pp. 91–8) about favouring type of unit as the key to distinguishing between international and world society, I cannot avoid the conclusion that individuals and transnational actors should <u>not</u> be bundled together. In terms of revising figure 3 this move has two consequences. First, it would seem to destroy the concept of world society as used in figures 1–3. This rather alarming development is balanced by the fact that in doing so, the separation of the individual and transnational worlds opens up ways around some of the dilemmas for English school theory posed by world society, and exposed most clearly in the examination of Vincent's work. Second, it creates strong reasons to divide the non-state into two, and thereby restore a triadic structure, but now with each of the three pillars defined by a distinct type of unit: individuals, TNAs, states.

Buried in all of this argument has been a major departure from the role that individual human beings play in the normative verson of English school theory.[3] In that tradition, individuals are of primary interest as the carriers of moral rights. It is the individual that matters, whether singly as him or herself, or collectively as humankind. In the structural version of English school theory emerging here, the focus is not on the

---

[3] I am grateful to Lene Mosegaard Madsen for pointing this out.

individual as such, but on the patterns of shared identity that group human beings into various forms of community. A structural approach does not do well at dealing with individual units. It necessarily seeks patterns on a larger scale.

At this point, everything is in place to undertake the revision of figure 3, and to reconsider the meaning of both international and world society.

Conclusions: reconstructing the English school's triad

To sum up, the argument above has defended the following propositions.

- That there are strong reasons for keeping a distinction between state and non-state as a feature of the analysis (figure 2);
- That the physical–social distinction should be largely set aside in English school theory. Given the heavy overlap between them, the two should be considered together within the context of a range of types of social system (figure 3);
- That society and community need to be considered as distinct forms of social relationship, nearly always linked but with little or no determinate causality in either direction;
- That the individual and the transnational have such different ontological foundations that bundling them together as a collective 'non-state' or 'world society' category is not sustainable.

The task in this section is to work out the consequences of the last two of these conclusions for reconstructing the English school's triad, and to apply these to revising figure 3.

Recall that in constructing figure 3, I followed Wendt, James and others in abandoning the idea of a purely physical, mechanistic 'international system'. The consequence of that move was extending the range of international society to cover a wider spectrum than pluralist to solidarist. This spectrum went from asocial (very rare) and Hobbesian at one extreme, through pluralist and solidarist, to Kantian, with (con)federative forming the borderline with hierarchical modes of political order at the other extreme. In line with Wendt, I accepted that enemy and rival were as much forms of social relationship as friend. I also accepted the Wendtian move of separating out the type of international society from the mode/depth of its internalisation (coercion, calculation or belief). I noted that Wendt's formulation left quite a bit of ambiguity as to where and how the society/community distinction as discussed above (pp. 108–18) fitted into his scheme, and that thread is one of the keys to designing figure 4.

Wendt's scheme rests on a distinction between the type of society (i.e. <u>what</u> values are shared) and the mode/depth of internalisation of the values (i.e. <u>how and why</u> they are shared). I can see no reason why this distinction should not apply to any kind of society, whether a primary one composed of individuals, or a second-order one composed of states or TNAs. If one accepts the distinction between *what* and *how/why*, as is done in figure 3, then the society–community distinction clearly belongs in the *how/why* dimension. The *what* dimension identifies the form, or type, of social structure as determined by the character of the norms, rules and institutions that make it up. The society/community distinction does not address the range of values that define the differences between the various positions along the spectrum of international social structures shown in figure 4. Following Wendt's logic, society and community are about the binding forces which hold <u>any</u> type of social structure together. The first step in revising figure 3 is therefore to locate the society/community distinction within Wendt's *how/why* dimension.

Note that this move has the result of co-locating society and community with coercion. This is a radical departure from those traditions which have tended to see coercion and violence as the <u>absence</u> of society/community, as the problem that society/community should in some way address. Yet coercion is never far from the surface of discussions about society. Think of Hobbes's Leviathan, or of Marxian understandings of capitalism. It is also the case that if one follows the constructivist logic of treating all human interactions as social, then violence and coercion have to be counted as forms of society and investigated as such. Wendt (1999: 254) thus rightly puts coercion into the *how/why* dimension <u>alongside</u> society and community and forming a spectrum with them of 'degrees of cultural internalization'. This move also occurs as a consequence of extending the domain of international society to cover what was seen previously as physical and mechanistic conflict dynamics at the Hobbesian end of the spectrum. Enmity is also social, and coercion is one of the ways in which collective behaviour can be shaped. Following this logic, society becomes synonymous with Wendt's 'calculation', which as noted above is a very comfortable fit. Wendt's presentation of calculation is closely parallel to the rationalist, instrumental, modernist understandings of what society means in the sociological debates. Community then has to become synonymous with Wendt's 'belief'. At first glance, this is not such an immediately comfortable fit, though neither is it all that jarring. If community is understood as shared identity, it might be thought to represent something similar to, but narrower than, shared belief. Shared identity is of course a form of shared belief, viz. Anderson's (1983) famous 'imagined communities'. But does shared belief necessarily generate shared identity? On reflection, and with the caveat that good communication is also required in order to establish as common knowledge that belief is shared, it is difficult to imagine that it doesn't. In discussing their logic of appropriateness, March and Olsen (1998: 951) also make this link, noting that for this type of motive, 'the pursuit of purpose is associated with identities more than with interests'. I conclude that calculation and society, and belief and community, are substantively close enough to confirm that the distinction between society and community does belong in the *how/why* dimension of Wendt's scheme, and not in the *what* dimension.

Society and community (and coercion) thus represent the binding forces by which social structures of any sort can be created and sustained. They do not determine the values defining the social structure and in principle each can apply to any type of social structure. Wendt is clear that he wants to see his types of social structure in mutually exclusive terms: either Hobbesian or Lockean or Kantian, but not mixtures. He goes in a similar direction about the disposition of the three components of the *how/why* dimension. That each can apply to any social structure is a powerful insight, set up in a 3 × 3 matrix of coercion, calculation and belief with his Hobbesian, Lockean and Kantian types of social structure (Wendt 1999: 254). Wendt's assumption that the types of social structure in the *what* dimension will always have a sufficiently clear pattern of enemy, rival or friend to give them clear and mutually exclusive designations is already bordering on heroic simplification (Buzan and Wæver 2003), though it might just about be sustainable for analytical purposes. But to assume the same about the three elements of the *how/why* dimension is not sustainable.

Almost any social structure one can think of will be held together by some mixture of coercion, calculation and belief. The necessity of mixture, and how to deal with it, is what defines politics. Empires might mainly be held together by coercion, but one could not understand either the Roman or British empire without adding in substantial elements of calculation (the economic advantages of being in the empire), and belief (local elites sharing some of the values of the empire). Similarly, liberal democracies might be held together mainly by belief, but the substantial role of calculation is indicated by fears about whether democracy can be sustained without economic growth. No democracies have been able to do without some coercive institutions that have primarily domestic functions. Much of Westphalian pluralist international society rests not just on the society/calculation element of agreed norms, rules and institutions, but also on the community/belief acknowledgement amongst the states that they are the same type of (sovereign) entity, and thus share an identity. The issue of community/belief emerges even more strongly for solidarist international societies, where an ever-extending range of cooperative norms, rules and institutions is likely both to reflect, and encourage, a move towards increasing similarity in the domestic structures and values of the states concerned.

The case for treating coercion, calculation and belief as simultaneously present in all but a few extreme cases of theoretically possible types of social structure is reinforced by the nature of the sociological and political theory debates about society and community. Recall that in these debates society and community are generally held to represent distinct forms of social relationship, that are nevertheless nearly always found chained together in some degree. They are distinct as ideal types, but in practice they are found mixed together in complex and fundamentally indeterminate ways, sometimes in tension with each other sometimes complementary. The nature of the relationship between society and community is much disputed, but the fact that there always is a relationship is generally accepted. There is a recurrent disposition in the literature to see this link in terms of layering or hierarchy. Those of a more historical disposition (much of the sociological debate reviewed in chapter 3) put community as the earlier, primitive form and society as the later, more sophisticated (though not necessarily better), development. By contrast, those of a more structural inclination (Brown's formulation discussed in pp. 112–14, also the WSRG's approach, and Wendt) tend to see society as the simpler, more basic, less demanding form, and community as the more difficult (and usually desirable) thing to develop as the deep form of social integration.

Understanding society and community as elements of the *how/why* dimension helpfully keeps in focus that neither society nor community is necessarily nice. That they are part of the means that hold any set of shared values together, and do not determine what those values are, untangles some of the problems revealed in the discussion of global civil society in chapter 3. Social structures that can be characterised as societies or communities in the traditional usage of those terms can just as easily be sites of conflict as well as zones of cooperation and harmony, as any reflection on the experience of family, clan, nation or religion quickly reveals, and any study of civil war underlines. Putting society and community into the *how/why* dimension makes it less easy to lose sight of that dual character.

In the formulation adopted here, I am therefore following Wendt in adding coercion into the society/community mix, but not following him in treating coercion, calculation and belief as mutually exclusive features. In dealing with the *how/why* dimension, the English school's 'three traditions' approach of assuming that all elements are always in play, seems much more appropriate, complementing the conclusion reached above (pp. 118–28) that the three types of unit that compose society are likewise always in play to some degree.

With these qualifications, figure 4 can thus build on the strength of Wendt's insight that the issue of mode/depth of internalisation applies across the whole range of types of international society. Sticking with Wendt's scheme as begun in figure 3 offers an interesting way of taking on board the society/community distinction. It also has the advantage of separating out, and bringing into clearer focus, the question of <u>what</u> the shared values are that compose international and world societies. This issue has major implications for the English school's pluralist–solidarist debate, which has not investigated sufficiently the question of what the values are that can constitute solidarism, and not really investigated at all how the issue of mode/depth of internalisation bears on the under-standing of solidarism. More on this in chapter 5.

Given the cumulative shifts and refinements of definition, what do the traditional concepts of international and world society now represent? The necessary revisions to figure 3 can be summarised and explained as follows:

(1) The elevation view representing Wendt's mode/depth of internalisa-tion remains the same, and I stay with Wendt's language for labelling the *how/why* dimension. As noted, applying the *how/why* classifica-tions of coercion, calculation and belief to interhuman and transna-tional societies does not seem to pose any problems.

(2) The top half of the pie in plan view, representing the *what* spectrum of types of international society, remains the same subject to a change of label set out in point 4 below.

Plan View = *What* Dimension

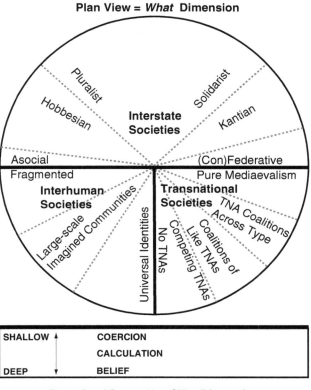

Figure 4. The 'Three Traditions' third revision: a social structural reinterpretation of the English school's triad

(3) The bottom half of the pie, previously representing world society, gets cut into two quarters representing the distinct domains within the scheme occupied by individuals and TNAs. This returns to an approximation of the original English school triad, but now based on type of unit and linked by the common substrate of the *how/why* dimension. The three domains are now separated by the hard boundaries resulting from defining them in terms of different types of constitutive unit. They are <u>not</u> a spectrum as the three traditions of the classical English school model were generally taken to be (Mayall 2000: 13). Consequently, interest shifts from what defines

these borders (now clear) to how the three domains as so constituted interact with each other. Because the boundaries are hard, no
significance now attaches to the placement of the interhuman and
transnational segments of the pie: they could be reversed, or perhaps
even better, given as three separate, self-contained, circles. The key
English school idea that the three traditions are understood to be
simultaneously in play is preserved, but now on the grounds that
social formations involving the three types of unit are always expected to be present in international systems to some degree. At a
minimum, each domain in the triad constitutes part of the operating
environment for the other two. At a maximum, conditions in one domain may determine what options are possible in the others (more
on this below). Although the triadic structure is restored, the domains no longer represent equal proportions of the pie, as they did in
figures 1 and 2. This might be thought to privilege the state over the
other two, and if so, that would be consistent with the arguments on
pp. 91–8 for doing so. It might also be thought to diminish the place
of the state, because in figures 1 and 2 the state-based elements occupied two-thirds of the pie (international system and international
society), and that thought is also justified. In the background of the
relationship amongst these three domains is Vincent's (1988: 210)
sharp observation 'that authority must reside somewhere if order is
to obtain anywhere'.

(4) In figure 4, the three domains represent <u>pure</u>, or ideal type, forms
of society based on different constitutive units (as discussed on
pp. 118–28). To reflect this, and also to underline the shift to defining the domains more clearly in terms of their constitutive units,
they are labelled *interstate societies, transnational societies* and *interhuman societies*. Societies is given in the plural to reflect the point
made in chapter 1, and followed up in chapter 7 below, that international and world societies are not just phenomena found on
a global scale, but also ones found simultaneously in regional and
other sub-global forms. (Somewhat irritatingly, 'society' is used here
in its general sense incorporating all types of social cohesion. There
is no obvious escape from the confusion caused by 'society' carrying
both this general meaning and the more specific one discussed at
length above.) A key part of the argument in this book is that the
elements that make up international society are not found only at the
global level, but also, and simultaneously, at a range of sub-global
scales.

(5) As noted in point 2, the spectrum of interstate societies from figure 3 remains unchanged, but there is a need to consider the detailed contents of the *what* dimension for both transnational and interhuman societies. As argued on pp. 118–28, the differentiation between interhuman and transnational societies hinges on the distinction between primary and second-order societies, i.e. societies composed of groups of humans on the one hand, and of groups of TNAs on the other. The difficult bit in this distinction is that if interhuman societies achieve actor quality, they become TNAs. Interhuman societies are thus largely constructed in terms of shared identities, with networks posing the main ambiguity about classification. On this basis, the *what* dimension of the interhuman pillar runs across a spectrum from highly fragmented to highly integrated. In thinking about this, one needs to start with the range of scales on which human identity groups occur. The minimum interhuman society is the basic family / clan unit necessary for reproduction. In the middle of the range one finds large 'imagined communities' such as nations, religions and various kinds of functional networks. These may be defined in such a way as to always or necessarily exclude some section of the human race (such as *Gemeinschaft* concepts of nationalism, or supporters of a particular football club), or may be failed universalisms, which in principle could include the whole human race but in practice act as dividers (all 'universal' religions and political ideologies). At the maximum end of the spectrum would be universally shared identities which could vary from the minimum recognition by all humans of each other as like-units (paralleling pluralism among states), to the advent of a world civilisation linking all of humankind together in a complex web of shared values and elaborated identities. In simple terms, the spectrum from highly fragmented to highly integrated would represent the exclusive dominance of small-scale groups on one end and the exclusive dominance of a universal identity on the other. But since humans in more complex societies generally hold multiple identities this spectrum cannot in the real world represent a spectrum of staged, mutually exclusive positions. All, or at least many, will exist simultaneously. The minimum position will always exist. The maximum, universalist one, may or may not exist, but if it does, it will not eliminate the ones in the rest of the spectrum. Therefore the spectrum from highly fragmented to highly integrated will almost always represent a complex mixture, the most interesting question being whether anything at all exists towards the highly

integrated end of the spectrum, and if it does, how strong it is, and how deeply rooted? Again, to reiterate, because the boundaries are now hard, <u>no</u> significance attaches to the placing of 'Fragmented' next to 'Asocial' or 'Universal Identities' next to 'No TNAs'.

The question of how to characterise the *what* dimension for a pure transnational society is a more consciously artificial exercise because as argued above pure transnational societies are rather difficult to imagine. Easiest is to start thinking in terms of a weak-to-strong spectrum of global civil society defined in terms of TNAs. At one end of the spectrum, it is perfectly easy to imagine an international system in which no TNAs existed, though historical examples of this might be difficult to find. The requirement would be a domineering interstate society in which the states either suppressed non-state actors altogether, or contained them tightly, each within its own borders. Next would come fragmented transnational societies in which similar types of TNAs build up shared norms, rules, institutions and identities among themselves. In the middle of the spectrum one would find coalitions involving links among different types of TNAs, such as one often finds in peace movements that tie together 'pure' peace groups with religious, political and trade union organisations. At the strong end would be a kind of pure transnational neomedievalism in which many different types of TNAs recognised each other on the basis of principles of functional differentiation amongst the different types of units, and agreements about the rights and responsibilities of different types of unit in relation to each other.

As already argued, in this scheme each domain is at a minimum, part of the operating environment of the other two, but is there any more systematic relationship among the three domains? Notwithstanding the widespread tendency to privilege the state, the three are ontologically distinct. Both TNAs and states can reproduce themselves in the absence (or presence) of the other, and being collective units, they are distinct from individuals. But it does not require much hard thinking to show that the societies formed by each type of unit quite quickly begin to play into each other. Although it is true that patterns of shared identity among human beings can and do occur on large scales, the historical record shows pretty clearly that the creation of the larger 'imagined communities' such as nations and religions depended heavily on states and TNAs to promote them (the Christian churches, the later Roman Empire, the Abassid Caliphate, etc.). And while it is possible to imagine states and TNAs being composed of entirely atomised human individuals, the historical record again makes abundantly clear that the developmental potential of both states and TNAs is closely linked to their ability to integrate themselves with the shared identity of the people who compose them. As Ahrne (1998: 89), notes: 'How to make people participate with a moral enthusiasm and at the same time follow orders and rules is in fact a common problem in much organisation theory.' Obsession with nationalism as the key to linking the three domains is very evident in the attempt common to both IR and political theory, and very much alive in the mythology of modernist real-world politics, to tie the human sense of shared identity/community into the state. But as many postmodernists and globalists of various stripes celebrate, and as increasingly acknowledged even in *realpolitik* circles post-Cold War, there is a new world disorder defined by the degree to which interhuman identities, whether kinship, ethnonational, religious, political–ideological, cultural or epistemic have spilled out of state containers, often with the encouragement of the state, though frequently also against its will. World history, with its migrations of peoples and its comings and goings of states and empires, has bequeathed humankind a thoroughly mixed condition in which there are both strong overlaps and strong disjunctures between the interhuman and interstate social structures.

If one blends TNAs into this picture, it is clear that the interesting question is less about ideal-type transnational societies, and mostly about how TNAs relate to the society of states. The main development at present is the trend for TNAs to form functional networks among themselves (the Bank for International Settlements (BIS), the International Political Science Association (IPSA), the International Chess Federation (FIDE), the European Roundtable (business CEOs), and innumerable others representing everything from football clubs to trade unions). But this trend is less interesting as a study of pure transnational societies than it is as a study of the interplay between the transnational domain and the interstate one. The least imaginitive and most politicised way of formulating this relationship is in zero-sum terms, where gains for one equal losses for the other, and the outcome has to be the elimination or subordination of one by the other (Risse-Kappen 1995a: 3–13). Much more relevant is to ask how these two domains of human society are redefining each other, and what problems and potentialities this development opens up.

That enquiry takes us away from the mostly static, definitional, conceptualisings of society that have occupied this chapter, and towards the question of social dynamics, and the forces that drive change and evolution in international social structures. I will have more to say about these driving forces in the chapters that follow. These questions take us beyond the limits of this chapter. To address them, one needs to look more closely both at what difference is made by variations in the *how/why* dimension across the different types of society, and at how the institutions of international society relate to each other. To get at this, one needs first to look more closely at the questions encompassed in the pluralist–solidarist debate. Just what are the kinds of shared values and identities that qualify for movement across the spectrum of types of interstate society? This will be done in chapters 5 and 6. Second, one needs to look at the geographical dimension. If the assumption that international and world society have to be global is abandoned, and sub-global levels of society are brought into the picture, then there can be no single answer to how interhuman, transnational and interstate societies interact with each other at any given point in time, and regional differentiation emerges as a key driving force for change. This will be the subject of chapter 7. Astute readers will also have noticed that the terms international society and world society are not present in figure 4. Do these key terms of classical English school usage disappear in a more structural interpretation, or if not, how are they to be deployed? This question too is best left until we have looked more closely at the pluralist–solidarist debate. In the meantime, I will use the three terms developed in this chapter (interhuman, transnational, interstate) when I want to confine the meaning to a specific domain, and the two traditional terms when referring to usage within the existing English school debates.

5 Reconstructing the pluralist–solidarist debate

On the basis of the arguments in chapter 4, and the progressive revisions to the English school's three pillars, I can now return to the pluralist–solidarist debate. In chapter 2, I argued that pluralism and solidarism should be understood not as mutually exclusive positions, but as positions on a spectrum representing, respectively, thin and thick sets of shared norms, rules and institutions. The basic differentiation between thin and thick was qualified by some discussion about the nature of the values shared, with pluralism associated with rules about coexistence, and solidarism potentially extending much beyond that. I used Bull's ideas about rules of cooperation and the centrality of positive international law to question the reasons behind his pluralism, arguing that these can be seen also as a powerful key to an understanding of solidarism wider than the one Bull himself employed. I argued against basing solidarism on cosmopolitanism, because that approach confines its meaning to a narrow band largely occupied by human rights and therefore excludes much that is of great empirical and theoretical significance to the concept. I also argued for allowing solidarism to be a feature of interstate societies, and not using it as a vehicle to imply some necessary conflation between international and world society.

In this chapter, I want to pick up these arguments and examine them in more detail. Since pluralism already has a fairly well-developed image, I will concentrate particularly on solidarism, the content of which has not been explored in anything like the same depth. The debate about pluralism and solidarism is absolutely central to English school theory, and how the debate is constructed makes a big difference to what can and cannot be done with the theory. In this chapter, the initial focus will be on pluralism and solidarism as the key to defining types of *interstate* society. This approach opens the way not only to the economic sector, but also brings in other features of solidarism for which substantial empirical referents can be found. It also turns one's attention to the question of the institutions of international society, which will be the subject of chapter 6. Classical English school writing discusses a set of pluralist institutions without offering much either in the way of criteria for distinguishing what does, and what does not, count as an 'institution' in this sense, or thoughts about how the institutions of international society change.

One way of cutting through the complexities of the pluralist–solidarist debate is to say that pluralism is what happens when pessimists/realists/conservatives think about international society, and solidarism is what happens when optimists/idealists/liberals do so. There is an element of truth in this view, but it is problematic for one big reason: pessimistic and optimistic evaluations do not arise only as a result of the predispositions of certain character-types. They can arise also as a result of how the things being evaluated are themselves defined and interpreted. As I hope to show in what follows, thinking more carefully about what pluralism and solidarism mean changes the basis on which they are evaluated. The detailed discussions of pluralism and solidarism in chapter 2 and in this chapter are thus necessary. It matters how things are defined.

If one accepts the 'thin–thick' characterisation of pluralism–solidarism developed in chapter 2, then the way forward in this enquiry is to first focus on developing an understanding of solidarism in interstate society, and then ask how this might relate to the interhuman and transnational domains. Recall that if one accepts the argument that all of international relations is social, that 'enemies' is just as much a social structure as 'rivals' or 'friends', then the term 'interstate society' covers a wide spectrum of phenomena ranging from Hobbesian social structures on one end, to Kantian at the other. In this perspective, the debate about pluralism and solidarism can be seen largely as a debate about types of interstate society, with pluralism representing a Westphalian model, and solidarism covering a swath of the spectrum from 'pluralism-plus' through Kantianism (homogenous state domestic structures on liberal lines), to the fringes of federation (at which point the 'international' dissolves into a single polity). Thinking along these lines might be construed as picking up Manning's (1962: 165) idea of international society as a game of 'let's-play-states'. What are the constitutive rules of the game of states (at the very least, sovereignty, territoriality, diplomacy), and how many basic variations (within the pluralist–solidarist spectrum) do these rules allow of the way in which the game can be played?

Where are the boundaries beyond which one is playing a game other than 'states'? Does the pursuit of solidarism eventually depart from the game of states and become some other game (empire, cosmopolitanism, federation)?

In the discussion of solidarism in chapter 2, some quite different interpretations were in play. Some, perhaps most notably Linklater, understand solidarism as a specifically liberal linkage between state sovereignty and individual rights. The link to human rights has played particularly strongly in English school thinking about solidarism. In Vincent, Bull, Mayall, Jackson and others one finds cosmopolitanism as the key to solidarism, and for Bull also one finds the question of provisions for enforcement. Suganami (2002: 13) sees the pluralist–solidarist debate as 'differing judgments about the extent of solidarity or potential solidarity' in international society, and I want to make explicit the criteria for differentiating judgements. At the risk of stating the obvious, solidarism rests on the idea of solidarity, which implies not only that a unity of interests and sympathies exists amongst a set of actors, but that this unity is of a type sufficient to generate capability for collective action. Two ideas are the key to unlocking the full meaning of solidarism: shared values, and the use of these to support collective action. In chapter 2, I argued that solidarism was crudely about the number of shared values, with many possible candidates for what those values might be. But there was already a hint in that argument that the type of values (coexistence or cooperation) was also a factor in the pluralist–solidarist distinction. In order to tease out this argument further, it helps to investigate three questions about solidarism.

(1) What type of values, if shared, count as solidarist?
(2) Does it make any difference to the question of solidarism how and why any given values are shared?
(3) What does 'thickness' mean in terms of type and number of values shared, and type and number of people and/or states sharing them?

These questions have so far only been addressed indirectly, if at all, in the pluralist–solidarist debate. They need to be examined in their own right.

In one sense, they can be seen as asking where the border is between pluralism and solidarism. At what point, and by what criteria, does an interstate society move from being pluralist to solidarist? Pluralist interstate societies are easy to visualise. Pluralism generally stands for the familiar Westphalian model based on mutual recognition of sovereignty and non-intervention. This model is widely used in both realist and English school writing, and has easy referents in much modern European and world history. Science fiction also registers here. One of the things that lifts the universe of *Star Trek* above its asocial compatriots in the genre from *War of the Worlds* to *Independence Day* and *Starship Troopers*, is its development of a pluralist galactic interstate society with diplomacy, alliances, rules of non-intervention ('the prime directive') and suchlike (Neumann 2001).

Contemplating solidarist interstate societies puts one on less familiar ground. The classic English school thinkers have not much developed this image except in terms of human rights, and those who have tried, most notably Vincent, quickly cross the border into world society by bringing in TNAs and individuals. Yet it is a useful discipline to start by confining the exploration of solidarism to interstate societies. The most obvious example of a solidarist interstate society that we have, albeit only as a subsystem, is the EU, and the English school has only just begun to engage with this regional development (Diez and Whitman 2000; Manners 2002). If one accepts the argument from chapter 2 that positive international law is the key to interstate society, then there is scope for a progressive development of interstate society in which the states work out agreed norms, rules and institutions covering various functional areas such as trade, finance, property rights, human rights, pollution and health and safety standards, standards of calibration and measurement, and suchlike. The EU example suggests that progressive solidarism of this sort must necessarily involve major parallel developments in the transnational and interhuman domains, and that the liberal version of interstate society as international society is certainly one possibility. But it is not the only possibility. One could imagine, for example, an interstate society that is solidarist in the sense of being based on a high degree of ideological uniformity, but where the shared values are nationalist rather than liberal. In such circumstances, governments might well develop a quite solidarist interstate society based on their shared view of the political ideal, while still also agreeing that each had the right and the duty to develop and foster its own distinctive national culture insulated from the others. Intimations of a benign nationalist scenario along these lines can be found in Herz (1950). For theory purposes, it is important to keep open the idea of solidarism as something that can happen purely within state systems (interstate societies), without necessarily requiring the spillovers into the interhuman and transnational domains that inevitably, at some point, become a feature of the liberal vision of solidarism. As I will show later, starting out with the focus on interstate societies is crucial to the subsequent move of asking how developments in the interstate domain relate to those in the interhuman and transnational domains.

What type of values, if shared, count as solidarist?

Since the image of pluralism is relatively clear, and since pluralism is the foundation on which solidarism has to be built, it makes a good place to start thinking about the criteria that distinguish solidarism from pluralism. Much of the writing about pluralism stresses the centrality of rules of coexistence as the essence of what pluralist international societies are about, with Jackson (2000) providing perhaps the strongest statement. Because it privileges tolerance of difference, coexistence is a relatively undemanding social goal. One of its enduring attractions is that, almost however understood, it does not threaten the constitutive rules of the game of states. Pluralism does not require moving much beyond the raw self-centredness and self-interest of egoistic sovereign actors – only that they recognise that their own survival and self-interest can be enhanced by agreeing some basic rules with the other actors in the system. Pluralist international societies thus encompass the first two of Bull's three types of rules discussed in chapter 2: constitutive principles (agreed as a society of states rather than a universal empire or a cosmopolitan community, or . . .); and rules of coexistence (which hinge on the basic elements of society: limits to violence, establishment of property rights and sanctity of agreements). Taken together, these provide the basis for Bull's conception of the *institutions* of classical European international society: diplomacy, international law, the balance of power, war and the role of great powers, to which should certainly be added sovereignty/non-intervention. Sovereignty is the designator of property rights and the basis for rules of recognition, and its corollary non-intervention sets the basic frame for political relations. As James (1999: 468) puts it, sovereignty is 'the constitutive principle of interstate relations'. The balance of power, war and the role of the great powers are about how the system is managed to put some limits on violence. Diplomacy and international law are about communication, negotiation and the sanctity of agreements. These institutions all play into each other, and as Mayall (2000: 94) notes, international law is 'the bedrock institution on which the idea of international society stands or falls'. This classical view of the institutions of international society pretty much sums up the modern European historical experience of a pluralist interstate society seeking order through rules of coexistence.

I will return to the question of the institutions of international society in chapter 6, but at this point one has to ask whether the classical portrait of pluralism just given represents the maximum that pluralism can encompass without spilling over into solidarism? In other words, how far does the logic of coexistence stretch? Bull's (1977a: 67–71) formulation wants to draw a line between constitutive rules and rules of coexistence on the one hand, and rules of cooperation on the other, defining the latter (1977a: 70) as prescribing 'behaviour that is appropriate not to the elementary or primary goals of international life, but rather to those more advanced or secondary goals that are a feature of an international society in which a consensus has been reached about a wider range of objectives than mere coexistence'. As noted in chapter 2, Bull's rules of cooperation suggest one way of defining solidarism, by drawing the line between it and pluralism's limitation to rules of coexistence. Alas, even a brief reflection on the modern history of pluralist interstate society suggests that Bull's distinction between rules of coexistence and rules of cooperation is too problematic to serve as the way of distinguishing between pluralist and solidarist interstate societies. The unquestionably pluralist, and mainly European, interstate society of the later nineteenth century, for example, was distinctive for setting up the first wave of intergovernmental organisations (IGOs). These aimed mostly at smoothing technical interoperability between states and peoples: the Universal Postal Union, the International Telecommunications Union, the International Bureau of Weights and Measures and suchlike. These would certainly have to count as 'rules of cooperation' fitting with the idea of 'more advanced or secondary goals that are a feature of an international society in which a consensus has been reached about a wider range of objectives than mere coexistence'. Yet they also seem, in essence, to be about coexistence. Like diplomacy, they are about reducing unnecessary frictions and inefficiencies in the intercourse of states and peoples. They do not threaten sovereignty, and they do not represent any substantial collective project at odds with a pluralist structure. One can see the present-day equivalent of these more advanced arrangements of coexistence in the bodies that allocate radio frequencies and orbital slots for geostationary satellites. Such arrangements, like their nineteenth-century precursors, reflect the pursuit of coexistence in a more technically advanced environment.

Examples of state behaviour from the Cold War suggest that the principle of coexistence might even be pushed into rules about dealing with shared dangers and common fates. Given the lamenting in English school classics about the deterioration of international society resulting from the Cold War rivalry of the superpowers, there can be little doubt that the interstate society of that time, at least at the global level, counted as pluralist (or even sub-pluralist, Hobbesian). Yet the US and the Soviet Union were able to sustain a dialogue, and establish a significant array of norms, rules and institutions, in areas where their fates were linked and they saw common dangers. The whole process of détente between them rested on a dialogue about arms control and the need to avoid unstable military configurations and unwanted crisis escalations. A limited amount of inspection was eventually allowed, though this issue was always deeply controversial. So even between enemies, fear of nuclear war made it possible to establish quite extensive cooperation around a shared interest in survival, adding its own nuance to the meaning of coexistence. It is not difficult to imagine other such grounds for cooperation: for example in response to a clear and present global environmental danger for which countermeasures were within reach. The measures taken to preserve the ozone layer fall comfortably within a logic of coexistence, where the emphasis is on measures necessary to maintain the conditions of existence for the members of the society. All such developments would be compatible with a pluralist international society committed to preserving its differences and taking a hard view of sovereignty and non-intervention. So, perhaps, would the array of cooperations observed by those neoliberal institutionalists who work with rational choice theory, and seek to derive the logic of international cooperation from the calculations of egoistic actors in pursuit of their own self-interest (Milner 1997; Snidal 1993).

Under pluralism, coexistence is rooted in the self-interest of the states composing interstate society. Self-interest certainly stretches to cooperation in pursuit of a livable international order, but it keeps the focus on differences among the states and does not require that they agree on anything beyond the basics, or that they hold any common values other than an interest in survival and the avoidance of unwanted disorder. It nevertheless needs to be noted that pluralism does not exclude the members of interstate society from sharing a degree of common identity. The institution of sovereignty serves as a kind of bottom line for shared identity inasmuch as the states are required to recognise each other as being the same type of entity with the same legal standing (Buzan 1993). But classical European interstate society also shared a conception of itself as 'Christendom' or 'la grande république', and the idea that a shared culture of some sort was, if not necessary, then extremely helpful, in underpinning interstate society is a commonplace in the Wight/Watson historical side of English school thinking. Pluralism, therefore, does not rule out an element of community. States in a pluralist society may share a weak common identity, as the Europeans shared Christendom, and as the Atlantic states currently share the idea of being 'Western'. They may well use this primarily to differentiate themselves from non-members, as when nineteenth-century Europeans defined themselves as civilised and others as barbarian or savage, and now, when the West defines itself as the first world in distinction from various second, third and fourth worlds. But this useful differentiation between us and them does not stop the members of a pluralist interstate society from constructing strong differentiations among themselves. In Europe, this was done first in terms of rival monarchs and *raison d'état*, and later, and more notoriously, in terms of a social Darwinist reading of nationalism.

If neither shared identity nor Bull's rules of cooperation provide the key to differentiating pluralism from solidarism, what does? Obviously one cannot go on stretching the meaning of coexistence forever. Just as obviously, solidarism almost certainly builds on the foundations laid down by pluralism, or at least must do so in its early and middle stages, whatever it might evolve into in its more advanced forms. At least some of Bull's essentially Westphalian institutions can easily be envisaged as operating in, and contributing to, a solidarist interstate society, most obviously diplomacy and international law, but also great power management and war. The portrait of pluralism painted above suggests two principles on which a departure into solidarism might be constructed. Both could be added to coexistence, yet both also move away from the key defining qualities of pluralism.

(1) States might abandon the pursuit of difference and exclusivity as their main *raison d'être*, and cultivate becoming more alike as a conscious goal. One might expect that there would be a correlation, on the one hand, between solidarism and a substantial degree of homogeneity amongst the domestic constitutions of the members, and on the other between diversity in the domestic constitutions of members and pluralism.

(2) States might acknowledge common values among them that go beyond survival and coexistence, and which they agree to pursue by

coordinating their policies, undertaking collective action, creating appropriate norms, rules and organisations, and revising the institutions of interstate society.

The first of these principles reflects a Kantian logic of convergence. The second is suggested by Mayall's (2000: 21) idea of 'an enterprise association . . . that exists to pursue substantive goals of its own'. Mayall clearly thinks that 'pursuing substantive goals of its own' transcends an understanding of pluralism as based on coexistence, and I imagine most pluralists would agree. He links this idea to cosmopolitanism, but that link is not necessary to the idea, and in what follows I will take it as being only one among several possibilities underpinning solidarism. In practice, convergence and pursuit of a joint project will often overlap, sometimes substantially, but this overlap is not a necessary one for all possible scenarios.

For convergence among states to move into the realm of solidarism, it would have to grow beyond the basic acknowledgement among them that they are all the same type of sovereign entity, which is the baseline of pluralism. This additional commonality might be thought of as a conscious move towards greater homogeneity in domestic structures and values among a set of states. It might be a Kantian community of liberal-democracies, as most existing discussions of solidarism presuppose. Or it might equally be a community of communist 'peoples' republics', or Islamic states, or monarchies, or any other form of ideological standardisation. It is essential for a sound theoretical development of solidarism to keep these non-liberal options open. The human rights focus of most solidarist writing has obscured them from view and generated a too narrow and too controversial understanding of what solidarism is about. I do not include here the cultivation of instrumental commonalities such as all landlocked states or all developing countries. Those can occur under pluralism as a matter of forming alliances on particular issues. Convergence in the sense necessary for solidarism has to involve a deeper sort of 'we-feeling'. It has to involve a package of values that is associated not just with belonging to the same civilisation (which was true for the states of classical pluralist Europe), but also with a substantial degree of convergence in the norms, rules, institutions and goals of the states concerned. Pluralism is abandoned when states not only recognise that they are alike in this sense, but see that a significant degree of similarity is valuable, and seek to reinforce the security and legitimacy of their own values by consciously linking with others who are like-minded, building a shared identity with them. Convergence in this sense begins to look like a form of community, and in its stronger forms will involve acceptance of some responsibility for other members of the community. The literature on pluralist security communities (Deutsch *et al.* 1957; Adler and Barnett 1998) explores exactly this type of development.

Although convergence is still hard to find on a global scale, on a sub-global scale it shows up rather strongly. The EU is a pretty advanced case of conscious convergence among states, and many of its stresses and strains result from the continuous necessity of adjusting to this process. The so-called 'Atlantic community', or in slightly wider form 'the West', or 'the liberal democracies' represent weaker, but still significant, instances of convergence around liberal democracy. Outside the West, one might see such bodies as the Arab League, the Gulf Cooperation Council and the Organisation of the Islamic Conference as representing at least aspirations in this direction, though mostly not backed up by much substance. Even globally the picture is not entirely bleak. Recall the argument made in chapter 2 about the apparent overdetermination of homogeneity of units in the international system. If the many theories that point in this direction are right, then the underpinnings of convergence are built into the operation of interstate society in several different ways. They may not yet have manifested their strength sufficiently to underpin any global solidarism, but they might be given some credit for pushing things along to where the logic of like-units is strong enough at least to support Coexistence forms of pluralism. Indeed, if homogenisation is overdetermined in the international system, then it should work in favour both of solidarist society and international and world community. But homogenisation is a tricky element in human affairs. While it may serve as a necessary condition for the development of both society and community, it is not therefore a sufficient one (Wendt 1999: 353–7). Groups of similar entities are prone to the notorious 'narcissism of small differences' that afflicts everything from religious communities to academic associations, and can lead to extreme social polarisations and violence. Wendt tried to tackle the question of homogeneity by distinguishing two types: *isomorphic*, which he sees as similar to Waltz's idea of like units (structural and functional similarity – see Buzan and Little 1996), and *ideological* (difference or not in the constitutive principles of political legitimacy). But it is not clear why there are only these two, since one could easily head the way of Rosenau's (1966) pre-theory, and the failed 1960s project of comparative foreign policy to construct typologies of states. This approach tends to be defeated by the huge number of significant variables on which states may or may not be alike. Homogeneity emerges as a subject in need of much more thinking. It could well be that increasing homogeneity amongst the dominant social units in the international system, rather than the processes of globalisation, is actually the main key to developments in international and world society. But what kinds of likeness are crucial, and how intense do they have to be?

The second principle on which an advance into solidarism can be constructed is that states might cooperate in one or more joint projects in pursuit of one or more common values. Such projects can of course come in as many different forms as there are common values that might be taken up in this way. And joint projects also raise the issue of enforcement. At the pluralist end of the spectrum, where international society is thin, collective enforcement of rules will be difficult and rare. Towards the solidarist end, where international society is thicker, a degree of collective enforcement in some areas might well become generally accepted and common. Bull's original idea of seeing collective security as a form of solidarism certainly seems right. But collective security usually comes attached to a universalist condition: anything less than universal participation is not true collective security but mere alliance-making. This definition sets an impossibly high standard, and therefore contributed to pluralist pessimism and rejection of solidarism as utopian. A softer understanding of collective security, which allowed sub-global developments such as NATO, opens up a more positive view. Surely NATO's development of joint command structures and extensive interoperability of forces, not to mention its agreement that an attack on one shall be treated as an attack on all, has a solidarist ring about it (Jackson 2000: 351–5).

The joint pursuit of human rights is by far the best-developed theme in the solidarist literature. From Vincent's (1986: 146) call, quoting Henry Kissinger, that: 'all governments should accept the removal of the scourge of hunger and malnutrition . . . as the objective of the international community as a whole', to Wheeler's (2000), Knudsen's (1999) and others' calls for greater protection of human beings against violent abuse by their governments, solidarists have campaigned both to promote the development of a human rights project by interstate society, and to increase awareness that a legal basis for this is already emergent (Weller 2002: 700). Because it is heavily aspirational and promotional, much of this literature depends on linking solidarism to supposedly universalist cosmopolitan values. As noted above, pursuit of a human rights agenda raises difficult questions about ends and means that have not been adequately explored. If observance of human rights has to be imposed on those who do not share belief in the value, and/or do not calculate observance of it as being to their advantage, then one faces the problem that this project can, in the short term, only be expanded by coercive means. Here, as elsewhere, solidarists cannot escape the dilemma, apparent in the whole story of the expansion of international society, that rules about a 'standard of civilisation' are generally spread from a sub-global core by a mixture of means in which coercion is often prominent. This problem is what animates the more extreme defenders of tolerant, non-interventionist pluralism such as Jackson (2000). The universalist requirement also means that too little attention has been given to substantial solidarist developments on a sub-global scale (for example, in the EU).

As Jackson (2000: 176–7) points out, environmentalism is another distinctive area for solidarist development. The idea that states (and/or citizens) should have trusteeship or stewardship of the planet itself is a value quite distinct from human rights. As I have argued above, elements of environmentalism can develop, and have done so, within the pluralist logic of coexistence. But this agenda readily spills over into a much more ambitious collective project encompassing everything from the preservation of particular species and their environments to management of the planetary climate. It could easily be argued that, as with human rights, the environmentalist agenda represents a leading aspirational element of solidarism, but also one in which not insignificant practical measures have already been accomplished (e.g. restraints on trade in endangered species or products derived from them; restraints on various types of pollution).

Collective security, human rights and environmentalism still represent the aspirational more than the empirical side of solidarism – a campaign for collective self-improvement of the human condition. There have been some practical developments, but these are small in relation to what most solidarists would like to see. What strikes me as peculiar, is the way in which the focus on human rights has resulted in the almost complete ignoring of two other areas in which real solidarist developments have been most spectacular: the pursuit of joint gain and the pursuit of knowledge.

It is long past time to begin repairing the English school's neglect of the economic sector. The most obvious exemplar of solidarism in the pursuit of joint gains lies in liberal understandings of how to organise the economic sector. In order to realise joint gains, a liberal international economy has to be organised around a host of rules about trade, property rights, legal process, investment, banking, corporate law and suchlike. Unless states can cooperate to liberalise trade and finance, so liberal theory goes, they will remain stuck with lower levels of growth and innovation, higher costs and lower efficiencies than would otherwise be the case. In order to realise these gains, states have both to open their borders and coordinate their behaviours in selected but systematic ways. In other words, they have to agree to homogenise their domestic structures in a number of quite central respects. Over the past half-century this has in fact been done to a quite remarkable degree, though still short of what the more strident neoliberals continue to demand. Although initially subglobal, this development of solidarism is now nearly global in extent. What is more, it is held in place by an elaborate mixture of belief, calculation and coercion, and displays all the complexities of 'thickness' surveyed below (see pp. 154–7). These qualities make it an ideal case study for both the *what* and the *how/why*, of solidarism in action, and provide excellent leverage on the question of (in)stability in solidarist arrangements. The liberal economic project even includes some significant enforcement measures, thus meeting the hard test of willingness to support the collective enforcement of international law that was one of Bull's (1966a: 52) benchmarks for solidarism. There is a pressing need for the English school to bring its perspective to bear on the work in IPE.

Also neglected is the collective pursuit of knowledge, again an area in which the actual record of solidarist achievement is quite impressive. International cooperation in 'big science' projects such as physics, astronomy and space exploration now has a substantial record, from the multinational projects to pursue high-energy physics, through global coordination of astronomical observations, to innumerable joint space probes and the international space station. Some of this lies in the transnational domain, but a great deal is interstate. In contrast to the economic sector, coercion plays almost no role. Belief not only in the pursuit of knowledge for its own sake, but also in the means by which such knowledge can be pursued, is sufficiently widespread in the world to underpin cooperation motivated by belief and the calculation of joint gain. It is worth noting that this kind of joint project is highly constrained under pluralism, where it might cut too closely to concerns about technologies with military applications.

All of these joint projects threaten sovereignty if it is defined in strict pluralist terms. As the solidarists have long recognised in relation to human rights, such projects require states to redefine how their sovereignty and their boundaries operate, and this is what differentiates solidarist societies from pluralist ones.

Does it make any difference to solidarism how and why any given values are shared?

Since pluralism is rooted in the survival instincts and self-interests of states it does not raise serious questions about either what values are shared or how and why they are shared. If there are shared values they will either be instrumental, technical ones, such as those to do with communication and common standards, or ones closely related to survival questions, such as those associated with arms control or environmental management. Solidarism, by contrast, rests on the idea that states share values that are beyond concerns about survival and coexistence, and significant enough to underpin the pursuit of joint projects and/or convergence. For solidarism, therefore, the twin questions of what values are shared, and how and why they are shared, become central. Because the pluralist–solidarist debate got hung up on the particular issue of human rights, the English school has not investigated sufficiently the question of what the range of values is that can constitute solidarism, and not confronted directly the difficult questions about the binding forces that underpin shared values. Given both the background of English school work on the expansion of international society, and the particular nature of the human rights issue, this neglect is surprising. The general history about how a European interstate society became a global one is a story in which persuasion and conversion played some role, but coercion was the main engine by which a 'standard of civilisation' was imposed (Gong 1984; Bull and Watson 1984a). As noted in chapter 4 (see pp. 98–108), similar, though usually less militarised, coercive practices continue today, and the war against Iraq in 2003 could easily be read as old style coercive imposition of a 'standard of civilisation'.

The human rights issue likewise features coercion. Solidarists would prefer it if all states came around to accepting the values of human rights. But they do not shy away from advocating military intervention on humanitarian grounds, and they advocate making recognition of sovereign rights conditional on observance of a human rights standard of civilisation rooted in cosmopolitan values (Wheeler 2000: 288–310). Solidarists, therefore, cannot avoid confronting the double normative implication inherent in their stance of human rights advocacy. Moral questions arise not only in relation to *what* values are shared, but also in relation to *how and why* they are shared. In its bluntest form, the moral issue here is whether it is right to use 'bad' means (coercion) to impose observance of 'good' values (human rights). In principle this moral dualism applies to any shared values that might define the *what* dimension of solidarism explored above (pp. 143–52). As Hurrell (2002a: 149) argues, the decline of consent-based adherence to international society gives rise to tensions between 'sets of rules that seek to moderate amongst different values and those that seek to promote and enforce a single set of universal values'.

Recall the discussion from chapter 4 of Wendt's degrees and modes of internalisation (coercion, calculation and belief) and how these were incorporated as the *how/why* dimension in figure 4. Wendt's insight is that the different means by which social structures of any sort can be created and sustained do <u>not</u> determine the values defining the social structure. In principle any type of social structure can be supported by any type of means. The upshot of this argument is that one has to ask of any type of solidarist international society whether the shared values on display rest mainly on coercion, calculation or belief. Solidarist/Kantian social structures could be deeply internalised as a result of shared belief in liberal principles, and/or they could be a result of instrumental calculations of advantage, and/or they could be a result of a coercive suzerain able and willing to impose its values on others. If understood in terms of sustained patterns of behaviour, solidarism is not necessarily about belief. Hurrell (2002a: 143–4) opens the way to this interpretation with his argument that norms encompass both 'regularities of behaviour among actors' and a prescriptive sense of what ought to be done. But note the ambiguity of 'ought'. It seems to imply beliefs that differentiate right from wrong in an ethical sense, but could also be read in a more rational, consequentialist mode of the need to respond to the imperatives of calculation or coercion ('you ought to behave properly or you will be punished . . .'). In this view people share the value of human rights (or economic liberalism, or . . .) so long as they behave appropriately to the value, and regardless of why they do so. The key to solidarism is what values are shared, not how/why they are shared, which will always be a mix of coercion, calculation and belief. Belief is the preferable form of solidarism, but not the necessary one, especially where solidarism is based on pursuit of joint gain. The pursuit of joint gains in the economic sector might be based in part on shared belief in the tenets of economic liberalism, but its mainstay is more likely to be calculations of advantage, and some weaker players will simply be coerced into going along. The projection of a 'standard of civilisation' will also rest on some mixture of coercion, calculation and belief. As the solidarist literature on human rights makes clear, coercion is not ruled out in the pursuit of solidarist international society: that the right values <u>are</u> observed is more important than how/why they are observed. Thus Wendt's question about depth of internalisation is highly relevant for understanding solidarism. Where solidarism is based mainly on belief, it will be most durable. Where based on calculation or coercion, it will be much more vulnerable to changes of circumstance. These variations in binding forces matter, but they do not define what solidarism is.

What does 'thickness' mean in terms of type and number of values shared, and type and number of people and/or states sharing them?

I have argued that pluralism and solidarism should be seen as a spectrum ranging from 'thin' to 'thick' in terms of the values shared amongst the states composing interstate society. The implication in figure 4 was that relative thinness and thickness along these lines could be used to set benchmarks for demarcating progression from pluralist through solidarist to Kantian international societies. As noted above, this approach is in harmony with the several writers (Almeida 2001; James 1993; Watson 1987: 151–2) who observe that even the most primitive international systems have some elements of international society (in terms of shared norms, rules, institutions). I share Almeida's (2002) understanding that pluralism and solidarism are not necessary opposites, but can coexist. The argument above (pp. 143–52) suggested that qualitative factors to do with the type of shared value should be one criterion for judging the thinness or thickness of interstate societies. Values relating to the survival and self-interest of the states, and to coexistence, defined pluralism and therefore thinness. Values to do with convergence and the pursuit of joint projects defined solidarism and therefore thickness.

But if one accepts the general idea of a spectrum from thin to thick defined in terms of the type of value(s) shared, this still leaves some questions about what 'thin' and 'thick' mean. The argument above (pp. 152–4) reinforced the primacy of *what* values are shared by making the case that the *how/why* of shared values (coercion, calculation, belief) applies to all the types of values across the spectrum. So the type of values shared does matter. Since solidarism builds on pluralism it is also pretty easy to make the case that the number of shared values also matters. Moving into the solidarist part of the spectrum will mean adding new values to those already accumulated under pluralism, which could, as explained above on the logic of coexistence, encompass quite a wide range of cooperation. It is not difficult to envisage that international societies pursuing convergence will pursue extensions in the number and type of values shared. This still leaves the tricky questions of who holds the values and how strongly they do so.

When one says that a state shares a given value with other states, what does this mean? At a minimum, it means that the present leadership of that state holds that value. At a maximum, it means that the value is widely diffused throughout the elites and the mass of ordinary citizens. In between lie innumerable configurations of contestation and indifference. The value may be strongly supported by one political party and its followers, and strongly opposed by another and its supporters. Or it may be widely supported among the elites, but regarded with suspicion or hostility by a substantial part of the population (the Davos culture versus the anti-globalisation movement). If this pattern extends across state borders, such that a set of ruling elites support a value, but their citizens mostly oppose it, one finds the grounds for tension between international and world society that so worries some English school writers. As with the *how/why* dimension discussed above, variations of this kind will make a difference to the stability of international society, opening up the possibility that even quite advanced, seemingly solidarist international societies may in fact be quite fragile, and vulnerable to sudden reversals because of domestic political changes in key countries. Thus a value such as human rights, or economic liberalism, might be quite widely held if viewed simply as a matter of current government policy across a set of states, but be fragile because of the way it is held within some or all of those states.

On top of who holds the value, there is the additional question of how strongly those who hold it do so. Any person can hold any value with a degree of commitment ranging from passionate and overriding to a rather mild and marginal acceptance. One may hold oneself to be a Christian (or a Japanese, or a Manchester United supporter or whatever) with a strength positioned anywhere on this spectrum. Some values (most notably fundamentalist religion and hypernationalism), are associated with attempts to cultivate a single overriding commitment. Others will usually be found in an array of overlapping beliefs (the famous layers of postmodern identity ranging from member of the human race to supporter of local football team). This question is not the same as Wendt's one about mode/depth of internalisation, though the two may interact with each other. Belief may range from overriding to mild. It is easy to find, for example, fanatical Christians (or Muslims, or . . .) whose whole lives revolve almost entirely around their religious beliefs, and Muslims (or . . .) for whom their faith is still belief, but of a very background sort. It is also the case that coercion might induce a high degree of conforming behaviour in some individuals, and only very superficial conforming in others, a spectrum that could be observed in relation to communist ideology in what during the Cold War were called the Eastern European states. Although not the same as the *how/why* dimension, this variable also affects the stability of a solidarist international society.

One useful perspective on this question of how strongly values are held can be found in the special issue of *International Organization* on legalisation (2000, 54:3, see also Ratner 1998). The argument there is that legalisation of international agreements among states varies on a spectrum from 'soft' to 'hard'. How soft or hard any particular arrangement is depends on a combination of how binding its terms are on the participants, how precise the terms of the agreement are in terms of prescriptions and proscriptions on behaviour, and how much power is delegated by the signatories to institutions or third parties to monitor, manage and enforce the terms (Goldstein *et al.* 2000; Abbott *et al.* 2000). The argument is that soft and hard legalisations do not necessarily correlate with soft = bad/weak and hard = good/strong. Soft legalisation is better for some kinds of circumstances, hard for others (Abbott and Snidal 2000). This approach gives a nice insight into the thickness or thinness of institutionalisation. Another useful perspective is Krasner's (1999: 44) spectrum of high-to-low conformity with principles and norms.

Adding in the variables of how many shared values, held by who, and how strongly held, and how legalised, makes the question of thin/thick quite complicated. It is easy to imagine many combinations and permutations that could present themselves as solidarist in terms of the type and number of values shared amongst states. These would vary not only as regards the particular character and number of values shared, but also in terms of how widely and deeply they were shared within, and therefore between, the states concerned. A solidarist interstate society might hinge mainly on shared values to do with economics, or mainly on human rights. These values might be held widely or narrowly and/or strongly or weakly. What this scope for variation suggests is that degree of thinness or thickness of interstate society does not offer the type of simplification necessary for it to be theorised and used as a benchmark to define either causes or effects in formal theory. The possible variance <u>within</u> any given position on the spectrum requires that cases be looked at individually, and analyses made according to the particular balance of these factors within them. There is scope here for comparative method.

What this discussion of thinness and thickness most usefully reveals is that analysts of interstate society need to focus as much on the <u>stability</u> of sets of shared values among states as on <u>what</u> the shared values are. Krasner (1999: 44) comes close to this with his discussion of the durability of institutions – the degree to which they change with change of circumstance. Recall that what values are held is not affected by the *how/why* dimension (Wendt's mode/depth of internalisation). Especially when one is dealing with societies of states, this variable has to be considered separately. It is entirely possible to envisage interstate societies that in a day-to-day operational sense share a sufficient number and type of values additional to coexistence to count as solidarist, but that are largely held together by coercion and calculation. The former Soviet bloc gives the flavour, as do some of the great empires of history. Adding to this *how/why* argument the *thin/thick* issues raised here make the stability of interstate societies a separate question from their degree of advancement in terms of a pluralist–solidarist spectrum. <u>Any</u> given interstate society will be more stable to the extent that its shared values are internalised more by belief than by calculation or coercion; are held broadly rather than narrowly within states; do not inspire widespread and/or substantial opposition within the state; and are held strongly rather than weakly by those who do hold them. It will be less stable to the extent that its shared values are internalised more by coercion than by calculation or belief; are held narrowly within the states; attract widespread and/or substantial opposition within the state; and are held weakly by those who do hold them. Crucial to the stability or not of any interstate society as a whole will be whether these things are true within and between the leading powers.

Conclusions

Whether or not people agree with the interpretation I have put on the pluralist–solidarist debate in this chapter, I hope it at least challenges them to make their own positions clearer, and provides a benchmark against which to do so. I hope I have demonstrated that although solidarism may be linked to cosmopolitanism the link is not a necessary one, and pretending that it is has large costs in terms of how solidarism is understood. I hope also to have made a strong case that pluralism and solidarism can be used to think about societies of states, and that they are best cast as defining the basis for a typology of interstate societies. All I have done here is to establish that solidarism does not necessarily have to be seen as a mixture of international and world society. This move opens up analytical space for a range of non-liberal solidarisms. Certain, mainly liberal, forms of solidarism will automatically involve extensions of rights, responsibilities and recognitions to individuals and TNAs, and thus tie together interstate, interhuman and transnational society in important ways. But some will not. Those campaigning in the name of solidarism need to be aware that they are advocating a particular type of solidarist international society, and not solidarism *per se*. They also need to add to their concerns about *what* values are shared an equal concern with those variables that affect the stability of solidarist international societies: *how* and *why* are values shared, by whom, how strongly and with what degree of opposition.

Taking all this into consideration, figure 4 requires some further revision. First, pluralism and solidarism need to be repositioned so that they define the spectrum of types of interstate society rather than being positions within it as they are in figures 1–4. This move reflects the conclusion that solidarism is determined largely by the type of value shared, and within that, the number of values shared. It allows for the idea that solidarism at least initially builds on pluralism to become pluralism-plus, but can then develop into a variety of thicker versions. Second, having withdrawn pluralism and solidarism from the role of identifying only two types of international society, I relabel the spectrum with a set of benchmark positions identifying types of interstate society. At this point it seems appropriate to abandon the English school's and Wendt's tradition of linking types of interstate society to iconic political theorists. Tying types of interstate society to Hobbes, Locke, Grotius and Kant has some appeal, but it is fundamentally Western-centric, and for non-Western cases easily gets in the way. Instead I will adopt a set of

158

Plan View = *What* Dimension

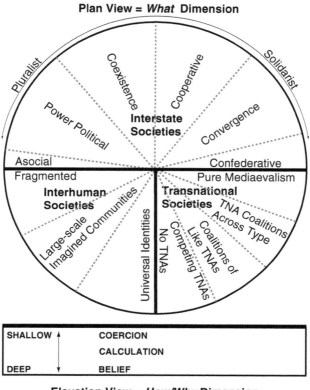

SHALLOW ↑	COERCION
	CALCULATION
DEEP ↓	BELIEF

Elevation View = *How/Why* Dimension
(Mode/Depth of Internalisation)

Figure 5. The 'Three Traditions' fourth revision: repositioning the pluralist and solidarist spectrum

more neutral, functionally based labels. These changes are set out in figure 5.

The new set of positions along the spectrum of interstate societies can be summarised as follows.

- *Asocial* is confined to the rather rare condition, found mostly in science fiction, where the only contact between states is wars of extermination unaccompanied by diplomacy or any other form of social contact.
- *Power political* represents here much the same as Hobbesian does for Wendt and the traditional English school's 'international system' pillar, namely an international society based largely on enmity and the

possibility of war, but where there is also some diplomacy, alliance-making and trade. Survival is the main motive for the states, and no values are necessarily shared. Institutions will be minimal, mostly confined to rules of recognition and diplomacy.

- *Coexistence* occupies some of the zone taken by Wendt's (1999: 279–97) uncomfortably broad Lockean category, focusing on the exemplar of modern Europe, and meaning by it the kind of Westphalian system in which the core institutions of international society are the balance of power, sovereignty, territoriality, diplomacy, great power management, war and international law. In the English school literature this form is labelled pluralist and incorporates the realist side of Grotian.
- *Cooperative* requires developments that go significantly beyond coexistence, but short of extensive domestic convergence. It incorporates the more solidarist side of what the English school calls Grotian, but might come in many guises, depending on what type of values are shared and how/why they are shared. Probably war gets downgraded as an institution, and other institutions might arise to reflect the solidarist joint project(s) (more on this in chapter 6).
- *Convergence* means the development of a substantial enough range of shared values within a set of states to make them adopt similar political, legal and economic forms. The range of shared values has to be wide enough and substantial enough to generate similar forms of government (liberal democracies, Islamic theocracies, communist totalitarianisms) and legal systems based on similar values in respect of such basic issues as property rights, human rights and the relationship between government and citizens. One would expect quite radical changes in the pattern of institutions of international society. This definition makes clear the divorce of solidarism from cosmopolitanism. In a society of states the Kantian form of solidarism around liberal values identified by the English school and Wendt is one option, but not the only one.
- *Confederative* defines the border zone between a solidarist interstate society and the creation of a single political entity (between anarchy and hierarchy in Waltz's terminology). It is a convergence international society with the addition of significant intergovernmental organisations (EU model).

The idea that each of these types (with the probable exception of asocial) can be held in place by any mixture of coercion, calculation and belief remains unchanged.

6   The primary institutions of international society

The debate about pluralism and solidarism leads into the question of the institutions of international society. It seems safe to say that there will be a close relationship between where an international society is located on the pluralist–solidarist spectrum, and either what type of institutions it has, or how it interprets any given institution. A number of authors have, for example, tracked the evolution of sovereignty, relating it, *inter alia*, to changes in the internal character of the dominant states (Keohane 1995; Reus-Smit 1997; Barkin 1998; Sørensen 1999). The concept of institutions is central to English school thinking for three reasons: first, because it fleshes out the substantive content of international society; second, because it underpins what English school writers mean by 'order' in international relations; and third, because the particular understanding of institutions in English school thinking is one of the main things that differentiates it from the mainstream, rationalist, neoliberal institutionalist, study of international regimes. Quite a bit has been written about the similarities and differences between the English school approach to institutions and that of regime theory (Keohane 1988; Hurrell 1991; Evans and Wilson 1992; Buzan 1993; Wæver 1998: 109–12; Alderson and Hurrell 2000). There is general agreement that these two bodies of literature overlap at several points, and that there is significant complementarity between them. The essential differences are:

(1) regime theory is more focused on contemporary events while the English school has a mainly historical perspective;
(2) regime theory is primarily concerned with 'particular human-constructed arrangements, formally or informally organised' (Keohane 1988: 383), whereas the English school is primarily concerned with 'historically constructed normative structures' (Alderson and

Hurrell 2000: 27); the shared culture elements that precede rational cooperation, or what Keohane (1988: 385) calls enduring 'fundamental practices' which shape and constrain the formation, evolution and demise of the more specific institutions. Onuf (2002) labels this distinction as 'evolved' versus 'designed' institutions.

(3) Closely tied to the previous point is that the English school has placed a lot of emphasis on the way in which the institutions of international society and its members are mutually constitutive. To pick up Manning's metaphor of the game of states, for the English school institutions define what the pieces are and how the game is played. Regime theory tends to take both actors and their preferences as given, and to define the game as cooperation under anarchy. This difference is complemented and reinforced by one of method, with regime theory largely wedded to rationalist method (Kratochwil and Ruggie 1986), and the English school resting on history, normative political theory and international legal theory;

(4) regime theory has applied itself intensively to institutionalisation around economic and technological issues, both of which have been neglected by the English school which has concentrated mainly on the politico-military sector;

(5) regime theory has pursued its analysis mainly in terms of actors pursuing self-interest using the mechanisms of rational cooperation; while the English school has focused mainly on common interests and shared values, and the mechanisms of international order (Evans and Wilson 1992: 337–9);

(6) *de facto*, but not in principle, regime theory has mainly studied sub-global phenomena. Its stock-in-trade is studies of specific regimes, which usually embody a subset of states negotiating rules about some specific issue (fishing, pollution, shipping, arms control, trade etc.). The English school has subordinated the sub-global to the systemic level, talking mainly about the character and operation of international society as a whole.

The fact that there are two schools of thought within mainstream IR (not to mention others outside IR) both claiming the concept of 'institutions' is in itself a recipe for confusion (Wæver 1998: 109–12). This situation is not helped by a pervasive ambiguity in what differentiates many of the associated concepts such as norms, rules and principles. The first section takes a brief look at the definitional problems with these concepts. The second reviews how the concept of institutions is handled in the English school literature. The third examines the concept of institutions through the lenses of hierarchy and functionalism, with a particular look at the distinction between constitutive and regulatory rules. The fourth surveys the relationship between the range of institutions and the types of international society. The fifth section concludes by reflecting on three questions: the relationship, if any, between institutions in the English school sense, and more materialist structural interpretations of the same phenomena; and the two questions left hanging in chapter 4 – one about how the interhuman, transnational and interstate domains relate to each other, and the other about the fate of the concepts 'international' and 'world' society in my structural scheme.

Definitional problems

The terms 'norms', 'rules', 'values' and 'principles' are scattered throughout the literature of both regime theory and the English school, yet it is seldom clear what, if anything, differentiates them, and in many usages they seem interchangeable. All are linked by the idea that their existence should shape expectations about the behaviour of the members of a social group. But what are the differences among shared norms and shared values and shared principles? Are norms and rules just shaded variations of the same thing? Perhaps the best-known attempt to confront this is Krasner's (1983: 2; see also Kratochwil and Ruggie 1986: 769–71) definition of regimes as:

> implicit or explicit principles, norms, rules and decision-making procedures around which actors' expectations converge in a given area of international relations. Principles are beliefs of fact, causation, and rectitude. Norms are standards of behaviour defined in terms of rights and obligations. Rules are specific prescriptions or proscriptions for actions. Decision-making procedures are prevailing practices for making and implementing collective choice.

This is quite helpful, but does not really produce clear, mutually exclusive concepts. There does not, for example, seem to be much difference between a principle understood as a belief of rectitude, and a norm understood as behaviour defined in terms of rights and obligations. Principles might serve as general propositions from which rules can be deduced, but inductive reasoning might also lead from rules to principles. Krasner's distinction between norms and rules seems to hinge on the degree of formality. Both aim to regulate behaviour, and both carry the sense that they are authoritative, though neither can be seen as causal (Kratochwil and Ruggie 1986: 767). In Krasner's scheme, norms feel more like the customs of a society, with rules occupying the more formal, written, possibly legal end of the spectrum. Yet norms could also be written down, and the general understanding of rules includes customary practices. It is fundamentally unclear how (or whether) these two concepts can be disentangled. The task is not made easier by Krasner's opening move of declaring that all of these concepts can be 'implicit or explicit' which weakens the basis for a distinction between norms and rules on grounds of degree of (in)formality. It is also unclear what the standing of 'decision-making procedures' is in this scheme. Identifying them as 'prevailing practices' simply disguises the fact that they could be principles, or norms or rules. They do not seem to be something that falls outside the first three concepts. Krasner does not mention values, and this term is much more important in the English school literature than in the regime theory one. A conventional understanding of values in the social sense is: the moral principles and beliefs or accepted standards of a person or social group. 'Moral principles and beliefs or accepted standards' easily embraces principles, norms and rules.

The unavoidable entanglements among Krasner's concepts perhaps explain why these terms are so often grouped together: 'norms, rules and principles' or 'norms, rules and institutions'. Even Kratochwil (1989: 10) uses rules, norms and principles as synonyms, and though he promises to distinguish them later in the book it is far from clear that he ever does so. Despite the difficulties, Krasner's formulation does suggest some helpful distinctions that are worth keeping in mind. The idea that norms represent the customary, implicit end of the authoritative social regulation of behaviour, and rules the more specific, explicit end, can often be useful, and I will try to retain that sense when I use the terms separately.

The concept of institutions shares some of the ambiguities that attend 'rules'. In common usage, 'institution' can be understood either in quite specific terms as 'an organisation or establishment founded for a specific purpose', or in more general ones as 'an established custom, law, or relationship in a society or community' (Hanks 1986). As noted above, these different meanings play strongly into what distinguishes English school theory from regime theory. Regime theory is mostly concerned with the first sense, though, as noted, regimes go beyond the idea of intergovernmental organisation. Keohane (1988: 383–5) is keen to draw a distinction between 'specific institutions' understood as things 'that can be identified as related complexes of rules and norms, identifiable in space and time', and 'more fundamental practices' providing 'institutionalized constraints at a more . . . enduring level', a distinction also pursued by Wæver (1998: 109–12). Keohane puts particular emphasis on rules, arguing that specific institutions exist where there is a 'persistent set of rules' that must 'constrain activity, shape expectation, and prescribe roles'. This confines his meaning of institution either to formal organisations with 'capacity for purposive action' or international regimes comprising 'complexes of rules and organisations', a distinction also made by Kratochwil and Ruggie (1986). This comes close to making the meaning of institution synonymous with intergovernmental organisations and legal frameworks.

Some IR definitions of institution act to blur these two meanings. Krasner (1999: 43), for example, sees institutions as: 'formal or informal structures of norms and rules that are created by actors to increase their utility'. This formulation seems to lean towards designed rather than evolved institutions, but since 'created' is unmodified, could be read either way. A more elaborate blurring is offered by March and Olson (1998: 948): '"institution" can be viewed as a relatively stable collection of practices and rules defining appropriate behaviour for specific groups of actors in specific situations. Such practices and rules are embedded in structures of meaning and schemes of interpretation that explain and legitimize particular identities and the practices and rules associated with them'. Here the first sentence seems to speak to Keohane's specific institutions, the second to his more fundamental practices. From the Stanford school (Meyer *et al.* 1987: 13) we get a definition that leans quite definitely towards the fundamental practices side: 'We see institutions as cultural rules giving collective meaning and value to particular entities and activities, integrating them into larger schemes. We see both patterns of activity and the units involved in them (individuals and other social entities) as constructed by such wider rules.'

Although Wæver (1998: 112) thinks that the English school operates across these meanings, and is confused about its position, a case can be made that in fact it largely takes the second, more general, sense of institution as its starting point. Bull (1977a: 40, 74) goes out of his way to make clear that when he talks of institutions he does not mean intergovernmental organisations or administrative machinery. Bull wants to get at Keohane's 'fundamental practices'. Keohane mainly discusses only one member of this category (sovereignty), which he also picks up in later work (Keohane 1995), though he acknowledges that there are others, including Bull's set (1988: 383). The English school has explored a range of candidates within this deeper sense of institution, and it is on this basis that much of its claim to distinctiveness rests.

Standing back from the IR debates, the English school's understanding of institutions feels close to that developed by Searle (1995). Searle argues that institutions are created when a social function and status are allocated to something but which do not reflect its intrinsic physical properties. A wall keeps people out physically, whereas markers can do so socially if accepted by those concerned. Money is the easiest example where an exchange commodity evolved into paper money which has no intrinsic value other than its status of recognition as money. Money, and much else in the social world, is kept in place by collective agreement or acceptance. Searle's idea is that human societies contain large numbers of institutions in this sense, and consequently large numbers of what he calls 'institutional facts' resulting from them (e.g. husbands and wives resulting from the institution of marriage). For Searle (1995: 2, 26) institutional facts are a subset of social facts, which arise out of collective intentionality. Social facts are distinct from 'brute' facts which exist without human thought affecting them. He notes (57) that 'each use of the institution is a renewed expression of the commitment of the users to the institution', which underlines the concern with 'practices' in the IR literature on this subject.

Both the specific, designed, and the deeper, evolved understandings represent legitimate interpretations of 'institutions', and there is no good reason for trying to exclude one or the other from its meaning. Neither meaning is contested, and since the essential difference between them is clear, the issue is simply to find a way of clarifying which meaning is in play. Given the influence of international law(yers) on Bull, it is perhaps worth pointing out that the distinction between primary and secondary institutions does <u>not</u> derive from Hart's (1961: 79–99) well-known formulation about primary and secondary rules. Hart's concern was to distinguish between primary rules (defining (il)legitimate activity in any society), and secondary rules (which are about transforming custom into a formal framework of law and justice). The institutions talked about in regime theory are the products of a certain type of international society (most obviously liberal, but possibly other types as well), and are for the most part consciously designed by states. The institutions talked about by the English school are constitutive of both states and international society in that they define the basic character and purpose of any such society. For second-order societies (where the members are themselves collective actors), such institutions define the units that compose the society. Searle (1995: 35) argues that 'social facts in general, and institutional facts especially, are hierarchically structured'. On this basis, and given that there is no disagreement about the English school's institutions reflecting something 'more fundamental', it does not seem unreasonable to call what the English school (and the Stanford school) wants to get at *primary institutions*, and those referred to by regime theory as *secondary institutions*.

The concept of primary institutions in English school literature

If the English school's focus is primary institutions, how are these defined, and what range of possibilities is encompassed? Regime theorists dealing with secondary institutions can make do with general definitions such as those provided by Krasner and Keohane. Within such definitions there are nearly infinite possibilities for types of formal organisation and regime. An indication of the type and range of diversity can be found in the discussion about 'hard' and 'soft' law referred to in chapter 5, and the three independent variables (obligation, precision, delegation) that produce degrees of hardness and softness in legalisation (Goldstein *et al.* 2000; Abbott *et al.* 2000). Dealing with primary institutions is a rather different proposition. Most English school writers spend little if any time defining what they mean by 'the institutions of international society', concentrating instead on listing and discussing a relatively small number that they take to define the essence of whatever international society they are examining. Since the idea of primary institutions is not controversial even for those who wish to focus on secondary institutions, the English school's neglect of definitions, though a shortcoming in its literature, does not weaken its general position. Usage of the term 'institutions' within the English school literature fits pretty well with the key features of primary institutions identified by others, viz.:

- that they are relatively fundamental and durable practices, that are evolved more than designed; and
- that they are constitutive of actors and their patterns of legitimate activity in relation to each other.

With this understanding in mind, and given that the English school literature is the main one making a sustained effort to develop the idea of primary institutions for international society, it is worth surveying its candidates for the primary institutions as a starting point for an investigation into what this universe might contain. It seems immediately clear, for example, that second-order societies, being simpler and having many fewer members than Searle's first-order human societies, will contain a relatively small number of primary institutions.

Wight (1979: 111) says that 'the institutions of international society are according to its nature', which implies that institutions will be different from one type of international society to another. This is consistent with his more historical work (Wight 1977: 29–33, 47–9) in which he identifies various institutions of premodern international societies including: messengers, conferences and congresses, a diplomatic language, trade, religious sites and festivals. Wight does not attempt any distinction between primary and secondary institutions, and his list could be boiled down to diplomacy, trade, and religious sites and festivals. Also looking backward, Reus-Smit (1997) notes arbitration as a distinctive feature of classical Greek international society, and Cohen (1998) could easily be read as a study of diplomacy as an institution in ancient and classical times. In a study of premodern China, Zhang (2001) looks at sovereignty, diplomacy, balance of power and a form of ritual analogous to international law during China's anarchic phase (770–221 BC), and adds the idea that the tribute system was an institution of the classical Sino-centric international society in East Asia. Warner (2001: 69–76) shows just how different from Westphalian models the institutions of classical Islamic international society were, in the process illustrating both the contradictions when the West imposed itself, and the range of possibilities within the idea of primary institutions. These ideas about premodern institutions suggest an evolution from the simpler arrangements of tribes, city-states and empires in the ancient and classical period, into the more sophisticated Westphalian criteria of the modern states system, with some overlap in the role of dynastic principles. Wight (1979: 111–12) goes on to enumerate those of (what from the context is) the international society of the first half of the twentieth century, as: 'diplomacy, alliances, guarantees, war and neutrality'. Somewhat inconsistently, he then says that: 'Diplomacy is the institution for negotiating. Alliances are the institution for effecting a common interest. Arbitration is an institution for the settlement of minor differences between states. War is the institution for the final settlement of differences.' Elsewhere Wight (1977: 110–52) puts a lot of emphasis on diplomacy, sovereignty, international law and balance of power as distinctive to European international society, but he does not anywhere draw together his various comments on institutions into a coherent discussion.

Bull puts institutions on the map for the English school, and his set of five institutions of 'international' (= interstate) society (diplomacy, international law, the balance of power, war and the role of great powers) occupies the whole central third of his 1977 book. Yet Bull never gives a full definition of what constitutes an institution, nor does he set out criteria for inclusion into or exclusion from this category. Neither does he attempt to explain the difference between his set and Wight's. Both by noting Wight's institutions for premodern international societies, and by himself setting out a variety of alternative possibilities for future international society, Bull appears to accept the idea that primary institutions can and do change, but he offers little guidance about how institutions arise and disappear. His core statement on institutions is firmly within the Westphalian straitjacket (1977: 74):

> States collaborate with one another, in varying degrees, in what may be called the institutions of international society: the balance of power, international law, the diplomatic mechanism, the managerial system of the great powers, and war. By an institution we do not necessarily imply an organisation or administrative machinery, but rather a set of habits and practices shaped towards the realisation of common goals. These institutions do not deprive states of their central role in carrying out the political functions of international society, or serve as a surrogate central authority in the international system. They are rather an expression of the element of collaboration among states in discharging their political functions – and at the same time a means of sustaining this collaboration.

The location of this set in the overall structure of Bull's argument is that they derive from the second of his three types of rules: rules of coexistence, which are those setting out the minimum behavioural conditions for society (see chapter 2). In Bull's scheme, rules of coexistence hinge on the basic elements of society: limits to violence, establishment of property rights and sanctity of agreements. This placing explains both the pluralist character of these institutions (which occurs by definition as 'rules of coexistence') and the curious absence of sovereignty (which falls under Bull's first set of rules about the constitutive normative principle of world politics). Indeed, Bull (1977a: 71) does say that 'it is states themselves that are the principal institutions of the society of states', but he does not develop this idea, whereas the other five get a chapter each.

Bull's presentation of institutions can be read in two ways: either it reflects his pluralist predisposition, or it reflects his understanding of the history and present condition of interstate society. As argued in chapter 2, there is scope in Bull's institutions for solidarist development. But he makes little attempt to explore this, or to develop a general definition of primary institutions, or to explore the range of possibilities that might be covered by 'institutions of international society'. One possible lead for such an exploration is suggested by the link between Bull's choice of institutions, and the explicitly functional quality of his understanding of society. Do his ideas about society being constituted by limits to violence, establishment of property rights and sanctity of agreements open a functional path into thinking about primary institutions? More on this below.

Bull's failure both to give a clear definition of (primary) institutions, and to relate to earlier work, continues into, and in some ways worsens within, the more contemporary English school literature. For example, Mayall (2000: 149–50) says:

> The framework that I have adopted describes the context of international relations in terms of a set of institutions – law, diplomacy, the balance of power etc. – and principles. Some of these – sovereignty, territorial integrity and non-intervention – have been around since the beginning of the modern states-system. Others – self-determination, non-discrimination, respect for fundamental human rights etc. – have been added more recently . . . do all these institutions and principles have equal weight, or are they arranged in a hierarchy? And if so, is it fixed?

Curiously, he does not mention nationalism, which might be thought to be his major contribution to the English school literature (Mayall 1990, 2000), and which clearly meets the criteria for primary institutions given above. Mayall (2000: 94) identifies international law as a kind of master institution: 'the bedrock institution on which the idea of international society stands or falls'. This view is supported by Kratochwil's (1989: 251) argument that: 'the international legal order exists simply by virtue of its role in defining the game of international relations', and Nardin's (1998: 20; see, contra Nardin, Whelan 1998: 50–1) that 'international society is not merely regulated by international law, but constituted by it'. The arguments made in chapter 2 about the centrality of positive international law to international society might also be taken as reason to privilege international law in this way. Aside from Mayall's exasperating etceteras, which leave one wondering what the full sets might look like, we are offered a distinction between institutions and principles with no explanation as to what the difference might be, or any clear setting out of which items belong in which category. His good questions about weight and change seem to apply to both together, and therefore to suggest that perhaps there is no difference, and Mayall in any case does not attempt to answer them.

Perhaps picking up on Bull's undeveloped point, and in contrast to Mayall's and Kratochwil's elevation of international law, James (1999: 468) says that sovereignty is 'the constitutive principle of interstate relations', though in earlier work (James 1978) he identifies diplomacy, international law and sovereignty as the key 'phenomena' indicating the presence of international society. Interestingly, James (1978: 3) also hints at a functional understanding of institutions by talking of sovereignty in terms of rules about who can be a member of international society. The emphasis on sovereignty is also shared by Jackson (2000: 102–12), who although he does not mount a direct discussion of institutions, also talks about diplomacy, colonialism, international law and war in terms compatible with an institutional view. Reus-Smit (1997) focuses on international law and multilateralism as the key contemporary institutions of interstate society, and Keohane (1995) also seems to lean towards multilateralism. To add to the mixture, some solidarists (Knudsen 1999: 39ff.) want to push human rights almost to the status of an institution, while others (Wheeler 2000) talk about it more ambiguously in terms of a norm of international society. As with Mayall's distinction between institutions and principles, it is not clear what, if anything, draws the line between institutions and norms of international society. Both carry a sense of being durable features (and in that sense social structures) of a society, and both are about constituting roles and actors, and shaping expectations of behaviour.

If the concept of primary institutions is to play a coherent role in English school theory, then we need to improve our understanding of what it does and does not represent. The existing discussion suggests several points needing further thought:

- that there is an urgent need to acknowledge the centrality of primary institutions in English school theory, to generate consistency in the use and understanding of the concept and to make clear what does and does not count as a primary institution;

- that Bull's classic set of five institutions is much more a statement about historical pluralist international societies than any kind of universal, for-all-time set, and that consequently there is a need to flesh out the wider range of primary institutions;
- that institutions can change, and that processes of creation and decay need to be part of the picture;
- that perhaps not all primary institutions are equal, and that some sort of hierarchy may need to be introduced;
- that a functional understanding of primary institutions is worth investigating.

A timely paper by Holsti (2002) has begun a systematic and stimulating attempt to take the taxonomy of primary international institutions in hand. Holsti's starting point is a concern to develop primary institutions as benchmarks for monitoring significant change in international systems. Holsti (2002: 6) sees institutions in this sense as embodying 'three essential elements: practices, ideas and norms/rules' in varying mixtures. He adds (Holsti 2002: 9–10) a key distinction between 'foundational' and 'procedural' institutions: 'Foundational institutions define and give privileged status to certain actors. They also define the fundamental principles, rules and norms upon which their mutual relations are based.' Procedural institutions are: 'repetitive practices, ideas and norms that underlie and regulate interactions and transactions between the separate actors', including 'the conduct of both conflict and normal intercourse'. Although Holsti divides institutions into two types, it is clear that he is not repeating the division between primary and secondary institutions: his procedural institutions are still primary in concept, not regimes or IGOs. Like Mayall, Holsti shies away from giving definitive lists, but he includes as foundational institutions sovereignty, states, territoriality and the fundamental principles of international law. Among procedural institutions he includes diplomacy, war, trade and colonialism. A similar move is made by Reus-Smit (1997: 556–66), when he identifies three layers in modern international society. The deepest layer he calls 'constitutional structures', which are similar to Holsti's foundational institutions. Constitutional structures reflect a hierarchy of 'deep constitutive values: a shared belief about the moral purpose of centalized political organisation, an organising principle of sovereignty, and a norm of pure procedural justice'. Picking up the functional theme he says that these structures 'are coherent ensembles of intersubjective beliefs, principles, and norms that perform two functions in ordering

172

international societies: they define what constitutes a legitimate actor, entitled to all the rights and privileges of statehood; and they define the basic parameters of rightful state action'. The middle layer Reus-Smit calls 'fundamental institutions', which he sees as 'basic rules of practice' such as bilateralism, multilateralism and international law. This does not feel quite the same as Holsti's procedural institutions, but the concept is not elaborated enough to tease out the difference either in principle or practice, and the difference is perhaps not large. Reus-Smit's third layer is 'issue-specific regimes', which brings us back to the distinction between primary and secondary institutions. Although they contain some embellishments, both Holsti's and Reus-Smit's definitions of primary institutions are broadly in line with the definitions discussed above.

Holsti's approach tackles the question of change and evolution in international institutions and thereby allows both entry into and exit from Bull's pluralist model. In this aspect, his work runs in parallel with others who have not only focused on institutions, but also on the process of institutionalisation. Krasner (1999: 44) raises the question of 'durability' which he defines as whether principles and norms endure or change with change of circumstances. The Stanford school (Meyer *et al.* 1987: 13) define institutionalisation as: 'the process by which a given set of units and a pattern of activities come to be normatively and cognitively held in place, and practically taken for granted as lawful (whether as a matter of formal law, custom or knowledge)'. March and Olsen (1998: 959–69) draw attention to the way in which the development of interaction and competence tends to lead to institutionalisation, and to the need to study how political history evolves in terms of institutions. I will look more closely at the process of institutionalisation in chapter 8.

Holsti shows how new institutions arise (trade), and some old ones drop out of use altogether (colonialism – see also Keene, 2002: 60–144), and it is apparent that any study of institutional dynamics must incorporate both the rise and consolidation of institutions and their decay and demise. He argues that war has decayed as an institution of contemporary international society, taking a similar view to Mayall's (2000: 19) remark that in the twentieth century war became regarded more as the breakdown of international society than as a sign of its operation. Other institutions have become much more elaborate and complicated (international law, dipomacy). In general, Holsti sets up a scheme that invites observers to look not just for the existence (or not) of institutions, but whether the trend is for those that do exist to strengthen, weaken

Table 1. *Candidates for primary institutions of international society by author*[c]

Wight	Bull	Mayall[a]	Holsti[b]	James	Jackson
Religious sites and festivals					
Dynastic principles					
Trade			Trade (P)		
Diplomacy	Diplomacy	Diplomacy (I)	Diplomacy(P)	Diplomacy	Diplomacy
Alliances					
Guarantees					
War	War		War (P)		War
Neutrality					
Arbitration					
Balance of Power	Balance of Power, Great power management	Balance of Power (I)			
International Law	International Law The State	International Law (I)	International Law (F) The State (F)	International Law	International Law
Sovereignty	Sovereignty	Sovereignty (P) Territorial Integrity (P) Nonintervention (P) Self-Determination (P) Non-Discrimination (P) Human Rights (P)	Sovereignty (F) Territoriality (F)	Sovereignty Political boundaries	Sovereignty
			Colonialism (P)		Colonialism

Notes: [a] for Mayall (I) = institution and (P) = principle
[b] for Holsti (F) = foundational institution and (P) = procedural institution
[c] words underlined are where the author identifies an institution as 'principal', or 'master' or 'bedrock'.

or evolve internally. Holsti's scheme, and Reus-Smit's, also address explicitly the question of hierarchy among primary institutions, and not just between primary and secondary ones, though more thinking is needed about this. Holsti's statement (2002: 13) that sovereignty is 'the bedrock for all other international institutions', reinforces the discord between, on the one hand, the seemingly similar positions of Alan James and Robert Jackson cited above, and on the other, Mayall's, Kratochwil's and Nardin's virtually identical statements about international law. The whole idea of 'bedrock institutions' seems to suggest a special status for some even within the foundational category. It is also unclear in these discussions whether the claims for bedrock status are general to any interstate society, or specific to the Westphalian one and its contemporary derivative. In addition, Holsti's inclusion of the state as a foundational institution alongside sovereignty and territoriality looks problematic. It is not clear that anything of consequence is left if one subtracts sovereignty and territoriality from the state. Neither is it clear that the state fits within Holsti's definition. If, as he says, 'foundational institutions define and give privileged status to certain actors . . . [and] the fundamental principles, rules and norms upon which their mutual relations are based', then actors cannot be primary institutions. This argument also undercuts Bull's unexplored classification of the state as the principal institution of international society. Primary institutions have to reflect some shared principle, norm or value. In this instance, states would be the actors constituted by the combination of sovereignty and territoriality.

Although not identifying all of the writers who have had something to say about primary institutions, the current state of play on primary institutions in English school literature is roughly summarised in table 1. One might want to add to it Reus-Smit's and Keohane's idea that multilateralism is an institution if not of interstate society globally, at least amongst the Western states and their circle.

This summary is inspiring because it is clearly getting at something basic and important about international social structure that is not covered either by secondary institutions or by Wendt's broad classification of basic types of social order. It is also both instructive and a bit depressing. It is depressing because it reveals something approaching indifference towards both conceptual clarity and cumulative debate. The English school's interest in primary institutions might be a candidate for the 'coherent research program' that Keohane (1988: 392) accuses the reflectivists of lacking, but to qualify will require much more systematic thinking than it has received so far. The summary is instructive on two grounds. First, because it suggests that there is a lot more to primary institutions than sovereignty. As Onuf (2002: 228) astutely observes, it is a feature of realist thinking that 'sovereignty is the only rule that matters for the constitution of anarchy'. A systematic approach through primary institutions would thus settle once and for all what it is that differentiates English school theory from realism. Second, primary institutions do have some kind of life-cycle in which they rise, evolve and decline, and this dynamic itself needs to be a focus of study (more on this in chapter 8). The summary also suggests a recurrent desire to differentiate primary institutions into some sort of hierarchy between the deeper and more constitutive, and the less deep and more procedural. Alongside this, and not clearly connected to it, are the hints about a functional understanding of primary institutions. How can one begin to transform the English school's lists into a coherent taxonomy? I will begin with ideas about hierarchy and then turn to the functional question.

Hierarchy and functionalism within primary institutions

What lies behind the persistent tendency in writings about primary institutions either to finger some one institution as 'primary' or 'master', or to make some more general distinction (Mayall's institutions and principles; Holsti's procedural and foundational institutions; Reus-Smit's constitutional structures and fundamental institutions). The idea of a 'primary' or 'master' institution implies that one deep practice essentially generates or shapes all of the others. The idea of two layers of primary institutions implies that some are 'deeper' than others.

Looking first at the notion of layers, Holsti's and Reus-Smit's distinctions are based on the idea that some (procedural/foundational) institutions are about repetitive practices and interactions, while others (foundational/constitutional structures) are about how the actors and the basic rules of the game among them are constituted. A distinction along these lines is similar to the one used by Ruggie (1998) and others (e.g. Kratochwil 1989: 26; Searle 1995: 27–8; Sørensen 1999) between regulative and constitutive rules. Since, as argued above (pp. 163–7), norms, rules, principles and values all overlap, and since institutions embody all of them, it seems reasonable to transpose the logic developed around constitutive and regulatory rules, to the discussion about different types of primary institutions. Regulative rules are intended to have causal effects on a pre-existing activity, while 'constitutive rules define the set of practices that make up any particular consciously organised social activity . . . they specify *what counts as* that activity' (Ruggie 1998: 22). Searle (1995: 114) argues that 'institutions always consist in constitutive rules (practices, procedures) that have the form X counts as Y in context C'. It seems that the strange status of the state in Bull's scheme, and his silence about sovereignty, reflect the positioning of his institutions within his 'rules of coexistence' category, which leaves out the institutions to be found under his constitutive rules. Bull thus comes close to falling foul of the criticism made by Ruggie (1998: 25) of neorealists and neoliberals, that they exclude constitutive rules, and that 'the scope of their theories . . . is confined to regulative rules that coordinate behaviour in a pre-constituted world'. Yet that would not be quite fair, since several of Bull's institutions do seem to fit under Holsti's 'foundational' category and Ruggie's 'constitutive' one. At first glance, it is not exactly clear how one would interpret Bull's three types of rules in the light of Holsti's and Ruggie's dyadic classifications. Bull's constitutive rules probably fit within Holsti's foundational institutions and Ruggie's constitutive rules. His rules of cooperation probably fit within Holsti's procedural institutions and Ruggie's regulative rules, and may also overlap with secondary institutions. But quite where Bull's rules of coexistence, and hence his five institutions, fit, is not immediately obvious. We are in the murky waters signposted by Hurrell (2002a: 145) when he noted the absence of any clear answer as to what actually are 'the most important constitutive rules in international relations'. One thing that is clear is that this debate is about a different concern from Hart's (1961) distinction between primary and secondary rules, which is more narrowly aimed at how custom is transformed into law.

Just what does count as constitutive in relation to interstate societies? Since the English school has in part justified its distinctiveness from (mainly American) regime theory by pointing to the constitutive quality of what it means by institutions, getting some sort of coherent answer to this question is essential to the standing of English school theory. As already noted, Bull's idea of constitutive rules is the social structural analogue to Waltz's first tier of structure, comprising the ordering principle of the system that defines whether it is a society of states, a universal empire, a cosmopolitan society or whatever. Bull's rules of coexistence are heavily shaped by the prior choice of sovereign territorial states within this first tier of constitutive rules. The rules of coexistence then set out the minimum behavioural conditions for society, in other words a kind of bottom line necessary for some sort of interstate society to exist. Holsti's and Reus-Smit's deepest layers define both the key actors and the fundamental principles, rules and norms upon which their mutual relations are based. Ruggie's idea is that constitutive rules define the set of practices that make up any particular consciously organised social activity, with the example of a game (e.g. chess – Searle 1995: 27–8) giving clear guidance. As in chess, the rules define the pieces, the environment in which the pieces act, and the ways in which they relate to each other and that environment. Taking all these ideas together, and staying with a game metaphor (chess, or Manning's game of states) it becomes apparent that there are two core elements in the idea of constitutive institutions: one is that such institutions define the main pieces/players in the game; the other that they define the basic rules by which the pieces/players relate to each other.

This sounds relatively simple, but is not. One problem concerns the separability of pieces/players on the one hand, and the rules of engagement on the other. These might be separate (as in chess), but they might also be linked, as in the mutual constitution resolution to the agent–structure problem. Sovereignty as the defining quality of states (pieces/players) cannot be disentangled from anarchy as the defining quality of system structure (and therefore the rules of the game). This link is dynamic, and as the several accounts of the evolution of sovereignty noted above make clear, both states and the game they play change over time. Sovereignty may stay constant as the key constitutive institution, but the practices that it legitimises are under continuous renegotiation. This changeability within a constant is less of a contrast to chess than might be imagined; the rules of chess have changed quite frequently without the identity of the game coming into question (Hassner 2003). A second problem lies in the conflation of 'pieces' and 'players'. In chess, the pieces are constituted by the rules, but the pieces are not the players, and although the activity of chess may be constituted by its rules, the people who play it are not (except in the very limited sense of being temporarily constituted as chess players). In the game of states, this distinction is much less clear. The pieces and the players are still separable (pieces = states, players = political leaders and diplomats), but they are closely interlinked, as captured in the distinction between 'role' and 'idiosyncratic' variables in the study of foreign-policy-making.

Where the pieces (states) are composed of sentient social actors, then what the pieces are and how they relate to each other will inevitably be connected. On this basis Holsti and Reus-Smit would seem to be correct in proposing that for the game of states, constitutive institutions must define both the main actors and the basic rules by which they relate to each other.

What does such a conclusion mean in practical terms? The clearest candidates for the status of constitutive institutions will be those that bear directly on the definition of the principal actors/players in the game. Taking the cue from Bull's discussion of constitutive principles, for the game of states in Westphalian form the key constitutive institutions would be sovereignty and territoriality, for the game of empires, it would be suzerainty, for a cosmopolitian community it would be human rights, and for a neomedieval system it would be the set of principles that differentiated the main types of actors and set out their rights and responsibilities in relation to each other. For something like the EU, the constitutive institution remains sovereignty, but accompanied by integration and 'subsidiarity' (the investment of authority at the lowest possible level of an institutional hierarchy – McLean 1996: 482). It is not impossible for some of these rules to coexist. During the colonial era, for example, the European states system was constituted by sovereignty, but the European powers related to the rest of the world on the basis of suzerainty, which defined a range of imperial entities from dominions through protectorates to colonies. Holsti (and Keene, 2000, 2002) are thus quite right to identify colonialism as a key institution of pre-1945 European international society. Thinking just about what constitutes the actors/players pushes one towards the idea of 'master' or 'principal' primary institutions, where perhaps one or two key foundational practices do seem to set up the rest of the game.

Moving to constitutive institutions focused on the basic rules of engagement is more difficult. Where is the boundary between what counts as 'basic' or 'fundamental' rules (coexistence for Bull, rules that define the game for Ruggie, fundamental principles defining relations for Holsti and Reus-Smit), and cooperation/regulative/procedural rules? Bull's idea of rules of cooperation being about secondary issues (those more advanced rules agreed by states beyond mere coexistence) looks immediately problematic. Such rules can include trade and human rights, both of which might well count as constitutive in the sense that they impact quickly and deeply on what practices are legitimised (or not) by sovereignty, and therefore how the key players are defined.

Both Holsti's and Reus-Smit's procedural rules and Ruggie's regulative ones are trying to define a level that is relatively superficial in the sense that it downplays or eliminates the constitutive element. Holsti's procedural institutions are: 'repetitive practices, ideas and norms that underlie and regulate interactions and transactions between the separate actors', Ruggie's regulative rules 'are intended to have causal effects on a pre-existing activity'. The idea here is to capture, as it were, the regular practices that sentient players engage in once the actors are established, the basic rules are in place and the game of states is under way. But this seemingly clear distinction is hard to sustain. Even at the level of secondary institutions there are plausible claims that the buildup of networks of regimes eventually entangles states to such an extent as to change quite fundamentally the nature of relations among them (more legal and institutionalised, less war) and thus to call into question the (neo)realist understanding of what anarchy means. Such claims are intrinsic to much of the discussion of globalisation and world society, and are not difficult to find in other literatures (Keohane and Nye 1977; Wendt 1999; Milner 1991). In effect, such claims connect even secondary institutions, at least in their cumulative effect as expressions of the primary institution of multilateralism, to constitutive status. Holsti counts both trade and war as procedural institutions, yet there are compelling arguments that both have major effects on the constitution and behaviour of states (e.g. Keohane and Nye 1977; Tilly 1990).

One key element in the difficulty of drawing a boundary between constitutive institutions and regulatory rules is the breakdown of the analogy between games such as chess where the pieces are <u>not</u> the players, and games such as 'states' where the pieces and the players are more closely intertwined. In the game of states, the players can reinterpret existing institutions as they go along. Ashley's (1987: 411) seemingly convoluted definition of international community is close to the sense of primary institutions, and captures this idea of essential fluidity well:

> international community can only be seen as a never completed product of multiple historical practices, a still-contested product of struggle to impose interpretation upon interpretation. In its form it can only be understood as a network of historically fabricated practical understandings, precedents, skills, and procedures that define competent international subjectivity and that occupy a precariously held social *space* pried open amidst contending historical forces, multiple interpretations and plural practices.

As Holsti's discussion makes clear, within the game of states, even quite basic institutions (colonialism in his set, which does define actors in the system) can disappear as the game evolves, or at least atrophy to the point where the label is no longer an acceptable way of characterising practices. Holsti tracks substantial changes of interpretation in other primary institutions as well, such as sovereignty (see also Keohane 1995; Barkin 1998; Sørensen 1999), war and international law. The shared norms or principles represented by primary institutions can endure in a general sense, while the particular rules and institutional facts that they legitimise undergo substantial change. The problem is how to distinguish between those institutions that change the nature of the game and the character of the key players, and those that don't. Drawing any such distinction in a definitive way is certain to be both difficult and controversial. There is endless scope for dispute as to what extent new institutions (the market, or human rights) change either the game or the players, and over what time periods they do so. In terms of the discussion in chapter 5, the question is: does solidarism change the game of states, and at what point do those changes add up to a new game for which the name 'game of states' is no longer appropriate? A suggestive answer to this question is provided by the tendency of EU studies to drift away from both IR and Politics, implying that at least in the minds of many of those who study it, the EU cannot be adequately understood either as a state or as a game of states.

Taking all of this into consideration, one can make the following general characterisation of the primary institutions of interstate society.

- Primary institutions are durable and recognised patterns of shared practices rooted in values held commonly by the members of interstate societies, amd embodying a mix of norms, rules and principles. In some cases these shared practices and values may be extended to, and accepted by, non-state actors.
- In order to count as a primary institution, such practices must play a constitutive role in relation to both the pieces/players and the rules of the game. There is probably not a useful distinction to be made between constitutive and regulatory (or fundamental and procedural) primary institutions.
- Although durable, primary institutions are neither permanent nor fixed. They will typically undergo a historical pattern of rise, evolution and decline that is long by the standards of a human lifetime.

Changes in the practices within an institution may be a sign of vigour and adaptation (as those in sovereignty over the last couple of centuries) or of decline (as in the narrowing legitimacy of war over the last half-century). One needs to distinguish between changes in and changes of primary institutions.

Although I have argued that a constitutive/regulatory distinction cannot be used as the basis for a hierarchy within primary institutions, the sense in the literature that there needs to be a hierarchy is strong. It is also uncontestable that there needs to be a better taxonomy of primary institutions. The simplest solution to the hierarchy problem is to treat it as an issue of nesting. Some primary institutions can be understood as containing, or generating others. International law, for example, can be seen as a general institution, a set of fundamental principles, and also as the container of the potentially endless particular laws about a wide variety of specific issues that can be built up within it, and which mostly fall under what I have labelled here as secondary institutions. The trick is to find primary institutions that stand alone. Looking again at table 1, it is clear that some of the candidates do stand alone, whereas others are derivative.

Sovereignty is a good candidate for a master institution of Westphalian international society. Within it one could bundle up Mayall's 'principles' of non-intervention, self-determination and non-discrimination. A good case could be made for seeing international law as derivative from sovereignty. Although there could, in principle, be international law without sovereignty, as Mosler (1980: 1) argues, before sovereignty, in ancient and classical times, there was no conception of a universal community of rules or laws (on this question see Onuma 2000; Zhang 2001). Without international law, it is difficult to imagine much international relations among sovereign entities other than war.

Territoriality, or territorial integrity, is distinct from sovereignty and not necessary to it. Sovereignty can in principle exist without being territorial, even though in practice that might be difficult to implement. Territoriality is therefore a distinct master institution of Westphalian interstate societies (Ruggie 1993). It might be argued that boundaries are a derivative institution from territoriality, though it could also be argued that territoriality and boundaries are opposite sides of the same coin. As argued above, sovereignty and territoriality together constitute the essence of the Westphalian state, and so eliminate Bull's and Holsti's attempt to see the state itself as a primary institution.

Diplomacy is another good candidate for a master institution. In historical terms, it predates sovereignty, and it easily bundles up Wight's messengers, conferences and congresses, diplomatic language, and arbitration and Reus-Smit's multilateralism.

Balance of power is a clear fourth Westphalian master institution. When understood as a recognised social practice, and shared value, rather than as a mechanical consequence of anarchy, balance of power contains alliances, guarantees, neutrality and great power management. It also contains war, again when understood as a social practice (Searle 1995: 89–90), which as Wight noted, is 'the institution for the final settlement of differences'.

Of the list in table 1, that leaves religious sites and festivals, dynastic principles, trade, human rights and colonialism as not clearly derivative or subordinate to any other master institution. Religious sites and festivals have dropped away as a feature of modern European international society, but clearly played a central role in ancient and classical times, and retain unquestionable importance in sub-global international societies, notably those of the Islamic, Jewish and Hindu worlds. Dynastic principles have also faded out of European international society, but they were crucial in its early phases, and were prominent also in ancient and classical times. Trade is another very old practice in human affairs and does not depend on any of the four master institutions listed above (Buzan and Little 2000). Whether trade as such is the institution, or particular principles applying to it, such as protectionism, or the market, is an interesting question needing more thought. A good case can be made that over the past century and a half, there has been a battle between these two principles of how to govern trade, and that since the end of the Cold War, the market has emerged clearly as one of the major primary institutions of contemporary interstate society. Even with that resolution, however, there remains a vigorous battle between 'economic' and 'embedded' liberals for the soul of the market. As noted above, human rights is a cosmopolitan institution, but it can also be picked up as a shared value in an interstate society. Probably it is not a master institution in itself, but derivative from the principle of equality of people established as part of decolonisation. Conversely, colonialism was a derivative primary institution of international society up to 1945, resting on the general principle of inequality of peoples.

Table 2. *The nested hierarchy of international institutions*

Primary Institutions	
Master	Derivative
Sovereignty	Non-intervention
	International law
Territoriality	Boundaries
Diplomacy	Messengers/diplomats
	Conferences/Congresses
	Multilateralism
	Diplomatic language
	Arbitration
Balance of power	Anti-hegemonism
	Alliances
	Guarantees
	Neutrality
	War
	Great power management
Equality of people	Human Rights
	Humanitarian intervention
Inequality of people	Colonialism
	Dynasticism
Trade	Market
	Protectionism
	Hegemonic stability
Nationalism	Self-determination
	Popular sovereignty
	Democracy

On the basis of this discussion, and setting aside religious sites and festivals, and dynastic principles on the grounds that they are mostly of historical interest, a simple logic of nesting generates a preliminary pattern of master and derivative primary institutions applying to modern interstate societies as set out in table 2. I am aware that some will find the dispositions in table 2 controversial, and I offer them more as a way of opening than of closing a debate about nesting as one way of dealing with the problem of hierarchy within primary institutions that is not resolved by the distinction between constitutive and regulatory rules.

Of course tables 1 and 2 do not contain all of the possible primary institutions, and neither do they tell us what the contemporary pattern looks like. Given the pluralist dispositions of the authors involved, these lists have not only an interstate, but also a specific Westphalian bias, and even there are not complete. One thing that is noticeable about trade, human rights and colonialism in relation to sovereignty, territoriality, diplomacy and balance of power, is that they don't fit comfortably together. Sovereignty, territoriality, diplomacy and balance of power are a harmonious set. They do not guarantee peace, but they complement each other comfortably and contain no necessary contradictions. The market, human rights and colonialism raise contradictions. The contradiction between human rights on the one hand, and sovereignty/nonintervention on the other is well developed in the English school literature (Bull 1977a; Mayall 2000; Jackson 2000). Colonialism contradicts sovereignty by creating a society of unequals, a mix of Westphalian and imperial forms (Keene 2002). The market principle creates tensions with sovereignty and territoriality, not to mention balance of power, in ways that have been well explored in the literatures of IPE and globalisation.

Given the problem of contradictions, it is not without significance that nationalism which, given its importance as the political legitimiser for sovereignty, might well be thought a quite longstanding master institution of interstate society, is not part of table 1. Like trade, human rights and colonialism, nationalism, and its corollaries popular sovereignty and the right of self-determination, create contradictions with some of the other master institutions (sovereignty, territoriality, trade, even at times diplomacy), a story well told by Mayall (1990). Nationalism, as Mayall (2000: 84) notes, sacralises territory by making sovereignty popular. It can also underpin the solidarist call, derided by Jackson (2000: 366) to make democracy a universal institution of interstate society. It is perhaps no accident that the English school classics avoided talk of trade and nationalism for fear of disrupting the harmony of their core Westphalian set of institutions. Bull, and more recently Jackson, put the pursuit of order as their first priority. A consequent disinclination to take on board disruptive institutions would be of a piece with their often fierce resistance to human rights, which creates similar tensions. Although the potential for contradictions among primary institutions is real, it is also sometimes overdone. The fear that the WTO regime degrades sovereignty by imposing rules and restrictions on states, for example, is a common part of the debate about globalisation. In defence, the OECD (1998: 13–14, 77–90) argues that since states agree to the rules in pursuit of what they define as their own national interests, the trade regime is an exercise of sovereignty, not a surrender of it. This line is close to Manning's, cited in chapter 2, that 'What is essentially a system of law *for* sovereigns, being premised on their very sovereignty, does not, by the fact of being strengthened, put in jeopardy the sovereignties which are the dogmatic basis for its very existence. Not, at any rate, in logic.' Those classics of the English school that subordinate the exploration of tensions among primary institutions to the concern for order, block one of the most interesting insights to be gained from the study of primary institutions: that tensions among them are a key driving force in the evolution of interstate society. More on this in chapters 7 and 8.

Another missing primary institution is environmentalism, discussed by Jackson (2000: 175–8) as a fourth area of responsibility (after national, international and humanitarian) involving stewardship or trusteeship of the planet. This was little, if at all, discussed by earlier English school writers, in part because the issue was not then as prominent as it later became. As discussed in chapter 5, environmental stewardship can, up to a point, be fitted into a pluralist logic of coexistence, but it can also become a solidarist project. It might be argued that environmentalism as a master institution is generating derivative institutions such as the right to survival for all species.

Taking these additions into account, and focusing in on the particular pattern of contemporary international institutions, is the task of table 3. Here it is also possible to begin seeing roughly how primary and secondary institutions relate to each other, though I have not tried to trace all of the cross-linkages where secondary institutions might well link to, or express, more than one primary institution (e.g. the UNGA linking to sovereignty, diplomacy, self-determination). Note also how in this more specific focus the market and great power management move to the status of primary institutions with their own derivatives. Again, as with table 2, I offer this interpretation as a way of opening a discussion that the English school, and others interested in international institutions, need to have.

I will look in more detail at the institutions of contemporary international society, and the dynamics that drive them, in chapter 8. There remains the question of exploring the path opened by Bull, James and Reus-Smit towards a functional understanding of primary institutions. One could also derive functional leanings from the discussion about constitutive rules being what define the players and the rules of the game. Heading in that direction requires abandoning the empirical, inductive approach with which I started, and turning towards a more deductive

Table 3. *Contemporary international institutions*

Primary Institutions		Secondary Institutions
Master	Derivative	(examples of)
Sovereignty	Non-intervention	UN General Assembly
	International law	Most regimes, ICJ, ICC
Territoriality	Boundaries	Some PKOs
Diplomacy	Bilateralism	Embassies
	Multilateralism	United Nations Conferences
		Most IGOs, regimes
Great power management	Alliances	NATO
	War	UN Security Council
	Balance of power	
Equality of people	Human rights	UNHCR
	Humanitarian intervention	
Market	Trade liberalisation	GATT/WTO, MFN agreements
	Financial liberalisation	IBRD, IMF, BIS
	Hegemonic stability	
Nationalism	Self-determination	Some PKOs
	Popular sovereignty	
	Democracy	
Environmental stewardship	Species survival	CITES, UNFCCC,
	Climate stability	Kyoto Protocol, IPCC, Montreal Protocol, etc.

approach. Jack Donnelly (2002: 21–3) has made a preliminary start down this path, choosing a functional logic as a way both of building on Bull's understanding of society, and of addressing the manifest shortcomings of the English school's simple lists. Without giving much explanation as to why, he offers five types of political functions as 'likely to be performed in any international society' and begins to allocate institutions to them: *communicating and interacting* (diplomacy, heralds and messengers, the ancient Greek practice of *proxeny*), *making and applying rules* (international law), *regulating the use of force* (war, 'just war' rules, various practices specifying the right to bear arms) *aggregating interests and power* (alliances, spheres of influence, IGOs, feudal obligations, religious solidarity), and *allocating jurisdiction and establishing status* (sovereignty, suzerainty, universal empire). Donnelly's paper is his first cut at a large project, and while understandably unsatisfactory in some respects at this early stage, is nevertheless usefully suggestive, not least in starting from the requirements of second-order ('international') societies rather than assuming (as Bull does) that one can start from the requirements of any form of society.

Unlike first-order societies, second-order societies do not have to deal with some basic human functions such as sex, birth and death. But because, unlike the individual humans who compose first-order societies, their entities are both collective and socially constructed, they do have distinctive problems about communication and recognition. As James and Reus-Smit emphasise, second-order societies have a particular need to specify what kind(s) of collective actors are allowed membership, and what not. Since the entities are collective, they also need rules about how communication is to be conducted, and which voice from within is to be treated as authoritative. Beyond that, the obvious historic core concerns of second-order societies are with war and commerce, which are captured by Bull's emphasis respectively on constraints on the use of force, and allocation of property rights. To pursue either commerce or restraints on the resort to war, necessitates bringing in Bull's third element of society which is understandings about the sanctity of agreements. One could therefore start a functional analysis of the primary institutions of international society with these five. In terms of the institutions discussed earlier in this chapter the allocations might go as follows:

Membership – the importance of defining the membership of a second-order society was apparent in the discussion above about constitutive rules and who the players/actors are. Membership partly overlaps with Donnelly's category of 'allocating jurisdiction and establishing status', but also goes beyond it, potentially taking in such identity issues as feudal obligations and religious solidarity, which Donnelly places under 'aggregating interests and power'. It is thus not just about Bull's constitutive rules, but also contains equality/inequality of people (or not) and their derivatives, human rights/colonialism and dynasticism; nationalism and its derivatives self-determination, popular sovereignty and democracy, and other variations on the question of identity that would bear on the 'standard of civilisation' that determines whether entities are admitted to or excluded from international society.

Authoritative communication – this is close to Donnelly's classification, and is mainly about diplomacy and its antecedents.

Limits to the use of force – it is difficult to make a tight distinction between this function and membership. It would obviously include many of the classic Westphalian institutions emphasised by English school pluralists: great power management, war, alliances, neutrality and balance of power. But at least for Westphalian-type interstate societies, it would be difficult to exclude from this function some of the institutions that also determine membership, for example, colonialism, dynasticism, and human rights. As I have argued elsewhere (Buzan 1996) membership of international society has security implications in and of itself, not necessarily guaranteeing survival, but giving some protection against being treated as a *terra nullius* whose inhabitants can be treated as non-human.

Allocation of property rights – curiously, Donnelly does not pick up this aspect of Bull's functional approach to society, thereby perpetuating the English school's neglect of the economic sector. Allocation of property rights has both political and economic aspects, respectively about who governs where, and who owns what. Whether these aspects can be treated as distinct, as in Tilly's (1990) counterpointing of coercion and capital, or whether they are intertwined, as in Ruggie's (1983) argument that private property and sovereignty emerged together, remains controversial. On the political side, the obvious Westphalian institutions are territoriality and boundaries, though as the feudal model indicates, this kind of hard territoriality is not the only way of allocating property rights. On the economic side, property rights points towards the institutions associated with trade and finance. In societies where the environment has become an issue, institutions associated with stewardship would also come under this heading.

Sanctity of agreements – this is close to Donnelly's 'making and applying rules' and is mainly about international law and its antecedents.

This discussion does no more than open the door on the question of how to understand the primary institutions of international society in functional terms. I do not have the space here to develop this line of thinking further, but the desirability of doing so is apparent for at least two reasons. First, a functional framing is one way of giving theoretical grounding to the English school's so far rather *ad hoc* and empirical approach to institutions, and moreover doing so in terms that can be linked into Bull's work. Second, Donnelly is no doubt correct in thinking that a functional approach would greatly facilitate the Wight/Watson project of comparing international societies across space and time. In the meantime, it is useful to try to get a somewhat more systematic sense of the possible range of primary institutions beyond the Westphalian model. To do this one needs to look at different types of interstate society through the crude functional lens just established.

The range of institutions and the types of international society

First-order (interhuman) societies are typically complicated, and may well have large numbers of defining institutions (Searle 1995). Second-order societies will typically have fewer members and fewer institutions, but they can take many forms and shapes, and therefore even though the number of primary institutions within any given international society may be fairly small, the overall possibilities for such institutions are, if not infinite, at least very numerous. I am therefore unable to escape the 'etcetera' problem for which I earlier pilloried Mayall and others, although at least now one can see why. On the basis of the thin/thick argument in chapter 5, one would expect fewer institutions at the pluralist end of the spectrum and more at the solidarist end. Exactly what the primary institutions of any given international society are is a matter for close empirical enquiry conducted within functional guidelines. Holsti is quite right to link the question of how to benchmark change in international systems to the study of the institutions that define what the society is and what the rules of its game are. Especially in games where the pieces are the players, institutions are open to change, whether change of meaning and practice (e.g. sovereignty, war), or rise/decline of the institution as such (e.g. market, colonialism).

Even with a functional frame, one cannot set out a definitive list of primary institutions for all times and places, yet it is nevertheless interesting and instructive to try to think through the question of primary institutions in relation to the four types of interstate social order set out in figure 5. In particular, such an exercise enables one to revisit the issue of change in the context of the idea from the discussion of pluralism and solidarism above, that solidarist forms of interstate society at least initially build on pluralist foundations. One has to keep in mind that each model can in principle be held together by any mix of coercion, calculation and belief.

A *Power Political* interstate society was defined as based largely on enmity and the possibility of war, and therefore as thin in terms of primary institutions. Survival is the main motive for the states, and no values are necessarily shared. Secondary institutions are unlikely to

190

exist at all. At a minimum a Power Political society will require means of authoritative communication, even if only for alliance making, and therefore some form of diplomacy. By historical experience, there is also likely to be some institutionalisation around property rights. Trade becomes an institution when there is shared practice for granting particular rights to merchants, which was common even in ancient and classical times (Buzan and Little 2000). It is easy to find historical cases where diplomacy and trade existed without there being any shared political principle. It also seems likely that some sort of territoriality would be important because of its intrinsic relationship to the processes of war and conquest, though this might well not take the form of hard boundaries. Empires and tribes usually have fuzzy frontiers rather than fixed lines. In such a thin society, there may well not be much elaboration around the rules of membership. Sovereignty might or might not be an institution in a Hobbesian society, which could just as easily rest on suzerainty, or even on the simple pragmatic test of whatever kind of entity is able to field significant military force. In most of ancient and classical times, for example, international systems were composed of a mix of city-states, empires, nomadic barbarians and hunter-gatherer bands. This does not rule out that Power Political interstate societies could also feature shared political institutions such as dynasticism or suzerainty, as they did for much of classical history and also early modern European history. By definition, Power Political interstate societies are unlikely to feature major constraints on the use of force, though war may well be a strong candidate for an institution in the sense of a general acceptance of conquest as a legitimate way to establish political claims. Any society will require some method of establishing the sanctity of agreements, even if only the value placed on 'word of honour', but the ruthless survivalism of a Power Political one is unlikely to feature much in the way of developed international law.

A *Coexistence* interstate society was defined as based on the model of a Westphalian balance of power system in which the balance of power is accepted as an organising principle by the great powers, and sovereignty, territoriality, diplomacy, great power management, war and international law are the core institutions of international society. This is Bull's pluralist international society, close to the experience of modern European history up to 1945. In functional terms, these classic institutions already cover a quite well-developed means of authoritative communication (diplomacy), membership (sovereignty), limits to the use of force (war, balance of power, great power management), property rights (territoriality) and sanctity of agreements (international law). Yet the classical pluralist presentation of institutions in the English school literature does not exhaust the possibilities. In terms of membership, colonialism is an option for such a society provided that it has room to expand outside its core (Holsti 2002; Keene 2000, 2002), and so also is dynasticism, as it was in Europe well into the nineteenth century. A 'standard of civilisation' embodying other cultural and/or religious identity markers might well also be applied to membership, as it was by the Europeans before 1945. In terms of property rights, Coexistence interstate societies can also generate economic institutions more sophisticated than the basic trading practices that can be found even in Power Political interstate societies. Coexistence interstate societies might well keep the mercantilist practices and principles inherited from Power Political forebears, but they might also seek to improve on them. In the case of nineteenth-century Europe, the Gold Standard could be seen as one such development, as, perhaps, could the attempts to move towards liberal trading practices, such as agreed tariff reductions and most-favoured-nation agreements. As Coexistence societies move towards the Cooperative model, they may well begin to generate secondary institutions in the form of regimes and IGOs, as began to happen during the late nineteenth century.

The most important institution missing from the English school's essentially Coexistence set is nationalism, which bears on both membership and the political side of property rights. Mayall (1990, 2000) has long been the champion of giving full recognition to this as a constitutive institution, arguing that during the nineteenth century it melded with the institution of sovereignty and transformed it in a number of quite fundamental ways. National self-determination not only displaced dynasticism as the key to political legitimacy, it also sacralised territory (Mayall 2000: 84) and imposed limits on the legitimate uses of war. Hurrell (2002a: 145) reinforces Mayall's position with his suggestion that 'national self-determination is the most important constitutive norm of the modern era'. Nationalism, like sovereignty, has spread well beyond its European origins. It has been instrumental in the demise of colonialism as an institution of Western interstate society. It is part of the explanation for the decline of war as an institution, and through its link to popular sovereignty is also implicated in the rise of the solidarist agendas of human rights and democracy.

A *Cooperative* interstate society was defined as based on developments that go significantly beyond coexistence, but short of extensive domestic convergence. This definition implies a considerable carry-over of institutions from the Coexistence model, and it would be surprising if a Cooperative interstate society did not possess a fairly rich collection of secondary institutions. It is not difficult to imagine that sovereignty, territoriality, nationalism, diplomacy and international law remain in place, albeit with some elaboration and reinterpretation. Judging by the UN Charter, the practices within the EU, and the still vigorous and interesting debate about unipolarity and multipolarity, great power management can also remain in place. It seems highly likely, however, that Cooperative interstate societies will have more elaborate criteria for membership, more stringent institutions concerning the sanctity of agreements, and greater restraints on the use of force. Indeed, such societies may well downgrade or even eliminate war as an institution. Recall Mayall's (2000: 19) remark that in the twentieth century war became regarded more as the breakdown of international society than as a sign of its operation. If interstate society is engaged in solidarist cooperative projects, then allowing free scope for war as a legitimate way of changing political control becomes problematic. Neither the liberal economic project nor the big science one can be pursued, at least not universally, in an interstate society where war remains one of the core institutions. War may not be eliminated, but its legitimate use gets squeezed into a relatively narrow range closely centred on the right to self-defence, and not in violation of the right of national self-determination. The squeezing of war in this way seems likely to downgrade the balance of power as an institution, at least in the robust sense of its meaning in a Coexistence interstate society. In the contemporary international system, this whole nexus of questions is under test by the apparent desire of the US to reassert a right to war for the purposes of combating terrorism and containing rogue states.

Whether and how downgrading of balance of power happens may well depend on what kind of solidarist project(s) a Cooperative interstate society pursues, and the question of what other primary institutions such a society might have also hangs on this question. It will make a difference whether the joint project is big science, human rights, collective security, the pursuit of joint economic gain, environmentalism, universal religion or some combination of these or others. If contemporary Western interstate society is taken as a model for the possibilities, then the most obvious candidate for elevation to the status of primary institution would be the market. The market means more than just trade. It is a principle of organisation and legitimation that affects both how states define and constitute themselves, what kind of other actors they give standing to, and how they interpret sovereignty and territoriality. The market does not necessarily eliminate balance of power as an institution, but it does make its operation much more complicated and contradictory than it would be under mercantilist rules. I have elsewhere (Buzan and Wæver 2003) labelled this the liberal–realist dilemma, and it is most visible in contemporary Western, Japanese and Taiwanese relations with China. Realist, or balancing, logic suggests that it is unwise to trade with, and invest in, and thus empower, states one may later have to fight. Liberal, or market, logic suggests that one can reduce the probability of having to fight by allowing the operation of a market economy to democratise and entangle potential enemies.

A *Convergence* interstate society was defined as based on the development of a substantial enough range of shared values within a set of states to make them adopt similar political, legal and economic forms. This implies not only a thick development of institutions across all the functions, but also extremely exacting conditions for membership. Exactly what this type of society would look like depends hugely on what model of political economy its member states were converging around: liberal democracy, Islamic theocracy, absolutist hereditary monarchy, hierarchical empire, communist totalitarianism, etc. This choice would largely determine the practices and legal systems that would define the institutions. Some pluralist institutions might well still be in play, though it seems unlikely that war and balance of power would play much of a role. In a liberal (Kantian) version of Convergence interstate society, the market, property rights, human rights and democratic relations between government and citizens might well feature as primary institutions. But if the convergence model was Islamic, communist or some other, then the institutions would be radically different. All three of these forms would probably bring sovereignty and territoriality seriously into question, not necessarily, in Holsti's (2002: 8–9) scheme, by making them obsolete, but either by increasing their complexity or transforming their main functions. Convergence would almost certainly push non-intervention as a corollary of sovereignty towards obsolescence for many purposes. As Convergence developments moved towards *Confederalism*, and the border between international systems and unified ones, one would expect a change in the character of its secondary institutions. There would not just be significant IGOs of the forum kind, like the UN, but also secondary institutions of a more integrative sort, like those in the EU. By this stage, restraints on the use of force would have to be nearly total, diplomacy largely transformed into something more like the process of domestic politics, and international law transformed into something more like domestic law, with institutions of enforcement to back it up. One can draw from this discussion the following conclusions.

- That it is possible, using a functional frame, to go some way towards identifying the institutions that would go along with different forms of macro, second-order, societies, but that the possible range of such societies is large, and all of their particularities impossible to predict.
- That norms, and therefore institutions, can change. This change may be driven by changes in the domestic societies of the member states, or as Hurrell (2002a: 146–7) argues about contemporary international society, by promotion by TNAs, by the discursive tendency of norms to expand by filling in gaps, by analogy, by responses to new problems and/or by debate in IGOs.
- That there are 'master institutions' in the sense that some primary institutions nest inside others, but not in the sense that some are constitutive and others regulatory.
- That while solidarist evolution does build on pluralist foundations initially, it does so not just by direct accumulation, but as solidarism thickens, by dropping or downgrading or transforming some key pluralist institutions.
- That as Hurrell (2002a: 143–4) observes, the set of institutions constituting any given interstate society may well contain contradictions/tensions among themselves. These contradictions/tensions may well be a key dynamic in the evolution (or decay) of any given interstate society. More on this in chapter 8.
- That one needs to beware of the limitations of a purely politico-military approach to conceptualising institutions. Economic, societal and environmental institutions can be just as constitutive of players and rules of the game in interstate societies as can the narrow set of strictly politico-military ones.

Conclusions

Three issues remain to be discussed: (1) the relationship, if any, between institutions in the English school sense, and more materialist structural interpretations of the same phenomena; (2) the question left hanging in chapter 4 of how the interhuman, transnational and interstate domains relate to each other; and (3) the vocabulary question, also left hanging in chapter 4, about the fate of the concepts 'international' and 'world' society.

In the discussion of primary institutions above it was noted that war as an institution became more problematic as interstate society moved away from pluralist constructions and towards solidarist ones. This problematisation was not to do with technical issues such as the advent of weapons of mass destruction, which might well bring war into question even within Hobbesian or Lockean interstate societies. Rather, it concerned the contradiction between war as an institution, and the other institutions that might be cultivated by more solidarist interstate societies. War become increasingly incompatible with solidarist projects such as big science or the institutionalisation of the market. How is one to link this perspective to the more materialist one made famous by Tilly's phrase that 'war makes the state and the state makes war', which implicitly underpins much realist theorising about international relations? From this perspective, war is constitutive of states not in the form of a constitutive rule, but as a mechanical, Darwinian structure which favours the survival of units that are more like modern states, and drives into extinction or subordination other (older) types of unit that are less clearly organised around strict sovereignty and hard boundaries. If war itself gets driven towards extinction, what then becomes of the state? Although the logics driving this type of structural thinking are different from those underpinning primary institutions in the English school sense, the two do cross paths when one comes to consider the impact of the market. Like war, the market can be seen both as a mechanical structure and as an institution of interstate (and interhuman and transnational) society. In both perspectives there are some areas of overlap and complementarity between the two, but also an underlying contradiction that becomes more powerful as the market approaches global scale. War might, up to a point, support the market when the game is to grab control of sub-global shares. But when the market becomes global, war becomes a costly disruption to trade, production and financial markets. As institutions, war and the market become increasingly incompatible in solidarist interstate societies. As mechanical structures, they seem also to fall into a zero-sum game for what makes the state and what the state makes. It could well be argued that in contemporary interstate societies it is the market that makes the state and the state that makes markets. To the extent that this is true the shift in balance between these two constitutes not just a shift in the institutions of interstate society, but also a transformation in the Darwinian structures that shape the principal units in the international system (Buzan and Little 2000: 362–7).

The second issue is how the interhuman, transnational and interstate domains relate to each other. The main point I want to underline here is the need to remain aware that liberal models of solidarism are not the only option for thinking about this question. From a contemporary Western perspective, inside liberalism, it is all too easy to lose sight of this fact. The liberal model of solidarism offers a very particular, and quite compelling, answer to how the interhuman, transnational and interstate will relate to each other as solidarism develops. Liberal arguments contain a strong logic that although the three units of individuals, TNAs and states are ontologically distinct, the interhuman, transnational and interstate societies that they form will be closely interrelated in a quite particular way.

As I have argued elsewhere (Buzan 1993) there are grounds for thinking that interstate societies aspiring to solidarism, especially if their constitutent states are democratic, will have to be accompanied by matching elements of cosmopolitan world society among their citizens if the solidarist international society is to be sustainable. In other words, the twentieth century's obsession with nationalism as the link between the interhuman and the interstate domains has to be broadened out to incorporate the wider forms of interhuman society necessary to support a solidarist interstate agenda, whether in human rights, democracy or economic interdependence/globalisation. In addition, pursuit of the liberal economic project necessitates the creation and support of a host of transnational economic actors. In parallel with these developments in identity and economy, liberal interstate societies will need to promote (and/or allow) the development of a corresponding transnational civil society sufficient to carry the political burden created by moves into wider identities and more global markets. And while liberal solidarist interstate societies will need to encourage transnational <u>civil</u> society, the states composing them will need to adapt themselves by creating IGOs to deal with the forces of transnational <u>uncivil</u> society to which the processes of integration also give space. Amongst other things, dealing with transnational uncivil society can lead to reformulations of the institution of war, as visible in the post-2001 'war on terrorism' (Buzan 2003). Liberal solidarism will be unable to develop far unless the interstate domain can carry with it degrees and types of interhuman and transnational society appropriate to the degree and type of norms, rules, institutions and identities that they want to share amongst their members. A liberal interstate society will require parallel developments of cosmopolitanism in the interhuman domain, and of economic and civil society actors in the transnational domain. Without such developments the pursuit of the interstate project will be impossible beyond a rather basic level. In a liberal perspective, more interstate solidarism requires more cosmopolitanism in the interhuman domain and more TNAs, and cooperation amongst TNAs to support it. Conversely, the desired cosmopolitan developments in the interhuman and transnational domains cannot take place without the provision of law, order and security from the interstate domain. Liberal solidarism develops as a close nexus amongst the three domains.

The EU provides an instructive case for investigating this liberal nexus. Its ongoing debate about the tension between further integration of the EU (i.e. deepening of its international and transnational society) on the one hand, and the absence of any strong European identity amongst its citizens (i.e. lagging development in the interhuman domain), on the other (Smith 1992), and the endless debates about the EU's secondary institutions from police to parliament, all provide an advanced case study for looking at the development of liberal solidarism. Among other things, the EU case raises the question of where the driving forces for the development of international society are located. The EU has been primarily state-led, which explains why the interhuman domain is the laggard. In other cases one might find the driving forces within the interhuman or transnational domains.

Through liberal lenses, it looks to be the case that as one moves towards the (con)federative end of the interstate society spectrum ever more room is created for interhuman and transnational society. It also appears that the interstate development depends on progress in the other two, and at least in the minds of the more extreme sorts of globalists, that the process/progress might/should (if it has not already . . .) eventually topple the state as the dominant unit in the international system. That the three domains have historically interacted with each other is beyond question. For example, the present scale of interhuman societies was heavily shaped by the influence of earlier TNAs (the Catholic and Orthodox churches) and states/empires (Rome, China, Abbasid). In turn, these collective actors depended in their time on being able to tie their own organisation and legitimacy to the structures of interhuman society. In a realist world of competitive states, national states (those that make their subjects into citizens, and define themselves in terms of popular sovereignty) will outperform absolutist states both economically and militarily. The dynamics of the interstate society will thus work to make interhuman society conform to its political geography (both in terms of nationalism, and wider, interstate society developments such as the EU, the West, the Communist bloc etc.). But how the three domains interact with each other depends on what sort of values are in play, and where they are located. Liberal values encourage a broadly complementary relationship amongst the three, making developments in each dependent on matching developments in the other two. But even within liberalism more contradictory readings are possible. It can be argued that empowering transnational capitalist actors unleashes forces that not only assault patterns of identity in the interhuman domain, but also tend to atomise the interhuman world into individuals (consumers). Capitalist transnationals can also be seen as contradictory to the state, tending to hollow it out and shrink its domains of legitimate action. The liberal model, in sum, can raise a highly political agenda in which developments in one domain force quite extreme patterns on the other two, and the nature of these questions may well vary depending on the stage of development that liberalism is in (whether national, as in the nineteenth century, or globalist, as in the twenty-first).

Similar sorts of thought exercises could be conducted for non-liberal international societies. Islamic values, for example, could also be read as weakening the state domain by placing individual loyalty to the *umma* above the loyalty of citizens to states. The oft-told story of how a Westphalian states-system emerged out of European medievalism displays similar tensions between the demands of a universal religion on the one hand, and the demands of state sovereignty on the other. In the political sphere there was a zero-sum game between the emergent states and the Catholic church – between the interstate and transnational domains of society. It seems clear that in a communist interstate society there would be little or no room for TNAs, and strong assaults on religious and national identities in the interhuman domain. From the historical record, classical empires tended to constrain the development of transnational economic actors, and often did not care too much about patterns of identity in the interhuman domain (being more concerned with obedience than identity). In sum, the liberal model is not the only template on which one can and should think about the relationship among the three domains. Even within the liberal model, different interpretations of the relationship are possible according to which ideological perspective one takes on capitalism.

This brief look at alternatives also underlines the question about where the driving forces for the social structure of international systems are located. Physical interaction capacity obviously matters, for the technical ability to move goods, people and information around the system conditions the opportunities of actors in all the domains and across all of history. The work of tracing this factor across history has been done by Buzan and Little (2000). Beyond that, the question of driving forces turns to which, if any, of the domains dominates the other two. Is it that developments in the state pillar push and pull developments in the transnational and interhuman domains? Or is it that autonomous developments in the interhuman domain (the rise of a consciousness of being a member of humankind) and the transnational one (the rise of powerful TNAs of various kinds) force the state domain to adapt? Even within the liberal model, this chicken–egg problem presents itself. Most realists will take the view that states are the drivers, many globalists that the interhuman and transnational domains are taking over. Campaigners for solidarist developments will try to mobilise the interhuman domain to influence the transnational one, and use both to influence states. Or, depending on issues and circumstances, they may try to mobilise the state to influence the transnational and interhuman domains. Both the realist and globalist positions contain elements of the truth, but the argument between them is more interesting as a political phenomenon than as an analytical question.

What is interesting analytically are the constraints and opportunities that developments in any one of these domains pose for the other two. Embedded patterns in the interhuman domain might act as a brake on or a facilitator for, developments towards deeper forms of interstate society, the difference depending on the geographical overlap, or not, of the relevant patterns in the two domains. A good example of this is the classical English school question about the relationship between interstate society and underlying cultural patterns. The assumption was that an underlying civilisational pattern would facilitate the development of an interstate society (classical Greece, early-modern Europe) whereas the lack thereof would be a problem (the expansion of Western interstate society to global scale). Similarly, the character of interstate society very much conditions the possibilities for TNAs, but once they are established and powerful, TNAs also condition and restrain the possibilities for interstate society. The units in each domain have to operate in the conditions created by the units in the other two domains, but the units in each domain can, up to a point, and given time, also shape the nature of the other two domains. This is a highly dynamic universe in which agents and structure are engaged in a continuous game of mutual tensions and mutual constitutions. Both complementarities and contradictions are possible. Liberal solidarism must have supporting cosmopolitan and transnational developments. A communist interstate society is hard to envisage in a world in which transnational actors are strong, but a communist world society in which the communist party is the primary institution, and the state has atrophied, is just about possible to imagine. In this sense it is difficult to imagine developments in any one domain getting too far out of line with developments in the other two, and easy to see that some primary institutions necessarily extend beyond the strictly interstate domain. The range of possibilities is large. Some types of solidarist societies will require big developments in the transnational domain, others not.

Although I have argued that there is a lot of room for interplay among the three domains, it remains true in the contemporary world that states are still the most powerful and focused unit: states can shove and shape the others more easily than they can be shoved and shaped by them. But this is far from saying that states can shape the other two domains as they wish. Change is at best slow, and powers of resistance can be great. Politics, leadership, imagination and a host of other factors affect the way in which the three domains play into each other, and whether opportunities for change get taken up, or whether possibilities for resistance are effective or not. It is probably not possible to postulate a mechanical set of relationships among the three domains. What is possible is to set a mechanism of analysis that ensures that this relationship, and the changes in it, become a central focus of any examination of international social structures. I will have a first crack at this in chapter 8.

The other question left over from chapter 4 was the fate of the terms 'international' and 'world' society. World society disappeared in chapter 4 (p. 138) because of the decision to separate the interhuman and the transnational into two distinct analytical domains. International society has disappeared because the triad in figures 4 and 5 is now based on types of unit, making the term 'interstate' a necessary tightening up of usage (and reflecting more traditional English school formulations such as 'society of states' or 'states-systems'). The term 'international', though often used to mean interstate, has always carried a certain ambiguity (Buzan and Little 2000: 32–3) which makes it awkward to use as a label for the strictly state-based domain. But given that there does seem to be considerable institutional linkage among the three domains, the ambiguity of 'international' becomes useful. There is a need for terms to encompass the complex patterns that result when one looks at the interhuman, transnational and interstate domains all together.

My proposal is to use *international society* to indicate something like the arrangement that emerged during the twentieth century (Mayall 2000: 17–25), where the basic political and legal frame is set by the states-system, with individuals and TNAs being given rights by states within the order defined by interstate society. This would roughly accord with James's view cited above that individuals and TNAs are <u>participants</u> in international society rather than <u>members</u> of it, or with the arguments in chapter 2 about individuals being dependent 'objects' of international law rather than independent 'subjects' of it with standing in their own right. It also feels close to the alternative interpretation of Bull (given on pp. 95–6), where following his imperative about 'international order' in the conditions prevailing in the early twenty-first century, could lead one to a Davos-culture view of who it is that now provides it. This usage takes advantage of both the ambiguity and the state-centrism built into the term 'international'. Defining international society in this way means that the term cannot be applied to the classical Westphalian period of European history. The resolute pluralism of that period, the relative absence of TNAs and political nationalism, and the widespread disregard for the interhuman sector displayed by slavery, imperial expropriation and on occasions genocide, mark the Westphalian system as an interstate society well towards the Power Political side of the Coexistence model. There may well have been some institutions in the interhuman and transnational domains, but these would not have been closely tied into those in the interstate domain.

Following this reasoning, *world society* then becomes a vehicle for dropping the assumption that states are the dominant units, and interstate society the dominant domain. In world societies, no one of the three domains or types of unit is dominant over the other two, but all are in play together. This feels close to Bull's neomedieval idea, and to that one of Vincent's versions of world society that hinged on a rights-based community among states, individuals and TNAs (see chapter 2, and Gonzalez-Pelaez 2002: 38–41, 246–9). Buzan and Little (2000: 365–7, 414) discuss something close to it under the label *postmodern international society*. Given my criticisms of Vincent for his lack of clarity about the boundary between international and world society this move will strike some readers as sweetly ironic. But Vincent used world society in several senses, perhaps the main one taking off from the Wightian idea of opposition to international society. The usage proposed here does maintain the same blurring of boundaries between international and world society in traditional English school usage, but it proceeds from a position in which the traditional meanings of international and world society have been abandoned. Neither does it carry any of Vincent's and Wight's sense of opposition to, and/or exclusion from, interstate society. A world society in my sense would be based on principles of functional differentiation amongst the various types of entities in play, and agreements about the rights and responsibilities of different types of unit in relation both to each other and to different types. States and firms, for example, would have to accept the historical evidence that neither performs efficiently when it tries to do the other's job, and that their respective legal rights and obligations need to be clearly demarcated. Each type of unit would be acknowledged by the others as holding legal and political status independently, not as a gift from either of the others. Individuals and firms would thus become subjects of international law in their own right. Humankind has not yet seen a world society in this sense, though the EU may be heading in that direction. Such a development is certainly within the range of imagination, and it presents a far more plausible and engaging goal than the oversimplifications of anarchists, hyperliberals, hyperglobalists and dyed-in-the-wool realists who can only see the future in terms of the victory of one domain over the others.

Using these definitions, international and world society come back into play carrying specific, clearly defined meanings and representing an important distinction of relevance to contemporary world politics. That said, one might still complain, rightly, that my definitions leave gaps in the labelling scheme. Logically, one would also have to have labels for situations in which either of the non-state domains dominated over the other two. It might also be possible to imagine situations in which one would simply need to discuss the three domains separately, without bundling them together in some linking classification. For the reasons already argued in chapter 4, scenarios of non-state dominance are hard to imagine, and seem unlikely. Unbundled scenarios probably require introduction of the geographic variable, which is the subject of chapter 7. On reflection, therefore, it seems to me that interstate, international and world society, plus the option to discuss interstate, inter-human and transnational separately, cover almost all of the interesting cases whether historical, contemporary or foreseeable within the next few decades.

7 Bringing geography back in

Throughout the previous chapters I have registered a steady drumbeat of dissatisfaction with the combination of neglect and resistance that marks the attitude of most classical English school writers towards the subglobal/regional level. Sub-global and regional manifestations of international social structure have either been marginalised by a focus on global scale and universal principles, or resisted because seen as threats to the development of global scale international society. Wight's and Watson's explorations of historical states-systems do not count because most of those systems were substantially self-contained, and not part of a global scale interstate-system.

I am not the only dissatisfied customer of the classical English school tradition in this regard. Zhang (2002: 6) notes that:

> A cursory survey of the existing literature reveals a strange silence on the part of International Society scholars on regionalism. Deliberations by scholars of the English School on regional levels of international society in the twentieth century are until very recently muted, if not entirely invisible. Such silence is best reflected in an important essay on regionalism in 1995 by Andrew Hurrell. The comprehensive survey of *Regionalism in Theoretical Perspective* conducted by Hurrell contains no specific mentioning of either the English school or International Society perspective. It is remarkable that Hedley Bull is mentioned only once towards the end of his book as 'that arch-regional sceptic' (Fawcett and Hurrell 1995: 327). Even critical International Society as summarized nicely by Dunne (1995) does not seem to have made much dent on the studies of regionalism.

Zhang's point is underlined by the fact that Hurrell is a leading figure among contemporary English school writers. Zhang (2002: 7) goes on to note that the main concern of English school writers has been to study 'how a group of states come to form a society when they develop distinctive norms, common rules, and institutions and when [they] perceive themselves to have common purpose in international life and to share the workings of common institutions for the conduct of their relations'. Since there is nothing in this definition that excludes the regional, he puzzles, quite rightly, as to why interest has not been applied at the regional level when there are many interesting and distinctive cases to be found there.

It is certainly fair to point the finger at Bull as mainly responsible for this state of affairs. But it is worth noting that his often-cited 1982 article on 'Civilian Power Europe' should not be taken as exemplary for that attitude, either generally, or in relation to the English school's neglect of the EU. Bull's argument was not about regional international society at all. It was about global Cold War power politics. His aim was to reject the idea of 'civilian power Europe' as a significant actor on the global stage, and to call for <u>more</u> development of the EU, particularly in foreign and defence policy, in order to give it the wherewithal to distance itself from the US.

Despite its importance, the question of sub-global manifestations of social structure in the international system has had to be left until near the end of this book because it was necessary first to develop the analytical tools that I propose should be used to examine such structures at any level, global or regional. Now it is time to bring geography back in. At this point it will come as no surprise to readers that I plan to make a strong case for reversing the neglect of sub-global developments in interstate and interhuman society that has marked English school analyses of the contemporary international system. In the next section I make the case that exclusion of the sub-global is simply not necessary within the terms of English school theory, and that taking the regional level on board opens up a rich set of cases both for comparative purposes and to help in thinking about theory. In the second section I argue that confining the debate about second-order society to the global level has fed pessimistic, pluralist interpretations of interstate society, and starved optimistic, solidarist ones. In the third I show how this confinement has sealed off the possibility of exploring how differences in territoriality affect the classical literature's concerns about the interplay of international and world society. In the fourth I develop the idea that the sub-global level is essential for revealing what might be called a vanguard theory about how international society spreads and grows. Such a theory is implicit in the English school's account of the expansion of contemporary international society, but, with the exception of an oblique presence in Watson's concern with hegemony, absent from its main theoretical works. A reluctance to confront coercion as a mechanism explains some of this disjuncture, but much is also explained by failure to give the sub-global its proper place in the theory.

Exclusive globalism is not necessary

The question of whether international and world society must be considered only as universal, global scale phenomena has already been given a quite thorough airing in the section on 'levels' in chapter 1 (pp. 16–18). The underlying issue is the scale or scales on which it is appropriate to think about interstate, interhuman and transnational societies. In English school thinking, the assumption of global scale arose from a combination of the history of the expansion of European international society; the influence of universal normative principles in political theory; a fear, amplified by the Cold War, that sub-global developments would necessarily undermine global ones; and a blindness to empirical developments of international society in the world economy. In their defence, it might be argued that for most of the classical English school writers, decolonisation was a central event defining the context of their writing, and, at least initially, decolonisation seemed more a global-level event than a regional one. Among non-English school thinkers about world society, enthusiasm for global scale seems to stem mainly from a desire to generate a holistic conception of the international system broadly compatible with a globalisation perspective.

The first thing to note is that an attack on the global scale requirement is <u>not</u> an attack on holism *per se*. The goal remains that of building up a complete picture of the social structure of the international system, and the global level is a key component of that picture. But to restrict the concepts of macro-social structure to the global level is to crush the requirements of empirical and theoretical enquiry under the demands of a normative agenda. The classic English school definition of international society has as its referent 'a group of states (or, more generally, a group of independent political communities) . . .' which leaves entirely open the question of scale. Other traditions of theoretical enquiry within and around IR from balance of power and polarity, through regime theory, to Wallerstein's 'world systems' and 'world empires', all apply their key concepts to either the systemic or the sub-systemic level. Interestingly, Bull's infrequently cited definition of world society, unlike his frequently cited one of international society, <u>does</u> make the global requirement explicit, no doubt reflecting its origins in cosmopolitan thinking about the totality of humankind:

> By a world society we understand not merely a degree of interaction linking all parts of the human community to one another, but a sense of common interest and common values on the basis of which common rules and institutions may be built. The concept of world society, in this sense, stands to the *totality of global social interaction* as our concept of international society stands to the concept of the international system.
> (Bull 1977a: 279, my italics)

Whatever the reasons for it, this strong bias towards globalist/ universalist requirements for international and world society, and against the sub-global level, has to be discarded if English school theory is to develop its full potential. It is perhaps not going too far to say that blindness towards the sub-global level, whether in interstate terms, or in interhuman and/or transnational ones, is the most damaging legacy that the classical English school writers left to their successors.

Looking first at the interstate domain, it is perfectly clear that a global-scale pluralist interstate society exists on the basis of effectively universal acceptance of basic Westphalian institutions such as sovereignty, territoriality, diplomacy and international law. But it is just as clear that this global society is unevenly developed to a very marked degree. Moving on from Vincent's famous eggbox metaphor of international society (in which states were the eggs, and international society the box), one might see this unevenness as a pan of fried eggs. Although nearly all the states in the system belong to a thin, pluralist interstate society (the layer of egg-white), there are sub-global and/or regional clusters sitting on that common substrate that are both much more thickly developed than the global common, and up to a point developed separately and in different ways from each other (the yolks). The EU, East Asia and North America, for example, all stand out as sub-global interstate societies that are more thickly developed within themselves. Yet even though a great deal of their extra thickness arises from similar concerns to facilitate economic exchange, these three are quite sharply differentiated from each other in the modes and values that bind them (Helleiner 1994). The EU is heavily institutionalised, and pursuing both social market and single market objectives. Its attempt to move beyond Westphalian international politics has produced perhaps the only example of a convergence interstate society ever seen, and the only one that even begins to approach a world society as I have defined that term. NAFTA is less ambitious, organised mainly around a set of neoliberal rules, and has no commitment to equalisation or factor movement. East Asia has few institutions or formal rules and is largely organised by state-sanctioned private capital and a tiered system of development. Lesser attempts to create thicker, liberal, regional interstate/international societies by cultivating joint economic development can be found in Mercosur, and various other regional economic cooperations. Above some of these regional efforts one can find larger, looser, thinner, versions of the same thing labelled the 'West' or the 'Atlantic Community' or the 'Asia-Pacific'. A quite different form of relative thickness compared to the global common, reflecting concern with more political and/or cultural values, could no doubt be found by looking at the arrangements of ASEAN, or among the community of Islamic states, or the Arab League. Sub-global developments that are just different rather than thicker, are perhaps exemplified by the contested versions of human rights rooted in the West, Islam and various Asian cultures.

There is thus strong empirical evidence, particularly but not only in the economic sector, that distinctive development of interstate societies is flourishing at the sub-global level. What is more, this evidence suggests a rather balanced assessment of how sub-global developments might impact on global interstate society. As the fried eggs metaphor emphasises, there is no simple 'either/or' choice about global and subglobal developments. In the contemporary international system, the thinner global interstate society is shared by all, and the sub-global developments build on top of that. A second-order pluralism is possible when sub-global interstate societies seek rules of coexistence with each other at the global level. There are clearly no grounds for any automatic assumption that sub-global developments must fall into rivalry with each other and so weaken global social developments. This can happen, as the Cold War showed all too clearly, especially when rival ideologies are in play. Fear of conflict across levels can certainly be found in that body of (mostly liberal) concerns that regional economic blocs will undermine the liberal international economic order at the global level, creating some kind of replay of the 1930s. But against this is the argument that regional economic groupings are mainly responses to the global economic order, and that their existence may well serve to stabilise that order against the periodic instabilities that affect the trading and financial arrangements of all liberal economic orders. Short of that, such blocs offer options to strengthen the position of participating states within the global economy, so creating synergies rather than contradictions between the two levels.

The need to look at the sub-global level is just as obvious if one turns to 'world society', or what I recast in chapter 4 and figure 5 as interhuman and transnational society. Recall that interhuman society is largely about collective identity. Looking at the interhuman domain through this lens what one sees, in a very broad brush picture, is an inverse correlation between scale on the one hand, and the intensity of shared identity on the other. Families, clans, tribes and nations mostly shine strongly, whereas humankind, or members of the planetary ecosystem, are still little more than background glow (albeit up from nothing in the quite recent past). There are exceptions to this pattern. Some national identities embrace huge numbers of people and large territories. A handful of religions, most notably Christianity and Islam, have succeeded in creating vast subsystemic communities. Some civilisations (Western, Confucian) hold a similarly sized scale, but less intensely. In matters of identity, parochialism still rules. Despite some breakthroughs to larger scale, universal scale identity remains strikingly weak. In matters of identity, the sub-global 'yolks' rest only on the very thin substrate of 'white' provided by the general acceptance that all human beings are equal.

Transnational society is almost by definition less amenable to geographical classification than either interhuman or interstate society. Nevertheless, and again in very broad brush, the view is one in which higher intensities of norms, rules and institutions are found on the smaller scales than on the larger ones. Clubs, firms, lobbies, associations and suchlike are all more intensely organised locally than globally. But in the transnational realm of society, it is possible to achieve large, even global, scale in an extremely thin way. Some firms and INGOs do this, and behind them, and expanding fast through the internet, is a huge array of interest groups of many kinds now able to organise in real time on a global scale even for relatively tiny numbers of people. The network of scholars interested in the English school, for example, amounts to several hundred people at best, yet having 'members' on all continents can plausibly claim to be 'global'. In the transnational domain, however, these numerous globalisms tend to be separate rather than coordinated. In terms of the classifications in figure 5, the bulk of what one would find would be located in 'competing TNAs' (e.g. firms) and 'coalitions of like TNAs' (e.g. global umbrella bodies for all political science associations or all banks), with some development of 'TNA coalitions across type' (e.g. the anti-globalisation movement). There are thus many globalisms in the transnational domain, but the global level as such is interesting more for how these many TNAs interplay with interstate society, than how they interplay with each other.

In sum, the sub-global level is thickly occupied regardless of whether one looks at the interstate, interhuman or transnational domain. Interestingly, echoing the insight of Williams (2001), the global level is reasonably well developed <u>only</u> in the interstate domain. The diplomatic and political structure of global international society, and the regimes and institutions of the global economy, are altogether more substantial than either the faint glow of shared identity as humankind or the distant prospect of either a pure transnational society or a world society.

All of this suggests a serious need to take the sub-global level of interstate and international society on board in English school thinking. The combination of anti-regionalism and anti-economic predispositions in classical English school writing has meant that a rich array of empirical developments has been neglected. This is bad enough in itself, but it also represents three more serious losses. First, it means that a whole set of opportunities for the comparative study of contemporary international society has been ignored (Diez and Whitman 2000, 2002; Zhang 2002). Second, it means that the interplay between empirical studies and the development of theory has been substantially impoverished. As Ratner (1998: 71, 76–7) notes, for example, the regional level often generates much more robust mechanisms for enforcement, the key test of solidarism in the English school classics, than can be found on the global level. This impoverishment is most obvious in the neglect of the EU. If the EU is not the thickest, most ambitious and most highly developed interstate society ever seen, then it is difficult to imagine what it is. As such, study of it should be playing a leading role in thinking about how solidarist interstate societies, particularly liberal ones, can develop; what problems arise as they get thicker; and where the boundary is between a convergence interstate society on the one hand, and the creation of a new actor at the global level on the other. The EU not only raises many of the classical questions of English school theory about pluralism versus solidarism, and international versus world society, but also provides a mine of empirical cases and evidence against which the debates about theory can be sharpened. Better theory might then allow the English school to play a constructive role in the debates about the EU.

The third, and perhaps most serious, loss from the neglect of sub-global developments is that it has sustained an emaciated conceptualisation of what the whole idea of international/world society is about. Second-order society at the global level is almost inevitably thin, but sub-global developments may well be much thicker. The whole framework of interstate, interhuman and transnational societies needs to be understood as the interplay between sub-global and global levels. As I will show in the next three sections, bringing the regional level back in changes both the structural and the normative frameworks of debate about contemporary international society.

Unwarranted pessimism

I argued in chapter 1 that in several ways the pluralists within the English school have virtually determined a pessimistic evaluation of international society from the way they have set up the problem. Their ignoring of the economic sector and other areas of solidarist development was discussed in chapter 5. Given the predisposition of most English school writers to focus on the global level, and given that for much of the nineteenth century, and again increasingly so since the later twentieth century, the economic sector has functioned strongly at the global level, this omission is, to say the least, odd. It was perhaps understandable during the Cold War, when the principles of global economic organisation were a central part of what was under dispute, but this does not forgive its general neglect.

In this section I want to draw attention to two other sources of pluralist pessimism, both of which relate to an excessive focus on the global level, though going in quite different directions. The first is relatively simple, involving a privileging of the global level by either neglect of or hostility to sub-global societal developments. The problem generated by this move is that it makes the test for solidarist international society so hard that pessimism/pluralism becomes the obvious conclusion – especially so in the absence of the economic sector. Current examples of this mode of thinking are recent books by Jackson (2000) and Mayall (2000). Solidarism is firmly located in the idea that 'humanity is one' (Mayall 2000: 14), and then rejected on the grounds that there is too much diversity and too little democracy in the human condition to sustain solidarist goals. The second is more complicated, involving what seems to me to be a gross misreading of nineteenth-century interstate society as being thicker and stronger than it actually was. The consequence of this move is unwarranted pessimism in evaluations of how interstate and international society have evolved both globally and regionally since then.

Most English school writers have either ignored the regional level, or if they have paid attention to it, have seen it in negative, oppositional terms in relation to the development of global international society. Neglect seems to derive mostly from transposing a concern with universal values into an assumption that the relevant domain must be the global one. This screens out places where major solidarist developments have in fact occurred, most obviously within the EU and NAFTA, but also within the wider Western community, and not insignificantly in South America (Mercosur), South East Asia (ASEAN) and to a lesser exent among the Islamic states. As a result, it sets an extremely high standard for any sense of progress towards solidarism by demanding that it occur on a global scale. Following Zhang's reasoning, I can think of no good reason why this practice should be sustained.

Easier to understand is the fear that sub-system developments would necessarily, or even just probably, be subversive of international order. This fear was one of the themes that came out of the discussion of Bull and Vincent in chapter 2, and it can also be found in Brown (1995a: 195–6). Such fears perhaps made sense to those responding to the conditions of the Cold War, when interstate society was polarised into competing camps. It is certainly true that having two or more different sub-global interstate societies in play at the same time entails a risk that they will fall into conflict. But if it is posed as a general principle that sub-global developments in the social structure of the international system must necessarily or probably be in contradiction to global-level ones, then this idea needs to be questioned. As a general principle, it commits the same error as realist assumptions that powers must necessarily be in conflict. There are two other possibilities. One is that different sub-global interstate societies will find ways to coexist – a kind of second-order version of pluralism. This possibility is enhanced by the fact that sub-global interstate societies may well share a common substrate, building differences on top of certain shared norms, rules and institutions. Even the Cold War, particularly its détente phases, can be understood in this way. Neither side abandoned key shared primary institutions such as sovereignty, diplomacy, international law or the primacy of great powers, and together they pursued some significant measures of coexistence, most notably in arms control. The third possibility, that could overlap with either of the other two, is that sub-global developments of interstate society serve as the basis for a process of vanguard-led strengthening of interstate society at the global level. A very plausible case can be made that social developments are most easily nurtured sub-systemically, and spread from there to the global level. Indeed, the surprise here is that the English school's whole account of the expansion of interstate society over the last two centuries is quite hard to read in any other way, and the same goes for the Stanford school. Everything from anti-slavery to Westphalian modes of diplomacy and recognition followed a vanguardist pattern. It cannot be denied that such uneven development raises the possibility of conflict. But it also raises the opportunity for the mechanisms of socialisation and competition, with or without elements of coercion, to spread a variety of norms, rules and institutions up to the global level. Seen in this perspective, there is as much reason for optimism as pessimism in sub-global developments of interstate society. More on vanguardism in the last section of this chapter.

The second source of pessimism arises from an idealised reading of nineteenth-century interstate society, and a consequently bleak view of its twentieth-century successor (Miller 1990: 74–7). Bull and others see the nineteenth century as the high point of interstate society because the relatively coherent and well-developed interstate society of the European sub-system held sway over the entire planet. During the nineteenth century there was a quite strong commitment by the great powers to a set of shared values, and this was reinforced by a common European/Christian culture. On this basis, Bull and others take a rather depressed view of subsequent developments. They see decolonisation as not only bringing a host of weak states into interstate society, but also as undermining its civilisational coherence by the inevitable introduction of a multicultural social background. In this perspective decolonisation at best diluted and at worst corroded the stock of shared values on which interstate society rests. The descent of Europe into its civil war of 1914–45, and the fragmentation of the West into ideological factions representing opposed views about the future of industrial society (liberal democracy, communism, fascism) compounded the problem of weakened shared values, and shrank the area of consensus amongst the great powers. This process culminated in the Cold War, in which a zero-sum ideological confrontation between two superpowers drove global interstate society to the margins by unleashing and legitimising a host of mutually exclusive and competitive social values (Bull 1977: 38–40, 257–60, 315–17; Kedourie 1984; Bozeman 1984; Bull and Watson 1984b: 425–35).

In my view, this perspective is not only ethnocentrically narrow and misleadingly gloomy, but also fundamentally mistaken about what interstate society is and how it develops. It is certainly true that the European ascendency created a global imperium, and thus an exceptionally high level of societal homogeneity amongst the dominant powers. It is also true that this imperium set the conditions for a global interstate society, both by intensifying the density of the system, and by making all parts of it deeply aware that they were locked into a pattern of interaction powerful enough to shape the major conditions of their societal and political survival. But this imperium can only itself be called a global international (or even interstate) society at risk of ignoring the huge inequalities of political and legal status between the colonisers and the colonised. To assume that imposed values represent a strong society in the same sense that shared values do is to ignore Wendt's insight that it matters whether shared values are put and kept in place by coercion, calculation or belief. It is also to ignore the idea, essential not just to any progressive view of interstate society, but also to the more conservative Westphalian model of such societies, that some substantial perception of equal status must exist amongst its members. Keene's (2000, 2002) idea of 'colonial international society' and Holsti's (2002) idea that colonialism was, up to the Second World War, an institution of interstate society, both suggest a need to consider more of a disjuncture than is acknowledged in *The Expansion of International Society* between the interstate society that emerged after 1945, and the one that preceded it. At the very least, as noted in chapter 6, there was a major change in the core institutions of interstate society before and after the Second World War as colonialism became obsolete, and sovereign equality became universal. The lack of sovereign equality on a global scale until decolonisation occurred meant that there was no truly global Westphalian interstate society before 1945. The nineteenth century represented not a global interstate society, but a mostly imperial global extension of a largely regional European interstate society. On this basis, comparing late twentieth-century interstate society with its nineteenth-century predecessor assumes a false continuity at the global level and is not comparing like with like.

Seen from this perspective, many of the reasons for pessimism about the condition of contemporary interstate society disappear. There has been no great decline of coherence and homogeneity during the twentieth century because there was no real peak of these things at the end of the nineteenth. Colonial interstate society might have been more homogenous among the Western states, but half the world was coerced into a subordinate position. What we have witnessed during the twentieth century is a huge process of transformation. A narrowly based, coercive, global imperium collapsed, and was replaced by a thin global interstate society resting largely on voluntary acceptance of Westphalian primary institutions (Keene 2002). The sources of global interaction are now located all through the system rather than being located primarily in one part of it; and most of the units in the system relate to each other voluntarily as legal equals rather than as a coerced hierarchy of states, mandates, protectorates, dependencies and colonies. It might be objected that the formal position of legal equality still allows huge amounts of practical inequality between core and periphery. While this is true, there is nevertheless a profound difference between second-order societies in which the formal position is one of legal equality, and those in which it is not. Indeed, the shift from colonial interstate society to global Westphalian norms might be counted as a gigantic progessive step in twentieth-century international history. This new global interstate society was born out of the collapse of the old one, and in many important ways was created by it. The European imperium generated the need for a global interstate society and provided much of the political form within which it took shape. The question is therefore not how much ground has been lost since the heyday of European power, but what legacy was left by the old interstate society for the new? How much of European interstate society did the non-European states accept, and how much did they reject?

The main reason for thinking that interstate society is in relatively good shape by historical standards is the near universal acceptance of the sovereign territorial state as the fundamental unit of political legitimacy. This expansion can be seen as the great, though unintended, political legacy of the European imperium. So successful was the European state in unleashing human potential that it overwhelmed all other forms of political organisation in the system. To escape from European domination it was necessary to adopt European political forms. Some achieved this by copying, others had it imposed on them by the process of decolonisation. As even Bull and Watson (1984b: 434–5) acknowledge, much of European interstate society was accepted by the rest of the world when they achieved independence. The key primary institutions of sovereignty, territoriality, diplomacy, international law and nationalism became accepted worldwide. And this argument can be extended to tackle at least some of the concerns about multiculturalism weakening the cultural foundations of interstate society. Certainly there is less cultural cohesion underpinning contemporary global interstate society than there was behind the European colonial interstate society of the nineteenth century. But the European imperium left behind more than just a global acceptance of the sovereign state and pluralist interstate society. It also embedded nationalism, science, the idea of progress, and more recently the market, as more or less universally accepted ideas about human social organisation. Without adopting this wider set, almost no state can either compete effectively in power terms or establish a genuine legitimacy with its own population (Buzan and Segal 1998a). The existence of this 'Westernistic' culture does not eliminate the problems of multiculturalism. But it does represent a substantial transformation in the cultural underpinnings of interstate society that should not be ignored in assessments of progress.

Understanding the interplay among the interhuman, transnational and interstate domains

The argument for 'bringing geography back in' is essential if one is to pursue the layered understanding of international social structure developed in this book. The key point emerged in chapter 4, in the context of the discussion about differentiating society and community. Weller (2000: 64–8) noted that the relationship between society and community depends significantly on whether their geographical boundaries are the same or different. Bringing the geography of society and community into line has of course been the driving rationale behind the nation-state. Where community and society occupy the same space, as in a classical nation-state, the element of identity (e.g. nationalism) may well play a crucial role in balancing some of the divisive effects of society and politics (e.g. the class antagonism generated by capitalist economies; the need for political parties to play the role of loyal opposition when out of power). But where identity and society are not in the same space, as in the contemporary problematique of globalisation, they might well be antagonistic forces (e.g. nationalist reactions against economic liberalism). Similarly, in Wightian mode, the community element of civilisations represented by shared culture and identity may well facilitate the development of interstate and transnational society. It is less clear why the community elements of cosmopolitanism feared by Bull should contradict the society elements of interstate society unless values such as human rights are imposed by coercion on those not accepting them. The case that community facilitates the formation of a second-order society looks relatively easy to make. Whether or not second-order society necessarily, or even usually, leads towards the formation of community is a much more open question.

Weller's question is a neat way of formulating the many agonisings of the English school about the expansion of European interstate society into areas not sharing the history of European civilisation. It is also a way of addressing the English school's reluctance to talk about regional interstate societies as anything other than a threat to global interstate society. His insight, it seems to me, should be one of the starting points for enquiry about the contemporary condition of and prospects for the social structure of the international system. To understand the social structure of the international system at the global level requires that one also understand what is going on at the levels beneath. Translating Weller's question into the framework developed in this book requires not only looking at how geography operates within each of the three domains (interhuman, transnational, interstate), but also picking up his core concern about how it operates across the three domains.

Within the interstate domain, geography plays in two primary ways: first in the relationship between the global and sub-global levels, and second in the relationship between different sub-global interstate societies. Both of these types of relationship can range along the spectrum from antagonistic at one end, through indifferent in the middle, to complementary at the other end. Where the relationships are on the indifferent-to-complementary side, then geography will mostly be of descriptive use in identifying distributional patterns. For example, the sub-global Islamic interhuman society and the interstate society in East Asia are for the most part indifferent to each other, and both are broadly complementary to the global international society. But where the relationships are on the indifferent-to-antagonistic side, then geography becomes central to understanding the dynamics of the international social structure as a whole. One example of tension between the sub-global and global levels is the interplay between the economic and social liberal agendas of Western interstate society on the one hand, and the more Westphalian, pluralist norms of global interstate society on the other. Western liberalism threatens the sovereignty, territoriality and borders of those who do not agree with its values. Examples of antagonism between different sub-global interstate societies can be found in the story

218

of how European interstate society ran up against, and eventually over-whelmed, the imperial, suzerain–vassal societies of Asia, and also in the competition between 'East' and 'West' during the Cold War.

The interplay between sub-global and global interstate societies also allows a much more nuanced and useful view of the heated debate about intervention. The question of intervention blends elements of norma-tive and legal debate and connects both to current affairs. Is interven-tion a right or a duty, and for what ends and with what effects? Given the arguments around the US invasion of Iraq in 2003, the subject is as important, possibly more important, now than in the past, and is likely to remain a key focus of the English school agenda. If it is pos-sible to build distinctive subglobal/regional international societies on the common foundations provided by global international society, then this arrangement frames the issue of intervention in the form of three questions.

(1) How legitimate/legal is intervention within the global rules and norms: i.e. the lowest common denominator of interstate society?
(2) How legitimate/legal is intervention within the rules and norms of a given subglobal/regional interstate society such as EU-Europe or the Arab League?
(3) How legitimate/legal is intervention across the boundary between distinctive subglobal/regional interstate societies: e.g. from the West into Africa, Asia or the Middle East?

Questions about the legitimacy and legality of intervention relate so intimately to the issue of sovereignty that it is impossible to separate them. But sovereignty means different things at the pluralist and soli-darist ends of interstate society. In a pure Westphalian interstate society, virtually all intervention is both illegal and illegitimate (except against forces aiming to disrupt or overthrow the interstate order). In a thick, solidarist international society such as that represented by the EU, the agreed unpacking of sovereignty, and the establishment of agreements about elements of justice, and the rights of individuals and non-state ac-tors makes many more kinds of intervention both legal and legitimate. There may be many in-between cases where legality and legitimacy part company, as in aspects of the recent Western interventions in Iraq and the Balkans (Wheeler 2000). Since interstate society is *de facto* dif-ferentiated quite radically at the regional level, it is absurd to confine a discussion of the *de jure* aspects of intervention by imposing an as-sumption that interstate society is a single, global-scale phenomenon.

Each intervention has to be considered in relation to the specific characteristics of its location, and whether it is within a sub-regional society, or crosses boundaries between such societies. If NATO's intervention in former Yugoslavia had been presented and understood as an affair of European/Western interstate society, it would have triggered much less resistance from China and others who feared it might be setting a global precedent.

In the interhuman domain, geography also plays quite strongly, because patterns of collective identity often cluster. Most national identities are geographically clustered to a substantial degree, as, to a lesser extent, are most religious and civilisational identities. Since individual humans often hold more than one identity simultaneously, the question is how the patterns of distribution overlap, and which takes priority as a mobiliser or legitimator of political action. Some identities will fit inside others, like Russian dolls (e.g. Danish, within Scandinavian, within European, within Western), whereas others may be relatively diffuse, and have complicated patterns of overlap (e.g. religious identities in relation to ethnonational ones).

The transnational domain does not easily lend itself to geographical thinking. The key questions for TNAs is not about their geographical distribution, but about the thinness/thickness of their relationship to geography. As already noted, TNAs of various kinds might all be able to claim global (or regional) standing (the English school network, FIFA, Ford) yet with huge variation in the actual substantive content of that claim (quite large for Ford and FIFA, pretty thin for the English school network). For the transnational domain, the question of geography becomes more interesting in the relationship among the three domains.

It is when one turns to the interplay among the three domains that Weller's concern, about how patterns of identity interact with patterns shaped mainly by contractual bargains, comes mainly into focus. In the classical English school literature this concern took the form of three questions:

- was it a necessary precondition for the formation of an interstate society that it be underpinned by a pre-existing common culture? (as had been the case for ancient Greece and modern Europe);
- did the expansion of an interstate society beyond the area of its original common culture necessarily mean that expansion came at the expense of cohesion? (as the pluralists think about decolonisation); and

- did the rise of cosmopolitan values necessarily threaten the foundations of interstate society? (most particularly with respect to human rights).

These questions remain valid, and it is not difficult to fit plenty of other contemporary questions, about both policy and theory, into this heading. The problem of how to press on with European integration when the interstate mechanisms have outrun the rather weak sense of European identity amongst the peoples of the EU is one of the most obvious. Another – the globalisation problematique – is how to sustain the economic liberalisation being driven by the core states and firms, when its culturally homogenising consequences trigger nationalist reactions. Huntington's (1996) worrying 'clash of civilisations' thesis fits here, made all the more alarming by the escalation of securitisation between the Islamic world and the West that followed on from 11 September, the breakdown of the peace process between Israel and the Palestinians, and the US invasion of Iraq. So too do his incisive observations (Huntington 1996: 135–54) about 'torn states' such as Russia, Turkey, Mexico and Australia, unsure of which civilisation they belong to, and 'cleft states' such as Israel, Sudan and Sri Lanka, divided by starkly different identities in the interhuman domain. Also under this heading are things such as Asian values and the 'ASEAN way', pan-Arabism, pan-Islamism and pan-Africanism and any other attempts to ascribe a political quality to a cultural zone.

In a general sense, all of this can be understood as being about how political, economic and cultural geography play into each other. At the macro-level, interest focuses on the relationship between the larger patterns in the interhuman domain, and the sub-global and global social structures in the interstate domain. Do sub-global interstate developments follow the cultural patterns in the interhuman domain, as they appear to do, for example, with 'the West', and if so how closely tied are these two factors? How does the existence of only a very weak identity at the level of humankind constrain the possibilities for interstate and transnational society at the global level? Conversely, how does the operation of interstate and transnational society affect the rise and demise of identities in the interhuman domain? Does the existence of global TNAs and of a global interstate society cultivate the growth of universal human identity, or stimulate localist reactions and identity differentiations, or both?

Weller's implicit hypothesis is that identity, on the one hand, and the machineries of rational contractual relations, on the other, more easily reinforce each other when they occupy the same territorial space, and provide grounds for conflict when they do not. This idea, and its accompanying assumption that the three domains are generally present in any large-scale social structure, seems an excellent starting point for almost any enquiry into the social structure of the international system. More on this in chapter 8.

Conclusions: a vanguard theory of international social structures

A crucial reason for bringing the sub-global level into English school theory is to open up space for a *vanguard* explanation of the dynamics of international social structure. By vanguard I mean the idea common to both military strategy and Leninist thinking that a leading element plays a crucial role in how a social movement unfolds. As noted above, a vanguard theory of how interstate society expands is implicit in the way the English school has presented the story of the expansion of European/Western interstate society to global scale. In historical terms, the development of a global interstate society has been a function of the expansion of the West. From the fifteenth century onwards, the rise of European power first eroded, and then crushed, the longstanding configuration of four substantially self-contained civilisational areas in Europe, the Middle East, South Asia and East Asia (Buzan and Little 2000: 241–345). By the end of the nineteenth century, virtually the whole of the international system was either created in the image of Europe, as in the Americas and Australia, or directly subordinated to Europe, as in the African and Asian colonies, or hell-bent on catching up with Europe, as in Japan, Russia and, more slowly, China. The triumph of European power meant not only that a sharp and apparently permanent rise in the level of interaction (and thus density and interdependence) took place, but also that Western norms and values and institutions dominated the whole system. This mixture of coercion and copying and persuasion, as already noted, runs in very close parallel to Waltz's idea that anarchy generates 'like units' through processes of 'socialisation and competition'. Although the story of the expansion of interstate society is part of the English school's stock-in-trade, no attempt seems to have been made to develop a vanguard explanation about the development of interstate/international society as such. Suganami (2002: 14) hints at the sub-global possibilities with his talk of 'a solidarist core or pockets', and the idea that pluralism might evolve into solidarism, but does not attempt to link these two arguments.

Yet looking back on this history, it is difficult to come to any conclusion other than that Europe played the vanguard role for the development of contemporary interstate society. Vanguard explanations not only fit well with the history of interstate society, they also create grounds for opposing the assumption that sub-global developments of interstate society must necessarily be contradictory to global-level ones; regional developments might not be mainly problematic for global ones, but possibly essential to them. In addition, such explanations give open examination to the role of coercion in interstate society. The danger of accepting vanguard explanations is well known from the Marxist experience, namely that claims to be the wave of the future, and the justification of violent means on that basis, can be made by extremists of all sorts. In this application there is also a risk that vanguardism privileges the influence of the powerful (e.g. the West), and obscures the contribution of oppositional forces (e.g. anti-colonial movements).

Used in historical perspective, a vanguard explanation for the development of contemporary interstate society brings into focus a set of problematic normative issues surrounding the role of coercion. In so doing, it picks up the questions raised by Wendt, and discussed in chapters 4 and 5, about the binding forces that hold the shared values and practices of any society in place. Quite explicit in the vanguard story of global interstate society is the role of violence and coercion in spreading to global scale norms, rules and institutions developed in Europe. Also explicit in that story, despite the misgivings of many English school writers about the consequences of decolonisation for interstate society, is that several of the values that were carried outward by the force of Western military superiority have, over time, become internalised by those peoples on whom they were originally imposed. Nationalism, territorial sovereignty, international law, diplomacy and science are the most obvious examples, joined more recently, and perhaps still controversially, by the market. However morally distasteful it may be to acknowledge the efficacy of coercion in shaping values, it nonetheless remains true that most of these values are unquestionably now universally held values in interstate society. They are no longer held in place mainly, if at all, by force, but in many places have become internalised as widespread beliefs, especially diplomacy, science, nationalism, international law and sovereignty. The market is still held in place coercively in some parts of the system, and by calculation in others, but it too has a substantial worldwide constituency of believers, more numerous and more influential in some places than in others. What starts out as imperial imposition can become internalised and accepted by those on whom it was imposed, though there is nothing inevitable about this, and imposition can just as easily breed rejection (as the demise of the Soviet Union demonstrated). Where the values imposed by coercion bring improvement to the lives of peoples, whether in terms of wealth or power or social cohesion, then they have a chance of enduring beyond the coercion that originally carried them.

In addition to the obvious moral reservations, it might also be objected that this vanguard interpretation is of only historical interest. Can it be dismissed as a kind of one-off experience, no longer really relevant in an age in which imperial conquest has become not just unfashionable, but also substantially illegal? Any such opinion would, in my view, be mistaken. While it may be true that vanguardism will no longer be driven primarily by military conquest, the US occupation of Iraq in 2003, with its aim of promoting democracy in the Arab world, certainly fits in the vanguardist mould (and will be a very interesting test of whether coercion can change values). Yet unless there is a major breakdown of the present interstate order, the extension of interstate society by military means will be confined to relatively marginal cases such as Serbia, Afghanistan, Iraq and possibly North Korea. Vanguardism can work in other ways, especially so when the distribution of power in the international system remains markedly uneven. The neoimperial qualities inherent in the present condition of interstate society are noticed by Nye (1990: 166–7) when he argues that the US 'needs to establish international norms consistent with its society', and get 'other countries to want what it wants'. A more coercive interpretation of this view has emerged in the Bush administration post 11 September. A lopsided distribution of power enables the strong to impose themselves on the weak through all kinds of softer forms of coercion, usually labelled 'conditionality', and applied in relation to access to diplomatic recognition, aid, loans, markets, weapons and memberships of various IGOs (most obviously NATO, EU, WTO). This type of coercion is especially effective if the strong are not ideologically divided among themselves (as they were for much of the twentieth century), but all more or less on board in their own sub-global interstate/international society. If the social structure of the international system has a strong core–periphery form where the core is relatively homogenous, then imposition of a 'standard of civilisation' is much facilitated.

After the end of the Cold War there was some prospect that a fairly homogenous core would become a durable feature, but with the diplomatic disarray surrounding the war against Iraq in 2003 this looks, at the time of writing (April 2003), to be less likely. If the US persists in pursuing a project of neoimperial vanguardism it may have to rely more on the lopsided distribution of power than on a consensus backed by a concert of the great powers. The vanguard, whether composed of a concert of great powers or a single superpower, can try to impose its values by coercion (conquest or fear of takeover), but it can also operate more socially. Others might emulate the core, adopting its values, for several reasons. They might simply be overawed, and copy in order to conform and to obtain the same results. They might be persuaded by normative argument. They might emulate for competitive reasons, fearing loss of wealth or power if they fail to adapt, and hoping to outdo the vanguard at its own game. Whatever the mechanisms and whatever the rationales, the effect is one of a sub-global vanguard leading a global development. In the first, classical imperial round of this process, the main effect was to expand Westphalian interstate society from European to global scale. In the second phase, now in its early stages, the main attempt will be to increase the number and depth of shared values, both by elaborating the logic of coexistence within pluralism, and by inviting participation in solidarist joint projects such as liberal economics, big science and the pursuit of human rights. If this succeeds, it will push global interstate society towards a more solidarist formation (from Power Political, to Coexistence, to Cooperative, perhaps in places even to Kantian Convergence). If it fails badly, by seriously dividing the core, or by pushing too hard on contested values (most obviously democracy, human rights), or by failing to deliver promised effects (e.g. economic development and better distributed wealth), or by delivering damaging side-effects (environmental disaster, economic meltdown, political instability), it could give rise once again to oppositional sub-global interstate/international societies.

Between these two options lies a mixture of some movement towards solidarism at the global level, combined with some development of differentiated regional or sub-global interstate/international societies. The model for this is already apparent in the international political economy, where it is broadly accepted that regional economic groupings are both alternatives to a global economic order and ways of operating more effectively within such a global order (Buzan, Wæver and de Wilde 1998: 112–15). Sub-global structures play a delicate game both with each other (competitors in some senses, codependent in others) and with the global level (too much subglobalism will destroy the global level to the potential disadvantage of all).

A vanguard interpretation of how international social structures develop and decay draws attention to the domestic character of the leading powers as a key factor in understanding the dynamics of the international social structure. Recall the argument in chapter 4 (pp. 91–7) on the English school needing to make the internal evolution of the leading states, and the impact of their projection of their domestic values outward, a focus of historical and empirical work (see also Buzan and Little 2000: 374–7). Imperialism may or may not work as a way of expanding international social structures in space and depth, but whether it does or not will depend on the type of values projected, the methods by which they are projected, how they are evaluated morally by the recipients, and how well or badly they fit with other social values in play in the cultures either that are exposed to them, or on which they are imposed. All of this in turn will depend on the nature of the states and societies that lie at the core of the international system. Those with a taste for counterfactual history can explore this question by thinking through the likely consequences if Germany had won the First World War, or Germany and Japan the Second World War, or the Soviet Union and China the Third (Cold) World War. If fascist or communist powers now formed the core, what would interstate society look like? What would the main institutions be? Certainly it would not look at all like what we have today, and the degree of difference shows how much the question of the domestic character of the dominant power matters to what sort of international social structures do and do not get put in place. The process and outcomes of these wars can be seen also as aspects of the vanguard process in operation.

This line of reasoning ties up to the argument unfolded in chapter 5 (pp. 148–9) about homogeneity. I made the case there that one needed to be open minded about what sort of ideology underpinned interstate society. Much of the English school account tells only a liberal story, either because it is looking at European history becoming global history, or because it is specifically concerned with promoting liberal values. But other stories are perfectly possible, and some of them have real as opposed to counterfactual histories. The interstate societies of the ancient and classical world were driven almost entirely by the values of imperial ruling elites. The international social structures of the classical Islamic world, however one might best describe their mix of interhuman, transnational and interstate, were certainly not liberal. The absolutist phase of European interstate society was dominated by mercantilist and aristocratic values, not liberal ones. Fascism and communism had only rather brief historical runs, but a close look at how Germany, Japan and the Soviet Union operated within the spheres they did control would give some hints as to what would have happened had they come to dominate the whole of the international system. One could look also perhaps at China's long history as the core of an imperial system and glean some insights as to what the world would be like if an undemocratic China rather than the US was the sole superpower. From a theoretical perspective, and also a historical one, it is important not to lose sight of the fact that forms of international social structure other than liberal ones are possible, and that these too can be understood within the frame of English school theory.

Yet the historical legacy we have is that the three world wars of the twentieth century were about what form of political economy was going to shape the future of industrial society, and liberalism emerged victorious in all three rounds. It is thus not at all unreasonable to look closely at the particular character of the interstate and international societies generated by a liberal core. But one has to keep in mind that liberal values are not universally dominant. Other sorts of values are still in play worldwide, and at the sub-global level, for example in the Islamic world and much of East Asia, liberal values are not dominant within the local interstate societies. If one is going to bring the regional and the sub-global levels back into the study of international social structures, as I have argued should be done, then these non-liberal alternatives are of more than historical and theoretical interest. Some of them are still strongly in play at the sub-global level. How this mixture of the global and sub-global works in the contemporary world is the subject of chapter 8.

8 Conclusions: a portrait of contemporary interstate society

In chapter 1 I set out both my dissatisfactions with English school theory, and the reasons why I nevertheless thought it well worth pursuing. I committed myself to trying to shine some light on the important, but murky, relationship between international and world society, and to developing a structural interpretation of English school ideas, constructing them as a theory about norms rather than a normative theory. I also committed myself to using the methodological pluralism of English school theory, and its ability to look at several things at once, as a way of unpacking the problem of globalisation, and gaining more leverage on it. This agenda took me much deeper than I had originally intended, and with some help from various thinkers both inside and outside the English school, I have ended up with a rather radical revision of the classical three traditions. I hope I have also ended up with a plausible way of looking at the complex package of things that constitute the globalisation problematique.

Since misunderstandings seem to occur with frightening ease in academic debates, let me state very clearly for the record that <u>I do not intend that this structural rewriting of English school theory should replace or override the normative version of English school thinking which I labelled Wightian in chapter 1</u>. Wight's three traditions of debate about international relations, and the ongoing tensions between a prevailing orthodoxy and the various visions that challenge it, remains a valid and necessary understanding of English school theory. What I hope I have accomplished is to set up a structural interpretation alongside that normative one as an alternative but complementary way of understanding English school theory. I hope, of course, that some people will see merit in this alternative and take it up. I also hope that the more rigorous approach to taxonomy in the structural version will challenge various aspects of the debate in the normative version, and stimulate those pursuing that line to reconsider some of their assumptions. Perhaps the main theme throughout the preceding chapters has been that English school theory has not clearly enough distinguished between the structural and normative strands that weave through it, and that this practice has compromised the presentation of both elements. The structural element has never been clearly developed, and the normative element often flounders in conceptual confusion, as indicated by the nearly total incoherence about the central concept of world society. We need both the normative and the structural interpretations of English school theory standing side by side complementing and questioning each other.

Over the preceding seven chapters I have constructed what I hope is a clearer and more internally consistent English school lens through which to look at the questions posed by globalisation. This lens has several filters which select for the following:

- from chapter 4, the three domains (interhuman, transnational and interstate) and (from Wendt) the *how/why* dimension of shared values in terms of coercion, calculation and belief;
- from chapter 5, pluralism–solidarism and the spectrum of types of interstate society, plus the interplay among the three domains. Solidarism here includes a wider range of shared values, particularly economic ones, than are normally found in English school analyses;
- from chapter 6, primary institutions and the way these play into types of interstate society both as defining features and as benchmarks for change;
- from chapter 7, the distinction between global and sub-global (especially regional) levels, and the consequent question of how they interact, particularly the idea of vanguardism as a basic mechanism for the development of international social structure.

These filters are, I propose, the minimum toolkit that one needs in order to approach the issue of globalisation. They do not offer clean and simple hypotheses like those available from neorealism, but they do offer an escape from the severe loss of analytical leverage that results from bundling huge complexities into a single concept, whether it be god or globalisation. English school theory holds on to the obligation to think in holistic terms, and it is prepared to look straight into the eyes of the complexity that necessarily results. Although I have borrowed ideas from Wendt, and in some ways recast English school theory in Wendtian terms (although substantially modified ones), I have not followed him into the confines of state-centrism. If this book is read as a critique of Wendt, then the main point of departure is keeping the non-state domains in play alongside the interstate one. The social structure of the international system is very complicated, and I do not think that one can understand globalisation without taking into account both the state and the non-state domains. While I share Wendt's view that states are still the dominant type of actor in the international system, and likely to remain so for some time, I have aimed for a theory that in principle allows for this not to be the case. Doing that, it seems to me, is a crucial move if one is not to block off the ability to see fundamental changes of social structure (Buzan and Little 2001). If Wendt was aiming at the possibility of a social structural theory in parallel to neorealism, then I think this will eventually mislead more than enlighten. Any given international social structure will represent a complicated mixture of domains and levels, not to mention mixtures of coercion, calculation and belief, and much about its particular workings will depend crucially on how the mixture is composed. This opens the way to interpretive and comparative theory, but probably not to the hard cause–effect theory beloved of positivists.

In this last chapter it seems fitting to give this new lens a trial run by turning it towards the contemporary international system and seeing what kind of view it reveals. In one chapter it will not be possible to sketch more than a general portrait. One function of this portrait relates to the English school, and is to demonstrate the difference of view using this social structural lens as opposed to the constricted pluralist one that still dominates most English school writing, including the writing of the solidarists. My aim is both to fill in the gaps that have been the focus of criticism in preceding chapters, and to give a hint at what an English school take on globalisation looks like. The second function is to offer a contrast between an English school account of what the international system now looks like, how it got to where it is, and what driving forces it sees as the main movers of history, and the familiar accounts available from other mainstream IR theories. Here the emphasis will be on primary institutions as the main comparative advantage of an English school approach, combined with a commitment to always asking what mixture of coercion, calculation and belief holds these institutions in place. Neorealism cannot ask this kind of question, and by moving towards it (neo)liberalism largely follows suit. Constructivists can ask such questions, but so far lack a holistic and historical framework comparable to that developed by the English school.

In the next section, I will set out a static portrait of contemporary interstate society, looking at both the global and sub-global levels. Since I will be focusing on an interstate society whose core is mainly liberal (but some of whose periphery and semi-periphery is not), this view will contribute to investigating the features of the liberal form of a Co-operative interstate society, with a strong interplay among the three domains, and developments in the interstate sector being interdependent with those in the interhuman and transnational ones. The second section looks back briefly to the interstate societies before the Second World War. The purpose is to get some sense of how institutions have changed, and to take advantage of the powers of hindsight to look at the possible dynamics driving both the changes and the continuities. The third section focuses on the stability of contemporary interstate society. What are its internal contradictions? How do the interplays between global and sub-global levels, and among the interstate, transnational and interhuman domains, affect the stability of interstate society? How much do external developments in, for example, technology and environment influence its stability and development? Are there changes in the binding forces that hold it together, and is the global level stable in itself or dependent on a vanguard? The fourth section concludes with a speculation on what the pattern of dynamics at play in contemporary interstate society suggests about its possible futures, and some thoughts on 'where to from here' in the English school research programme.

A snapshot of contemporary interstate society

How would one set about characterising contemporary interstate society in terms of the ideas unfolded in the preceding chapters? Perhaps the most obvious point to begin at is the one underlined by literatures as diverse as Huntington's 'clash of civilisations' and the many interpretations of the post-Cold War international system as 'two worlds', or core and periphery. These literatures suggests that contemporary interstate society is a layered, diverse phenomenon. It certainly has significant standing at the system level, where there is a global-scale social structure, but this is accompanied by more diverse, and in places much deeper, sub-global structures. These levels need to be examined separately.

At the global level the dominant view in the English school literature is that interstate society is firmly towards the pluralist end of the spectrum, with not even the solidarists claiming much beyond that.

I have argued that this view is too pessimistic, both because it ignores sub-global developments (not strictly relevant here since I am considering only the global level at this point) and because it does not count developments in the economic sector as part of interstate society (which is relevant). In terms of the general spectrum of types of interstate society set out in figure 5, and elaborated in chapter 6 (pp. 190–5) above, it would be unreasonable to characterise contemporary interstate society as either Power Political or Convergence. Institutions are much too well developed, and war much too constrained, to see the world as Power Political; and the degree of structural and ideological diversity amongst states much too high, and resistance to the idea of homogenization much too strong, to see it as Convergence. The middle of the spectrum comprises the Coexistence model, which emphasises the primacy of states, and the limitation of interstate society to pluralist rules; and the Cooperation one, where many institutions will at least initially be carried over from the Coexistence model, significant downgrading of war and balance of power is likely, and some joint projects become a feature of shared values. If the economic sector is allowed in as a shared value of contemporary interstate society, then it is difficult to argue that it fits with the Coexistence model. For sure, much remains that fits a logic of coexistence, including some quite elaborate arrangements for arms control and environmental management. But the widespread acceptance of liberal rules for the world economy cannot reasonably be characterised as coexistence, and neither can more tentative acceptance of some elements of human rights. These represent a clear move into the Cooperative logic of collective pursuit of shared values (economic growth and development, human rights). So one can start this exercise by positioning contemporary global interstate society towards the pluralist side of the Cooperative model.

Picking up from table 3, and looking at the primary institutions of this global society, sovereignty and territoriality (and therefore the state) still feature strongly as master institutions. Of the derivatives from these, non-intervention is still quite robust, though no longer as absolute as it once was, being under pressure both from human rights and US claims to a broad right of preventive action in pursuit of its national security (Bush 2002). International law has become hugely elaborate, supporting many secondary institutions. Diplomacy remains a master institution with multilateralism the most significant derivative (though under threat from US unilateralism), and again a host of secondary institutions. Great power management remains robust as a general principle, but under stress from differences between unipolar and multipolar interpretations. Of its derivatives, alliances are no longer the most salient feature of the political landscape, and war is much hedged about with restrictions and largely ruled out amongst the major powers. Balance of power is somewhat harder to characterise. Certainly it does not operate in the same vigorous way that characterised it up to the end of the Cold War. The increasing adoption of liberal economic values has severely moderated anti-hegemonism, as exemplified *inter alia* by a quite widespread willingness among the powers to collaborate in big science projects. Nationalism and its derivatives, self-determination and popular sovereignty, remain strong, but democracy is not a globally shared value. Equality of people is strong as a master institution, but despite significant advances, its derivatives, human rights and humanitarian intervention, remain contested. It it still controversial whether to count them as global level institutions or not. The market has finally triumphed as a master institution, strongly tied into multilateralism, and with trade and financial liberalisation as its major derivatives. Environmental stewardship probably now registers as a master institution, but more with a logic of coexistence than with the force of a joint project.

Because this modestly Cooperative interstate society is dominantly liberal in character, one would expect, and one finds, a lot of interplay between the three domains (interstate, interhuman, transnational). With equality of people and the market as strong primary institutions, both individuals and, even more so TNAs of various kinds, are given substantial rights and standings within the secondary institutions of interstate society. Firms, political lobbying groups and interest groups are allowed, and often encouraged, to operate transnationally, and can acquire legal rights and responsibilities within the framework of interstate society. TNAs and individuals are allowed to accumulate and use huge amounts of capital and organisational resources, and to play openly (and covertly) in the political processes of bilateral diplomacy, conferencing and multilateralism. Powerful TNAs and individuals have a big enough role to justify labelling the global level an *international society*. They have been important movers of interstate society on human rights, environment and some arms control issues. Their position makes it reasonable to ask whether or not they are the dominant driving force behind the rise of the market to such a strong position among the institutions of contemporary international society.

If we live in a modestly Cooperative, and ideologically liberal global international society, what are the binding forces (coercion? calculation?

belief?) that hold it together, and how stable is it? Given the size and the complexity of this society (the number and variety of both its members and its institutions), it would almost certainly distort the truth too much to attempt a Wendt-style single overall characterisation. As I argued in chapter 4, coercion, calculation and belief will almost always come in mixtures. Without a much deeper investigation, it is not possible to give more than an impressionistic account of this aspect of contemporary international society, but common sense will perhaps save this from being too controversial. If one focuses on the interstate society, then many of the institutions appear to be held in place by belief. At the level of states, sovereignty, territoriality, non-intervention, diplomacy, international law, great power management, nationalism, self-determination (not all versions), popular sovereignty and equality of people(s), are all pretty deeply internalised and not contested as principles. Particular instances or applications may excite controversy, for example resentments of great power management, or opposition to some self-determination bids based on cultural nationalism. But the basic institutions of pluralist interstate society have wide support among states, and pretty wide support amongst peoples and TNAs. Most liberation movements seek sovereignty. Most TNAs want and need a stable legal framework. Although these institutions were originally imposed coercively by the West, it is far from clear that they are now held in place primarily by Western power and influence. Even if Western power declined, it does not seem unreasonable to think that most of these pluralist institutions would remain in place, as too might the modest level of commitment to environmental stewardship.

The same cannot yet be said for the more solidarist elements of contemporary international society. Should the backing for human rights and humanitarian intervention by the West weaken for any reason, it does not seem likely that they would retain much standing as global institutions, even though they would retain strong constituencies of interstate support regionally, and more widely in the transnational and interhuman domains. But at the global interstate level they are held in place more by calculation and coercion than by belief. Whether the same is true of the market and its derivatives is an interesting, important and difficult question. Until the end of the Cold War, the market was one of the core contested issues among the great powers, the rival principle being centrally planned economics. But with the collapse of the Soviet Union, and the abandonment of central planning by China, the market has become a global institution in the sense that most states conform to market rules, and powerful secondary institutions exist to support this (IMF, WTO, World Bank). While many states support this out of belief, it could be argued that many others adhere to it because of calculation or soft forms of coercion. One does not see much of gunboats being sent in to open markets as was done during colonial times, but for most periphery states, access to aid, loans and markets is frequently made conditional on compliance with market rules. Many calculate that their wellbeing or even survival depend on such compliance, and thus go along voluntarily. Others are subject to more direct forms of arm twisting such as sanctions. Because compliance is nearly universal, the market is a major institution of contemporary international society. Amongst many, adherence is rooted in belief, but for a significant number this institution is held in place by (and serves the interests of) Western power. If that power were to decline, weakening coercion, and changing the balance of calculation, it is not clear that the market would survive as a global institution.

In sum, although this is a modestly Cooperative international society, its Coexistence elements are quite deep-rooted and stable, whereas its Cooperative ones as yet have shallower roots, and could more easily (which is not to say easily) be swept away by changes in the distribution of power. An argument can be made that the interstate domain at the global level is increasingly supported by a global scale 'Westernistic' civilisation, or 'Mondo culture' which influences not just state elites, but also TNAs and popular culture (Buzan and Segal 1998a, b). Up to a century ago, relatively few people thought of themselves as members of the human race in any meaningful way. Empire was common, outright slavery only recently pushed to the margins, unequal treatment routine, and the idea of a common humanity very marginal except within some religious traditions. Few people knew much or cared much about what was happening on other parts of the planet. Now many more people do know at least something about what goes on elsewhere, and up to a point care about it, even if very unevenly and in ways heavily shaped by patterns of media attention. For the past half-century there has been a general acceptance that all humans are equal, even if this is still violated in practice in many ways and places. These things matter in that they contribute to the stability of a global interstate society by embedding its ideas not just in state elites, but in the minds of the peoples as well.

The picture at the sub-global/regional level is, as one might expect, much more mixed. The fried egg metaphor I floated earlier suggests that sub-global societies (seen as the yolks) would rest on, and share, the common 'white' representing the global level just described. This metaphor carries the important implication that there is a substantial degree of compatibility between the societal developments at the sub-global level and those at the global level (and for those attuned to racism, the idea of the substrate being 'white' will also carry some resonance!). If no such compatibility exists, then the global level itself does not exist. To say compatibility must exist is not to imply that harmony must exist amongst the sub-global societies, only that they must agree to share some institutions. In principle, the nature of the relationships both among the sub-global societies, and between them and the global level, remains open and historically contingent. It is possible for sub-global interstate societies to be strong rivals, as they were during the Cold War, and yet still share adherence to some global-level institutions (sovereignty, territoriality, diplomacy). I referred to this earlier as 'second-order pluralism'. Such pluralism could encompass intersocietal relations ranging from friendship through indifference to hostility. Sub-global international societies lose their point if there are no significant differences among them, and if the differences become too great then the global level disappears. I can see no reason to agree with the hypothesis assumed in some English school writings that sub-global societal developments must necessarily be rivals or necessarily degrade the global level. They might do so. Or they might not.

In the contemporary international system one can identify quite a few sub-global (mostly regional) interstate and/or international societies. Even a brief survey reveals that what is striking about them is that most are quite well in tune with the institutions at the global level, and that there are no fierce hostilities among them of the kind that defined the Cold War. There are, in other words, no competing universalisms of the type that so worried Bull and Wight. It can certainly be argued that the West, and particularly the US, sees itself as a universalism, but unlike during the Cold War, the other sub-global interstate societies are broadly concerned with maintaining their distinctiveness at the sub-global level, not trying to remake the global level in their own image.

Perhaps the most obvious candidate for a sub-global international society is the West. Because the West serves as the core for global level international society, there is no puzzle about its compatibility with the global level. The West is a clear case of the fried eggs metaphor where the yolk is thicker than the white because it represents a wider set of shared institutions. Within the circle of Western states, some of the things that are either hotly contested at the global level, or held in place by calculation or coercion, are deeply internalised and stable at this sub-global level. Within Western international society the market is broadly accepted, democracy even more so, and there is agreement on a substantial array of human rights. Individuals and non-state actors have well-established rights and responsibilities, and the whole sub-system is laced together with a dense network of secondary institutions and transnational networks. The West as a whole has achieved fully-fledged Cooperative status, and is often referred to as <u>the</u> international community (Gonzalez-Pelaez 2002: 47–59), though at the time of writing this development is coming under severe pressure from the unilateralist and in some ways imperial policies of the Bush administration.

The West is not monolithic. Some parts of it have distinctive Cooperative projects of their own, most obviously NAFTA, and more on the edges of the West, Mercosur. Although these largely embrace the same sorts of institutions as the West as a whole (the market, democracy, elements of human rights), they generate distinctive secondary institutions for the pursuit of those shared goals. Other parts of the West, most notably the EU, are progressing well into the Kantian version of the Convergence model by embracing both substantial elements of homogeneity in their state structures, and by constructing strong secondary institutions including some IGOs with a quasi-governmental character (the European Commission, the European Parliament, the European Court of Justice). The contrast between the Convergence goals of the EU, and the robust rejection of convergence by the US, has become much more visible under the Bush administration, even generating its own literature (Kagan 2002). Because the West is the core of the global interstate society, it cannot just be considered as a more thickly developed subsystem. It is also the centre of power that supports the global interstate society, and the repository of the more contested institutions which that core projects into global interstate society and to some extent supports coercively (the market, human rights, democracy). In this sense, the West generally is still playing the role of vanguard to global interstate society, pressing its own values and institutions onto societies that in varying degrees want to resist them, and which use the earlier round of pluralist institutions (especially sovereignty, territoriality, diplomacy) to do so. Although it is too early to judge at the time of writing, the 2003 war against Iraq by the US seems to suggest that the Bush administration has in mind a much more aggressive and imperial style of vanguardism, though whether this can be sustained, or will work, remains to be seen, as does the extent to which pursuit of it will undermine the cohesion of the West as the core of global international society.

There is a sub-global interstate society in East Asia which is mostly Coexistence in character. Unlike the West, and talk of 'Asian values' notwithstanding, East Asia enjoys little or no overall shared culture beyond that provided by the global level, and its interstate society is defined by strong adherence to sovereignty, territoriality and nationalism. The region as a whole is far from being a security community, even though within it the ASEAN states have built up quite a successful security regime. If it were not restrained by the ringholder presence of the US, East Asia would probably have war as a more prominent institution. Yet East Asia also has some Cooperative qualities. Mostly it resists the Western pressure on human rights and democracy, but many of its states have accepted a limited version of the market as necessary to their own power and stability. Economic nationalism remains strong, but with the understanding that the national economic development of each depends on a degree of openness to trade and investment, and acceptance of some market rules. Until the late 1990s, there was also acceptance of the distinctive Japanese model of capitalism. There is a common understanding among most of the leaderships that pursuit of economic interdependence both requires and supports restraints on the operation of the balance of power and war. East Asia has some still rather weak secondary institutions, and it is far from clear that as China grows strong this regional interstate society will be able to sustain a commitment to absolute gains in the face of relative ones that might change the distribution of power among the member states (Buzan and Wæver 2003: 142–80).

Turning to areas more clearly within the global periphery one finds a variety of other 'yolks' embedded in the global white. Russia is busy trying to adapt to the global institutions, having previously been the failed side in the Cold War's struggle of competing universalisms. South Asia strangely manages to be less on the regional level than the global norm – not so much a yolk sitting on the white, as a thin area of the white. Although it does have some (very weak) regional secondary institutions, South Asia is basically on the Power Political side of the Coexistence model. War is an ever-present possibility, India and Pakistan have trouble sustaining diplomatic relations, there is relatively little trade and investment within the region, and no parallel to the East Asian joint development idea.

238

Something of the same might initially be thought about the Islamic international society centred on the Middle East and West Asia. There too, war remains a vigorous institution, and there is little commitment within the region to joint economic development. There is also fierce resistance to Western impositions of human rights and democracy. Yet while in the interstate domain this might also look like being on the Power Political side of the Coexistence model, there are other things going on. As in South Asia, the states-system and basic Westphalian institutions are robust. There are some, mostly weak, secondary institutions, most notably the Arab League and the Organization of the Islamic Conference (OIC), as well as a variety of subregional IGOs (Arab Maghreb Union, Gulf Cooperation Council). And although the states-system has proved surprisingly robust, both Arab nationalism and Islam constitute powerful, and where they overlap, intertwined elements of collective identity within the interhuman domain. These strong interhuman components of this sub-global society are concentrated in the same area as the interstate component, but also reach out to a thinner global constituency. Among other things, they are powerful drivers of hostility to Israel and Iran. Although Islam is not organised as a hierarchical church, these patterns of identity support a substantial element of TNAs ranging from philosophical Sufi sects to al-Qaeda. While the interstate side of this sub-global international society is largely in conformity with the Westphalian elements of global interstate society, a case might be made that the interhuman and transnational elements are at least potentially, and up to a point in practice, in tension with it. Although most of the states in this society have succeeded at least partially in coopting Islamic legitimacy into their own structures, there remains a tension between the universalist claims and pulls of the *umma*, and the secular and sectional claims of the state. In some senses, the idea of an 'Islamic state' is a contradiction in terms. So long as those senses retain the capacity to mobilise people (as demonstrated by al-Qaeda) the Islamic international society will remain in tension both with itself and, as demonstrated most recently by the invasion of Iraq, with the global international society (Buzan and Wæver 2003: 185–216).

Africa is perhaps the most difficult of the periphery areas to characterise in these terms. On the one hand, so many of its states are weak or even failed, that it is hard put to meet Westphalian criteria in practice. Civil war of one sort or another is common, the dominant form of indigenous TNA is the armed insurgency group, and borders in many places are more notional than functional. On the other hand, Africa possesses a modestly impressive set of regional and subregional secondary institutions. Interstate wars are relatively uncommon. Its states are strong defenders of the principles of sovereignty, non-intervention and diplomacy, and there is at least rhetorical commitment to joint development. Because of the weakness of its local political, economic and social structures, Africa is heavily penetrated by both external powers and outside TNAs. It is the most peripheral part of the periphery, and the place where many of the local state structures would not survive if they were not held in place and supported by the institutions of global interstate society (Jackson 1990; Buzan and Wæver 2003: 217–51).

In sum, there is quite a lot of variation at the sub-global level. Some parts are more developed (or at least thicker, in the sense of more solidarist) than the global level, and act in part as a vanguard using their power to project contested values on a global scale. Other parts are less developed (or thinner, more pluralist), most notably in retaining war as an active institution less hedged about with restraints than the global level. Some parts are seeking to pursue their own variations within the broad framework of global level institutions, others seek to defend elements of cultural distinctiveness. At present, and with the possible exception of the US, there are no clashing universalisms where sub-global interstate societies seek to impose their norms on the whole planet. There are certainly tensions, most obviously around the 'war on terrorism', but more generally between the human rights and democracy vanguardism of the West, and the mostly African, Middle Eastern and Asian societies in which those values clash with indigenous cultural traditions. These tensions look enduring, and their outcome uncertain. But against them stand the really quite impressive, and quite stable set of interstate institutions that are common both to the global level and to most of the sub-global ones. While there is a lot going on in terms of globalisation in all three domains, there is also a lot going on in all three domains of a much more localist or regional character.

Looking back: what changed, what didn't and why?

I do not have the space here to conduct a detailed, step-by-step analysis of how the international social structure has evolved and changed over the last two centuries. It is nonetheless possible, and quite useful, to exploit the powers of hindsight by taking a quick look back. As set out in chapter 7 (pp. 214–17) above, there already exists a classical English school account of this period told as the expansion of European inter-state society to the rest of the world. I have argued that this account rests on an idealised view of the nineteenth century, leading to an unduly pes-simistic view of developments in the twentieth. This classical account therefore serves as one benchmark against which to develop an alter-native interpretation based on the theoretical framework developed in chapters 4–7. Picking up on Holsti's idea of using primary institutions as a benchmark for change provides another analytical tool. On these lines, and in contrast to liberals such as Ikenberry (2001) who use sec-ondary institutions to structure a historical account, it is also possible to build on the work of Mayall and Keene. Mayall's studies on nation-alism trace out, and up to a point explain, some of the most important changes in primary institutions during this period. Keene's (2002) dis-cussion of colonialism provides a similar service. One can ask whether these are changes within or between the main models that occupy the pluralist–solidarist spectrum? One can also look for significant changes and/or continuities in other elements of international social structure – the three domains, the question of binding forces, and geographical scope and subdivision.

In the previous section I argued that contemporary global level in-terstate society was modestly Cooperative. I gave its master primary institutions as sovereignty, territoriality, diplomacy, great power man-agement, nationalism, the market, equality of people and environmen-tal stewardship; and its derivative institutions as non-intervention, international law, multilateralism, balance of power, war (though now extremely hedged about with restrictions), self-determination, popu-lar sovereignty, and trade and financial liberalisation. Embedded in this global level, I identified a number of sub-global interstate societies, some much thicker than the global substrate, some a bit thinner, but most more or less in harmony with the pluralist end of the global level structure. A significant feature of this whole ensemble was its core–periphery structure in which the West played the role of past and present vanguard in creating, supporting, and in some respects pushing for extension of, the institutions at the global level. If this is a fair characterisation of what we have now, where did we come from, and what changed and what remained the same, to bring us to this point?

It is, I think, fair to accept the English school's classical assumption that the contemporary global international society evolved primarily out of developments in Europe. Since a global interstate society of any sort is difficult to trace much before the middle of the nineteenth century, it is thus reasonable to use European interstate society as the starting benchmark against which to track the changes that bring us to the present. If we take eighteenth-century Europe as representative of a classical Westphalian society of states, its primary institutions can be summarised as follows.

Table 4. *The primary institutions of eighteenth-century European interstate society*

	Primary Institutions
Master	Derivative
Sovereignty	Non-intervention, International law
Territoriality	Borders
Diplomacy	Messengers/diplomats, Treaties, Diplomatic language
Balance of power	Anti-hegemonism, Alliances, Guarantees Neutrality, War, Great power management
Inequality of peoples	Colonialism
Trade	Mercantilism
Dynasticism	Elite genealogy and marriage

Starting from this characterisation of eighteenth-century Europe, one can attempt to fill in the gap between then and now. Overall, we seem to be tracking a shift from a European interstate society located close to the Power Political side of the Coexistence model, and not global in scale, to the global scale modestly Cooperative international society of the present day. Obviously quite a lot of eighteenth-century institutions have survived, and the question is whether and how these have changed in terms of the understanding of what they represent and the practices legitimised by them. Earlier discussion already suggests that sovereignty, war and international law have undergone substantial internal changes. Just as obviously, some eighteenth-century institutions have dropped away (inequality of peoples, colonialism, mercantilism, dynasticism, elite genealogy and marriage, and more arguably alliances), and several additional institutions have been taken on board (nationalism, equality of people, self-determination, popular sovereignty, the market, multilateralism, environmental stewardship). Many of these exits and entrances are linked pairs occupying the same functional space (e.g. mercantilism and market, inequality of peoples and equality of peoples, colonialism and self-determination, dynasticism and popular sovereignty). For both the exits and entrances the question is when and why this happened. Table 4 also makes clear that the whole universe of secondary institutions came into being after the eighteenth century, and again the questions are when and why? It was probably the case that the institutions and operations of this eighteenth-century interstate society were largely detached from the interhuman domain except for the idea of Christendom. In the transnational domain the Roman church remained a player, and some banking and trading networks were also important, but apart from these, the transnational domain was thinly populated in comparison with the present day. Since eighteenth-century Europe had mainly colonial relations with the rest of the world, and an international system was not yet fully global in extent, and very thin in many places, it is hard to think in terms of global and sub-global levels of interstate society.

Because there has been no attempt within the English school to think systematically about primary institutions, there is almost no work that attempts to analyse the expansion and evolution of international society in this way. Holsti's (2002) paper has already been discussed in chapter 6. Watson (1992: 152–250) contains some hints, but since he is more concerned to highlight the role of hegemony within the anarchy–hierarchy spectrum, he does not deal systematically with institutions. He is nevertheless good at tracking the development of diplomacy, war and the balance of power as institutions, and touches on dynasticism, international law and nationalism. Mayall's (1990, 2000) work on nationalism brings in many other primary institutions, and provides not only a starting point, but also something of a model for how to approach the interplay and tensions among primary institutions as a key dynamic shaping how interstate societies evolve.

Mayall focuses his main effort on identifying the impact of nationalism on the interstate society into which it was introduced. For the purposes of this analysis I will accept the general understanding that nationalism came into vogue in Europe during the nineteenth century, having intellectual roots developed during the eighteenth. It can be explained multiply as a product of romantic thinking, as a political tool for peoples seeking to free themselves from empires (primarily Ottoman and Austro-Hungarian), and as a response by state elites both to military pressures (the use of the *levée en masse* by revolutionary France) and to the class tensions identified by Marx as arising from the practices of industrial capitalism. Whatever its source, during the nineteenth century nationalism was increasingly taken on board as a primary institution both by European interstate society and by the global interstate society that Europe was unintentionally making through colonialism. This process did much more than simply add another primary institution into the mix. As Mayall traces with some care, it played a key role in both the reinterpretation of some Westphalian institutions and the demise of others. Mayall's (1990; 2000) main observations are as follows:

- Nationalism underlay the shift from dynastic to popular sovereignty, and was also a strand leading into the development of human rights in the West (1990: 2). Nationalism supported self-determination, but introduced a tension about who constitutes any given nation (ethno-nationalism or political nationalism). This in turn confused the principle of self-determination adopted after the First World War, though also becoming one of the tensions that undermined colonialism (1990: 38–49; 2000: 39–66).
- Diplomacy survived the coming of nationalism, but nationalism modified the Westphalian primary institutions of sovereignty, non-intervention, war, territoriality and balance of power, without eliminating them. Even postmodern states still retain sovereignty and territoriality, though they use them differently (2000: 67–78). Nationalism weakened the principle of mutual recognition (by setting the nation-state ideal against the much more mixed reality) but strengthened commitment to sovereign equality. It created tensions between liberal inclinations to restrain the use of force, and interpretations of nationalism that elevated war to be the mechanism of social Darwinism. And it hugely deepened the relationship between governments and peoples (role of the state in society) (1990: 25–37). Nationalism challenged territoriality, not as such, but by hanging its legitimacy on national criteria, and generating problems of irredentism and secessionism (1990: 50–63).
- Dynasticism, political aggression and imperialism/colonialism were all delegitimised by nationalism (1990: 35).
- In some ways nationalism was entangled with liberalism, and thus developed as an institution alongside the market. Yet despite this shared parentage, nationalism and the market are often in tension, with nationalism challenging the market in ways ranging from cultural and political autarky projects, through imperatives of defence self-reliance, to labour mobility and migration (1990: 70–110). Economic nationalism was also a feature of both communist and many third world states (1990: 111–44). This general tension does not mean

that the nation-state idea is not also complementary to the liberal project in many ways, including defence, democracy, law and currency (1990: 150–1).

• Because international law is made by states, there are tensions between international law and democracy except where all states are democracies (Mayall 2000: 94).

Using Mayall's insights as a starting point, and adding in the exits and entrances already noted between eighteenth-century and contemporary interstate society, one can compile the following sketch about how, why and when the primary institutions of interstate society changed over the last two centuries.

During the nineteenth century nationalism consolidated as an institution of European interstate society, with resultant tensions between its derivatives, self-determination and popular sovereignty, and the stability of local (not overseas) empires (Ottoman, Austro-Hungarian, Russian). There was sustained tension between mercantilism and the market as to which would be the dominant derivative of trade. Later in the century came the first development of secondary institutions in response to growing trade and communication and the rapid shrinking of the world by technologies of transportation and communication. Interstate society became global in scale as European (and later US and Japanese) empires filled up the international system. This was a largely colonial interstate society with a European core. A Western hemisphere semi-periphery, and later East Asian developments centred on the rise of Japan, began to introduce a significant independent sub-global level, while most of Africa, Asia and the Pacific had subordinate political and social status. During this period, sovereignty, diplomacy, international law, territoriality, borders, the balance of power anti-hegemonism, alliances and war did not alter much, though the concert of Europe developed as an early form of multilateral great power management.

After the First World War, and in no small measure in reaction to its horrors, interstate war began to be downgraded as an acceptable general instrument amongst the members of interstate society, mostly because of fear that technologically driven powers of destruction threatened to wreck European civilisation. Diplomacy came under challenge in some European countries and the US because of its removal from popular sovereignty and public opinion, but it largely survived this turbulence unaltered. The mandate system began to question the legitimacy of colonialism and its derivatives (Mayall 2000: 17–25), and a major consolidation of self-determination and popular sovereignty within European international society (Wilsonianism) began the corrosive seepage of these ideas into the colonies. Dynasticism and its derivatives were largely eliminated as institutions of interstate society under the pressure of nationalism and popular sovereignty, though some dynastic practices remained as features of domestic politics in some states. There was a major development of secondary institutions, especially global forum organisations, and along with that the beginning of a major expansion of positive international law, foreshadowed by the two Hague Conferences on the laws of war late in the nineteenth century. During this period nationalism changed the understanding of territoriality and borders, and also completed the shifting of the legitimation of sovereignty from dynastic rights to peoples. The competition between mercantilism and market continued, as did central roles for alliances, balance of power and anti-hegemonism.

The Second World War, and the understanding of the processes leading up to it, likewise generated further changes in the institutions of interstate society. These reactions consolidated the market as an institution of Western international society, and linked this strongly to the shrinking legitimacy of war, which, under pressure from fear of nuclear weapons, was increasingly confined to an ultimate right of self-defence validated by sovereignty and nationalism. At the same time, the long tension between the market and (the communist version of) mercantilism entered what now looks like the last phase of the struggle for dominance, and democracy was consolidating as a primary institution of Western international society. After 1945 and outside the Soviet sphere, there was a rapid demise of inequality of peoples and its derivatives, colonialism and the right of conquest. This took place under pressure from the spread of nationalism, self-determination and popular sovereignty from European to global interstate society. Alongside this was a concomitant rise of equality of peoples as an institution of global interstate society. The winding down of colonialism meant that an interstate society based on sovereign equality became global in scale. This expansion opened up the way for a variety of sub-global/regional developments previously overlaid by colonialism, and it was during this period that the differentiation between global and sub-global international social structures spread to the whole system. At least within the Western sphere, multilateral diplomacy flourished as an institution, and many issues that might previously have led to war were handled in a variety of conferences and IGOs. This rise of multilateralism was accompanied by a rapid expansion of both secondary institutions and TNAs linked into Western interstate society. The rise of secondary institutions was linked to two things: first, the impact of decolonisation, which released dozens of weak states into the system, many not capable of fulfilling independently either their internal management or their diplomatic roles; and second, the rise of the market within the Western sphere, and the need for management of what was becoming a global economy. Within this context, international law continued to become more extensive and elaborate, not only among states, but also between them and TNAs, and to a lesser extent individuals. Within the West, and particularly so within the developing EU, sovereignty, territoriality and borders were adapted to meet the conditions created by a more extensive embracing of the market. In the wider global society, sovereignty and non-intervention remained robust, as did balance of power, anti-hegemonism and alliances. Environmental stewardship began to emerge as a new institution, and one substantially driven from the interhuman and transnational domains up into the interstate one.

After the ending of the Cold War, the market became a strong institution at the global level, and interstate war was pushed even further to the margins. The implosion of the Soviet Union created perhaps the last major round of decolonisation. One consequence of all this was a reduction in the importance of alliances, which while still present, no longer functioned within interstate society in the same central way that they had done traditionally. Another consequence was the weakening of anti-hegemonism, as exemplified *inter alia* by a quite widespread willingness among the powers both to open their economies and accept the risks of interdependence, and to collaborate in various big science projects. Asking whether the balance of power as a master institution was in decay was at least not an unreasonable question, though great power management remained strong. Nau (2001: 585), for example, argues that 'when national identities converge, as they have recently among the democratic great powers, they may temper and even eliminate the struggle for power'. There was room for thinking that in many ways the market, multilateralism and the host of secondary institutions associated with them, had taken over from war, balance of power and their derivatives as the institutions that now shaped how sovereignty and territoriality were to be understood. Yet with the US left as the sole superpower multilateralism came under some hard questioning as Washington adopted more unilateralist attitudes and practices, and turned against many of the secondary institutions it had been the prime mover in creating. So also, after 11 September, and more so after the invasion of Iraq, did the place of war, with the US claiming and exercising rights of preventive attack. With the West as a whole in a dominant position, the projection globally of its concerns about human rights and democracy raised tensions not only with non-intervention, but also with the problem that the social conditions necessary to sustain democracy and human rights as a 'standard of civilisation' simply did not exist in many parts of the world (Mayall 2000: 88–93, 106–20). Environmental stewardship continued to grow as an institution which, like human rights, had strong roots in the non-state domains.

This rough sketch of the development of interstate society over the past two centuries reveals both substantial continuity and a good deal of change. Perhaps diplomacy and non-intervention have been the most stable institutions, in the sense both of remaining in place and not being fundamentally reinterpreted. The practice of diplomacy has of course changed with better communications and more multilateralism, but its essential principles remain pretty much the same. Non-intervention has recently come under challenge both by human rights campaigners and by the new claims of the US for rights of pre-emption, yet this institution also has so far kept its basic shape rather well. By contrast, sovereignty, territoriality and borders, though remaining central, have been substantially reinterpreted to accommodate nationalism and the market. Both interstate war and the balance of power have been pushed towards the margins as institutions, not least by the rise of the market as a dominant institution.

Overall, this brief sketch presents a very different picture from the classical, rather pessimistic, account of the English school outlined in chapter 7 (pp. 212–17). It also provides a much fuller portrait than either neorealism (which tells the story in terms of changes in polarity) or neoliberalism (with its emphasis on secondary institutions). These theoretical approaches simply cannot generate the questions that animate the English school's approach. The development of global interstate society is of course susceptible to a variety of normative assessments depending on the values used. But it is difficult to see it as a story of retreat from some nineteenth-century pinnacle, and quite possible to interpret it as in many ways a progressive story, albeit one with ups and downs. Perhaps the really central change over the last 200 years has been the shift from a core–periphery mediated by imperial power and war, to one based on universalised Westphalian principles and multilateralism. Within that shift a greater scope for geographical differentiation has opened up as the process of decolonisation not only allowed the periphery to join a global interstate society on much more equal political terms, but also allowed sub-global interstate societies to form and develop in distinctive ways. If interstate society is understood only at the global level, and primarily as a phenomenon of great powers, then it is indeed possible to see the Cold War as a rather depressing time. But if one builds into the picture decolonisation as well as superpower rivalry, and looks not just at the global level but also the sub-global one, then even the Cold War has quite a bit to be cheerful about. The costs of losing a degree of cultural homogeneity underpinning interstate society are a legitimate source of concern, but need to be balanced both by the gains of losing colonialism and dynasticism, and by the development of elements of a global culture not just at the level of elites, but also, and increasingly, in the interhuman and transnational domains. In the West, and increasingly beyond it, we have an international and not just an interstate society.

Also clear from this story is that the changes in interstate society have many sources. War has been one of the key movers on both global and sub-global levels, though its central role now seems to be giving way to the market. Deeper developments in society, economy and technology, in the form both of revolutions and steadier incremental transformations, also motivate institutional change. So too does the interplay between different institutions and the tensions and contradictions among them, which lead to both reinterpretations of institutions that remain stable, and the atrophy of some old institutions and the entry of some new ones. And there is the interplay amongst the three domains already discussed in chapter 6. These driving forces are the subject of the next section.

Driving forces, deeply rooted structures and contradictions

Having looked at how things are in contemporary international society, and then at what changed to make them that way, the next step is to focus on the driving forces that kept some institutions stable, drove some from the field and inspired or pressed for the development of new ones. The focus on continuity and change of primary institutions provides a single frame of reference within which to capture the daunting array of variables that constitute the problematique of globalisation. The enormous complexity of globalisation means that any single dominant cause is unlikely. Both the dynamics and the statics of international society reflect interplays among a variety of (f)actors, some material, some social. In this section I will look briefly at the five main explanatory factors that arise out of the framework and analysis developed above: tensions and contradictions among primary institutions; the dynamics of societal geography and the distribution of power; the nature of binding forces and the character of leading powers; the interplay among the three domains; and the pressures of material conditions.

Tensions and contradictions among primary institutions

There was quite a bit of discussion of this in the previous section building on Mayall's contribution, and also in chapter 6, where I pointed out that while some primary institutions composed a relatively coherent, mutually supportive, set (notably the classical pluralist package of sovereignty, territoriality, diplomacy, balance of power and international law), others were both practically and intrinsically in tension both with some of these, and sometimes with each other (nationalism, human rights, the market). The basic point here is that there should be no expectation that the primary institutions composing any interstate or international society should necessarily or even probably all be in harmony with each other. Harmony should not be excluded as a possibility, and might have interesting implications for stability if it happened. But it is probably the exception rather than the rule. This should not be surprising. Contradictions within a set of values all held to be central are the everyday stuff of both individual morality and the practice of domestic politics in most states. If some of the primary institutions of any society are in tension with each other, then one must expect that tension to be a pressure for change both of and in institutions. That said, however, one should not underestimate the capability of powerful and generally successful societies to sustain and even profit from a degree of tension among their primary institutions. The merit of Mayall's analysis was precisely that he showed how the introduction of nationalism as a primary institution created tensions, and consequently changed the understanding of some other primary institutions (territoriality, sovereignty, market), and undermined others (colonialism, dynasticism). At the same time these other institutions affected how nationalism was interpreted (for example, in relation to self-determination). In contemporary international society there is a central tension between the market on the one hand, and sovereignty, nationalism and war on the other. The attempt by the Western core to promote human rights and democracy on a global scale produces tensions of a different sort, but should human rights and democracy be accepted as primary institutions of global international society, that would not entirely remove their tension with sovereignty and non-intervention (not to mention war), so creating pressure for adaptation and reinterpretation in both directions. Building on Vincent's idea of a basic right to subsistence, Gonzalez-Pelaez (2002) explores the tensions among human rights, sovereignty and the market. The point here is that such tensions are likely to be a common feature of interstate/international societies, and that in and of themselves they constitute an important dynamic of change. If one is curious as to why the pluralist package of sovereignty, territoriality, diplomacy, balance of power and international law, has proved so durable, both in practice and in its intellectual appeal, then the answer lies at least in part in the harmony amongst them. In practice, this harmony produces a degree of mutual support, allowing a degree of flexibility and reinterpretation which has enabled this package to adapt to the rise of new institutions. Intellectually, the harmony is naturally attractive to those whose main concern is order.

The dynamics of societal geography and the distribution of power

The relevance of societal geography and the distribution of power is obvious from three points already made above. First, the classical English school's story of the expansion of international society rests on a concentration of power in a specific geographical area, and the use of that power to expand control into weaker areas, in the process expanding international society. That whole process depends on strong differences in societal geography. Second, in the previous section it was possible to use the three world wars of the twentieth century as plausible benchmarks for significant turning points in the evolution of the institutions of interstate society. Since the outcomes of these wars both reflected and generated new distributions of power, there is a strong suggestion that this matters in the development of interstate society. Third, the idea that the distribution of power matters is an area of common understanding between realists and English school pluralists. Both emphasise the leading role of the major powers in defining the character of the international system: Waltz's poles of power taken up by neorealists, and Bull's 'great responsibles'.

The difficulty here is that we have two senses of 'distribution of power' in play: the neorealist and pluralist sense of polarity as number of great powers, and a more general sense of the overall distribution of power within the international system. What matters for the dynamics of interstate/international society is probably not the distribution of power in the sense of great powers and polarity as such. European interstate society expanded even though (or even to a degree because) the European great powers were fighting amongst themselves on a regular basis. More important for the dynamics of international society is the lineup between the distribution of power and the character of the leading powers: are the great powers strongly divided ideologically, as during the interwar years and the Cold War, or relatively tolerant of each other's domestic arrangements, as now? And of course it matters a lot what ideology is dominant among the great powers. It makes a difference that the liberal democracies and not the totalitarians won the wars of the twentieth century. More on this below (pp. 361–7).

The distribution of power within the international system more generally, points toward the distinction between the global and sub-global levels explored in chapter 7. It also points towards the idea that at least in terms of the historical record, a vanguard model is a prominent feature of how interstate and international societies develop. From Watson's (1992) many empires of ancient and classical times, to the expansion of European interstate society, it has been historically common for a centre of power to grow up in one part of the system and then to expand and in varying degrees impose its own social, political and economic order onto a wider realm. This centre of power might be a single political entity (Rome, the Han Empire) or it might be a sub-system of states (Sumeria, classical Greece, modern Europe) and Watson (1992: 316–17) notes the tension that this creates in contemporary international society between the norms of sovereignty and non-intervention, and the reality of hegemonic practice by great powers. This vanguard element explains the core–periphery structure of contemporary interstate society, which in turn opens the question of whether the global (or any systemic) level is stable in itself, or whether that stability depends on a vanguard to uphold it.

The nature of binding forces and the character of leading powers

I have argued strongly in earlier chapters in favour of Wendt's approach of separating the forces that bind societies together (coercion, calculation, belief), from the shared values that define whether and how a society is pluralist or solidarist. One major consequence of this move is to open up the possibility of both coercive Convergence societies and Power Political warrior cultures held together by belief. Another is to challenge the advocates of solidarist norms to come clean about what methods they will and will not accept in pursuit of their goals. The same challenge applies to historical and normative evaluations of how contemporary interstate society was made. I argued in chapter 5 (pp. 154–7) that among other things the particular composition of binding forces plays centrally into the issue of whether any given society is stable or not, with forces towards the belief end favouring stability, and forces towards the coercion end suggesting instability (or at least stability contingent on an ability to maintain a large difference in power at a manageable cost).

This approach means that the pattern of binding forces is itself part of the social structure of interstate society. In a crude way it suggests the hypothesis that, other things being equal, interstate and international societies based on coercion will be less stable than those based on calculation, which will be less stable than those based on belief/identity. This is a slightly more systematic way of formulating the fairly commonplace insight (Watson 1992: 127) that legitimacy is crucial to the stability of any political order. More agonisingly on the normative side, Wendt's approach raises the question of whether coercion is an effective or acceptable means for holding a value in place until it becomes accepted by calculation and/or belief. The historical record makes it perfectly clear that coercion has played a huge role in the making and breaking of interstate and international societies from Sumeria onwards. Empires that were ruthlessly coercive (Assyrian, Mongol, Soviet) collapsed totally even though their trade benefits would also have created some bonds of calculation. Those that offered more, whether through culture, religion or citizenship (Rome, China) were either more durable in themselves, or left behind durable residues that fed into subsequent interstate or international societies. The fact that Swedish kings were carving statues of Roman emperors onto the bowsprits of their warships a thousand years after the fall of Rome is testimony to the power of such legacies. Anti-slavery was initially imposed by the European powers (Watson 1992: 273), but eventually became a universal norm largely sustained by belief. Indeed, the whole edifice of European inter-state society was initially imposed by coercion, but has become universally accepted at least by calculation and in many places as belief (Buzan and Segal 1998a).

Watson (1992: 258:9) argues that by the nineteenth century many countries were eager to join European international society. Although some of this eagerness can be attributed to fear of coercion, calculation also played a part along the lines of Waltz's mechanism of socialisation. It was clear that the pluralist package of primary institutions generated power, both material and social, more effectively than any rival (Tilly 1990). Thus a combination of coercion, extinction and copying (calculation) brought more and more states into the Western interstate society, and over time, belief (in sovereign equality, in nationalism, in territorialty, in diplomacy) kept them there. Much the same might be said about the market, initially imposed by coercion, now held in place by a broad mixture of belief, calculation and coercion. Sometimes coercion works as a way of transplanting values, and sometimes (the Soviet experiment) it doesn't. The central political weakness of the fascist experiment during the interwar years was that its narrow ethnic/racist legitimising idea pretty much meant that beyond a fairly small sphere, it could only be held in place by coercion, and had little prospect for translation into support by calculation and/or belief. From a liberal perspective, the central threat of communism was precisely that, like liberalism, it had real potential to be accepted as a universal belief.

One can conclude from this discussion that both the nature of the binding forces (in the sense of their distribution at any given point in time) and the interplay among them in relation to any given value or set of values (in the sense of the actual or potential shifting either up or down the coercion-calculation-belief spectrum), are a key part of the dynamics of stability and change in the structure of interstate/international societies. As suggested above, this argument links the nature of the binding forces to the character of the leading power(s). There are two elements in play in this linkage. The first is to do with the particular nature of the values espoused by the leading power(s), and the way in which those values favour or moderate the use of coercion in promoting them. The second, assuming that there is more than one great power in the system, is about the degree of ideological homogeneity versus ideological difference/hostility among the powers – the Convergence model versus the divergence assumption that underpins pluralism.

The nature of the values espoused by the leading power(s), and how these relate to the dynamics of binding force is an extremely complicated question. At one end of the spectrum, one finds the fascist example, already mentioned, where the nature of the values espoused virtually guarantees a strong emphasis on coercion because of the lack of much basis for calculation and belief beyond a narrow ethnic/racial circle. In the middle of the spectrum one might place the case of the communist powers. Unlike fascism, communist values could be, and were, constructed as universal. In terms of the values themselves, it was an open question as to how they should be promoted, and in practice there was (for a time) a successful mixture of belief (the use of propaganda and example) and coercion (the imposition of communist governments by conquest or revolution). At the other end of the spectrum one might find at least some liberals, whose espousal of democracy and human rights would carry the conviction that these values cannot and should not be imposed by force. But here too there is much room for ambiguity. Other liberal values, such as the market, have quite frequently been imposed by force (the 'openings' of Japan and China in the mid-nineteenth century). Even democracy and human rights were successfully imposed on the Axis powers by conquest after the Second World War, and as I write an attempt to do the same thing is underway in Iraq. Liberal values are certainly not intrinsically immune from the lure of coercion, though they can be constructed in that way more easily than many other values.

The question of how values link to binding forces cannot be answered only with reference to the nature of the values themselves. Equally, or possibly more, relevant is the social context into which any value is projected. Fascist values will almost always have to be carried by force beyond the ethnic group that promotes them. Dynastic values might well carry fairly easily across quite different cultures, as demonstrated by many empires throughout history. Communist values might well carry more easily into societies with their own traditions of collectivism (as they did in parts of Asia) than into societies with more individualist traditions. And vice versa for liberal values, which might well carry more easily into cultures with individualist traditions than cultures with collectivist ones. This kind of positional analysis suggests something about how values will be evaluated morally at the receiving end, and therefore whether more, or less, coercion will be necessary to insert them. An easy or difficult fit of values will probably play a big role in how binding forces work or don't work. Regardless of this, there is also an efficacy factor, which is whether given values are seen to produce an advantage for one or more sectors of society. This element points towards calculation, and perhaps in the longer run, belief, and was/is a key part of the promotion of both communist and liberal values. Liberals assume that people will come their way because they will first see the advantages of doing so, and having entered into the practice, come to accept the values as a matter of belief. If adherence to some values does indeed make some wealthier, more knowledgeable, more powerful or more interesting than adherence to others, then this facilitates the move away from coercion towards belief. It was part of the crisis of the communist world in the later stages of the Cold War that its values visibly lagged in many of these practical respects compared with those of the West.

At present, one could apply this way of thinking to the concern about the US that it is moving sharply away from the practice of projecting its values by a logic of persuasion, and towards the coercive end of the spectrum. The US has been spectacularly successful over the last half-century not only in promoting the market, international law and multilateralism, but also in building a host of secondary institutions to reinforce the binding mechanisms of calculation (beloved of the rational choice approach) and belief (beloved of the normative theorists). Yet now the combination of unipolarity (a massive and for the time being quite easily sustained military superiority), 11 September (a national legitimising cause for unilateralism and extreme modes of securitisation), and the deeper strands of American exceptionalism (American values seen as universal truths), seem to be driving away from that tradition. The US vigorously attacks much of what it has created (the UN and many of its agencies), claims exceptional rights over international law and asserts the right to use force pre-emptively against targets of its own choosing (Iraq). If this trend continues, we may soon be concerned less about relative versus absolute gains, than about relative versus absolute losses.

On the impact of convergence versus divergence in the ideological character of the leading powers it is tempting, but almost certainly wrong, to propose that convergence equates with less coercion and divergence with more. The model case of convergence is the argument about democracy and peace. The twentieth century, with its three ideological world wars is a model case of divergence. But it is not clear that ideological convergence of any kind breeds harmony. Among fascist powers it almost certainly would not. Amongst communist powers it certainly did not, and neither did it amongst dynastic powers, or

Christian or Islamic or Confucian ones. Although ideological divergence easily can lead to conflict, it does not necessarily do so. Pluralism assumes that some common interests and values can be found amongst divergent ideologies on the basis of a logic of coexistence, but it is also the case that difference could breed indifference or tolerance. The current debate about whether or not Islam is, or must be, hostile to liberal values, and vice versa, or whether there are acceptable interpretations that make them more compatible, is an example of the room for manoeuvre available in second-order pluralism in this respect.

The interplay among the three domains

I opened this discussion in chapter 6 (p. 195), focusing particularly on the liberal model and its expectations and requirements of high interplay among the three domains. In terms of seeing this interplay as one of the driving forces affecting the international social structure, there are two ways, historical and ideological, of approaching the question. The historical route reflects the concerns of the Wight/Watson wing of the English school about the interplay between pre-existing cultures and the formation of interstate societies. This question generates the hypothesis that a shared culture is either a necessary, or at least a very advantageous, condition for the development of an interstate society (as in classical Greece, and early modern Europe). The historical approach awards a certain primacy to the interhuman domain. It sets up the larger-scale patterns of individual identity expressed in civilisations and the 'universal' religions as foundational for second-order societies. Doing this risks essentialising the social structures in the interhuman domain without asking where they came from. In the case of Europe, the civilisational substrate of Christendom on which the Westphalian interstate society was constructed, was itself a leftover of the Roman empire. Without the influence of Rome, it is far from clear that the European peoples would have become Christian. This creates a chicken–egg problem about whether interhuman social structures have to precede interstate ones, or vice versa. In the longer run, it seems clear that there is a process of mutual constitution between the social structures in the interhuman domain, and those in the interstate domain. Each feeds into the other through a series of cycles.

Perhaps the key dynamic identified by this approach hinges on the question of what happens when an interstate or international society expands beyond its cultural home base? Must such expansion necessarily weaken the interstate society? Many English school writers thought that decolonisation had done so to Western international society, and Huntington's (1996) 'clash of civilisations' thesis can be read as a more polemical version of the same argument. The underlying idea here is that when the social structures within the interstate and interhuman domains line up, then this reinforces their stability, and when they don't line up, the disjuncture undermines stability. This is close to Weller's (2000) discussion, cited at several points in earlier chapters, underlining the importance of social geography. Weller draws attention to the potential stabilities available where patterns of identity and patterns of rational contractual relations occupy the same territorial space, and the potential instabilities when they do not.

This is a hypothesis worth exploring through detailed case studies. Although it identifies a potentially important dynamic arising from the interplay between domains, it also carries a danger. While interstate society is regarded as being relatively fluid, and capable of expanding or contracting quite easily, the social structures in the interhuman domain are regarded as relatively static and fixed. If this is true, then expansions of interstate society will inescapably be challenged by disjunctures in the interhuman domain. Thinking in this way marginalises the possibility that expansions within the interstate domain are in themselves part of the mechanism by which social structures in the interhuman domain are created. Here the argument loops back to that made in the previous paragraph. It also connects to the discussions in chapter 4 about how 'society' and 'community' link together in a strong, but indeterminate way. Putting this idea in play casts the problem of expansion of interstate/international society into a different light. The question then becomes one not of an inevitable, existential, contradiction between the two domains, but a much more dynamic one about how quickly and how effectively the interstate society can remake the social structure of the interhuman domain on which it rests? Must there be a clash of civilisations as Huntington and some hard realists think, or do we already see elements of an emergent 'Mondo culture' as some globalists and world society advocates discern (and many anti-globalisationists target as McDonaldisation)? The greatest and most successful empires, such as Rome, China, and in different form the West, flourish by spreading their culture and changing how those within them think about their identity. They do this both by coopting elements of the local cultures (in classical times by absorbing their gods and festivals; now by commodifying local culture), and by offering attractive new practices. Patterns of identity may be slower moving than patterns of power, but they are not static. How this question is answered obviously connects quickly and strongly to the discussion of binding forces above. If developments in the interhuman domain lag behind those in the interstate one, is coercion an effective and legitimate means of holding things in place until the interhuman domain comes around in terms of calculation and/or belief? The historical record suggests that sometimes this works and sometimes not. The ethical questions are altogether more complicated.

By contrast, the approach through ideology tends to give primacy to the interstate domain. This approach focuses on how any particular type of interstate, international or world society incorporates the three domains into its governing ideas. As I argued in chapter 5, there are good reasons to think that states will generally be the dominant actors, as they have been within the frame of human history to date, and seem likely to be at least for some decades to come. Although it is possible to imagine world societies in which states are not dominant, it remains true in the contemporary world that states are still the most powerful and focused unit, and can shove and shape the others more easily than individuals and TNAs can shove and shape them, not least because of their dominant command of the instruments of coercion. It is nevertheless important, as argued in chapter 6, not to drift unthinkingly into the assumption that the only relevant model of interstate society, whether pluralist or solidarist, is a liberal one. There are many other models, and what the relationship among the three domains will be depends heavily on the type of interstate society in play. Liberal interstate societies will be ideologically disposed to give political and legal space to individuals and TNAs. Other types of interstate society, most obviously those based on totalitarian ideologies such as communism and fascism, will be ideologically disposed to give little or no political and legal space to individuals and TNAs. Yet other types of interstate or international or world society (e.g. Islamic, Sumerian, Mayan) might well have different mixtures.

The liberal model is of course of huge interest because it is the one we are living in, and by whose truth claims we are surrounded. Liberal international societies certainly open up enormous scope for interplay among the three domains by recognising and empowering individuals and TNAs. Yet liberalism can also be accused of feeding off the interhuman domain while at the same time undermining its structures of identity. Liberalism focuses on the individual both as the fundamental bearer of rights and responsibilities, and as the consumer encouraged to cultivate individualism, by differentiating him or herself through the acquisition of a unique portfolio of goods and services. It sets this focus on the individual into the context of universal values (human rights) and practices (the market) which easily cast as parochial and backward-looking many of the social structures in the interhuman domain, whether national, civilisational or religious. Looking at liberalism in this way links back to the argument just made about the interplay of the interhuman and interstate domains, posing two alternative views. Does liberalism's elevation of the individual serve well for the expansion of interstate society by offering attractive 'universal' foundations for wider social structures in the interhuman domain? Or does it just atomise, threatening the older patterns of identity in the interhuman domain? The former view is supported by the success of Westernisation/Americanisation in spreading its own fashions of dress, music, film and news reporting around the world. The latter view is exemplified by nationalist or religious fundamentalist reactions to globalisation in many parts of the international system. Liberal interstate societies should thus be expected to excite strong dynamics between the interstate and interhuman domains by mounting a fundamental assault on traditional cultural practices and identities. These dynamics will normally be played out by a mixture of coercion, calculation and belief.

But perhaps even more important is the way in which liberal interstate societies empower the transnational domain. In principle, liberalism favours a minimal state and the maximum liberty for individuals consistent with maintaining social order. In practice, this means the empowerment of civil society and the right of people to establish organisations for a wide range of purposes. Translated to the international sphere, this means that state borders have to be permeable to trade, travel, ideas, capital and a wide range of INGOs, including multinational firms, interest groups and lobbies. A liberal international society is likely to open up a substantial transnational space in which TNAs of various kinds have legal rights and considerable autonomy to act across state borders. This feature creates a strong pressure on states to harmonise their domestic arrangements on a wide range of issues from property rights and border controls to accounting practices and product standards. This pressure, in turn, underlies a tendency towards a Kantian Convergence model of interstate society. The logic of a liberal interstate society thus points towards international, and eventually even world society as I defined them in chapter 6 (pp. 201–4).

In a liberal international society, TNAs can (and have) become very powerful actors. Huge global corporations command wealth, resources and knowledge that surpass those of many of the poorer, weaker states in the system, and pressure even the more powerful states to compete for their investment. Transnational interest groups and lobbies can harass states directly over issues such as human rights and pollution, and a host of quieter TNAs can slowly leach away the authority and character of the state by providing alternative points of reference for its citizens. Because liberalism ties its political legitimacy and fortune to sustained economic growth, the rise of the transnational domain as a crucial element in the global economy, itself becomes a crucial element in the wealth, power and legitimacy of the core capitalist political economies. All of this is, of course, the stuff that drives the idea of globalisation. In the context of this discussion, however, the point of interest is that liberal interstate societies, perhaps more than any other, create a powerful dynamic between the interstate and the transnational domains. At a minimum, the transnational sector becomes a driving force in favour of reinterpreting primary institutions such as sovereignty and non-intervention, and promoting new ones such as the market and human rights. At a maximum, as thought by some globalisation enthusiasts, the transnational domain becomes the location of the vanguard driving the social structure of humankind towards some form of world society.

By this point in the discussion, any readers who had doubts about what happened in chapter 4, when I overthrew the classic English school triad and replaced it with the three domains, should be able to make up their minds. I hope I have shown how the three domains work as an analytical tool, and why they give a much clearer structural picture than would be possible by sticking with the traditional understandings of international system, international society and world society.

The pressures of material conditions: interaction capacity, human powers of destruction and the planetary environment

In thinking about the driving forces behind international social structures one cannot neglect a range of material factors that define the conditions in which the game of states is played. Changes in these conditions can be critical drivers of changes in the primary and secondary institutions of interstate society. One obvious example of this is the rise of awareness starting in the 1960s, but visible further back in Malthusian thinking, that the planetary environment is a finite resource, and that rising human numbers and capabilities have moved it from being an independent variable running on its own logic, to an increasingly dependent one affected by an increasing range of human activities. As the physical vulnerability of the planetary environment to human activity increased, so environmental stewardship rose in prominence as a primary institution of interstate and international society. Without that physical change of circumstance, it is hard to imagine that the institutional change would have occurred (though it is possible to imagine that the institutional change would not have occurred despite the physical change had international society been differently constituted than it was). A similar logic attends the rise in human powers of destruction, which fed a fear of war, and thus helped to weaken war and the balance of power as central primary institutions of interstate society. By fear of war here I do not just mean exhaustion from a particular war, as after the Thirty Years War and the French Revolutionary and Napoleonic wars), but existential fear of war <u>as such</u> arising from concern that the destruction involved would lead to the collapse or even extinction of the societies engaged in it. This fear was benchmarked by the First World War, which gave the first full experience of industrialised war, and reinforced later by the arrival of nuclear weapons.

A more general case can be made that the rapid, complex and universal growth of interaction capacity from the nineteenth century onwards is a key driver in the shaping of international relations. By interaction capacity I mean the physical and social technologies that determine the possibilities for transportation and communication within any social system. This case has been set out at length elsewhere (Buzan, Jones and Little 1993; Buzan and Little 2000). The physical technologies determine the size and degree of integration not only of the international system as a whole, but also of the units and subsystems within it. The social technologies that affect interaction capacity include some primary institutions (diplomacy, international law) and many secondary ones (forum organisations such as the UN). Once rising interaction capacity had created a fully global international system during the nineteenth century, its continued increase shaped both the speed and intensity of interaction within the system, and the number and type of people who had access to those capabilities. What started with the telegraph and the steamship as tools for government and business elites, evolved into the internet with its rapidly widening access to communication and information resources for all sorts of people. These social and physical technologies both make possible, and in some ways express, a liberal international society. They underpin the rise of the market as a primary institution, and it is hard to imagine that without them either equality of peoples or the beginnings of a global culture would have developed.

The social structures of humankind are substantially driven by internal logics and contradictions, but they are also shaped by the physical environment within which they operate. Mostly, that pressure comes from human impacts, as with interaction capacity; the capacity for destruction in war; and the alteration of the ecosystem both by various kinds of pollution and by direct destruction of life-forms and change of landscape. Sometimes it can come from nature, as would be the case with the return of the ice age, or the prospect of a large asteroid colliding with the planet.

Conclusions: where to from here?

There are two senses of 'where to from here?' that I need to address in this final section: first in terms of saying something about where the present-day international society might be heading; and second in terms of indicating the direction of the research programme implied by this book.

To gaze into the future means that one has to take the analytical framework set out above, and ask whether in terms of the various elements it identifies, there is a momentum, or discernible direction, to the evolution of contemporary international society? Do the dynamics explored in the previous section seem to line up in some coherent way, or do they pull against each other, making outcomes uncertain? This is not the type of theory that enables one to quantify the variables and seek statistical inferences. But it is the type of theory that enables one to combine a structural approach with a historical account, and so generate an analysis that is sufficiently simplified to make big questions about direction and momentum reasonably clear and approachable. One can look at the stability or not of the pattern of primary institutions, and explore its implications for movement along the pluralist–solidarist spectrum. Alongside that, one also has to look at the interplay among the three domains; at the stability or not of the geographical patterns of international social structure between the global and sub-global levels; and at the balance among the binding forces. I argued in the first section of this chapter that the contemporary global interstate society was modestly Cooperative and ideologically liberal, with its pluralist elements widely embedded by belief, but its solidarist elements presenting a much more mixed picture of coercion, calculation and belief. It could be classified as an international society dominated by states but giving rights to non-state actors. I also argued that the cultivation of difference in sub-global interstate and international societies was largely compatible with the global level.

Barring catastrophic interruptions, a case can be made that there is a lot of inertia in this general pattern. Much that has remained stable is likely to continue to do so, and much that has been changing will continue to move in the same directions. The general structure of a second-order pluralism in which sub-global interstate/international societies cultivate differences without either departing from global interstate society or trying to dominate it might well be robust, as might the overall core–periphery structure with the West as the dominant core. It is a more open question whether the incremental drift of the West into further Cooperative developments will continue, both generally, and in the more Kantian case of the EU. It could be that this process has for the time being reached its limits and will either stay relatively static or even fall back as a result of transatlantic political divergence, or within the EU, resistance to further integration. At the global level, the pluralist institutions look pretty stable, as does the continuance of controversy about human rights and democracy. The big question is about the stability of the market. Because the international politics surrounding the market are always fractious and turbulent, it is particularly hard to see whether the battles over trade and finance are essentially <u>within</u> a stable institution, or whether they are <u>about</u> the fate of the institution itself. Given that the global market delivers so much in terms of wealth and power, and given the huge costs of dismantling it now that most economies are structured towards it, the odds have to favour its continuance, almost certainly with no diminution of the associated disputes, and probably with a similar mix of coercion, calculation and belief. The market is sustained, *inter alia,* by the widespread belief that it is a major factor in the downgrading of war, and by its central role in fulfilling the liberal vision of international society. It is also sustained by its strong interlinkage with multilateralism, and the many secondary institutions they have jointly spawned. The principal material forces that play on international social structure – fear of war, concern about environment, increase of interaction capacity – all have strong momentum and are unlikely to change.

Other than catastrophic disruptions of some sort, there are two developments afoot in contemporary international society that have the potential to derail this inertia and produce some significant changes of direction: the 'war on terrorism', and the 'unipolar' distribution of power resulting from the US being the last superpower. These two developments are quite strongly linked. US superpowerdom does not depend on terrorism as such, but the exercise of it could be significantly shaped by the 'war on terrorism'. Terrorism, at least in its al-Qaeda form, is significantly dependent on US superpowerdom because that defines its main target. This link means that they have the potential to reinforce each other.

September 11 and the subsequent 'war on terrorism' can be seen as a serious turning in the interplay between the interstate and transnational domains. As argued above, liberal interstate societies encourage and empower the transnational domain, seeing the development of a global economy and a global civil society as good and desirable in and of themselves. In many ways, the market is the main expression of the liberal cultivation of the transnational domain. Extreme terrorism, prepared to resort to suicide attacks, and seeming to have no moral constraint about attacks on civilians or the use of weapons of mass destruction, exposes the darkest possible side of the transnational domain. The availability of communications, money and technologies of destruction to such groups exposes the contradictions of liberalism at their most extreme. Hate-filled fanatics wielding weapons of mass destruction not only threaten to change the balance of power between the state and transnational domains, but also threaten the practical sustainability of the liberal model itself. If (un)civil society becomes seen as the main source of threat, then as discussed in the third section of chapter 3, liberal logic gets pushed in a Power Political direction in which Leviathan is necessary to impose order and a civil sphere. Because the openness of a liberalised economy provides opportunities for transnational extremists of all sorts to operate on a global scale, the traditional Hobbesian domestic security agenda gets pushed up to the international level, becoming a problem for international society against global uncivil society. If the understanding of war as an institution of interstate society shifts in this direction, away from the state-to-state assumptions of the Westphalian model, then much more imperial approaches to world order easily follow. This logic is one of the most worrying aspects of the US–British invasion of Iraq.

Any such development, of course, depends on the practical seriousness of the threat; 11 September exposed the potential seriousness of this threat, but if the war on terrorism proves effective at preventing repetitions on that scale, then probably not much will change on this account. As anyone who lives in Britain or Spain can testify, modern societies can tolerate a certain level of terrorism without undergoing major structural changes. But if terrorists use weapons of mass destruction, then the scenario is quite different. That would cast 11 September as the opening round of a new clash of civilisations – or perhaps not a new one, but a taking up of the cudgels for a second round of the clash of civilisations that began several hundred years ago with the expansion of the West at the expense of other civilisations. As clashing expressions of the transnational domain, terrorism and the market become crucial factors in the fate of liberal international society. The effects of sustained terrorism could shrink and degrade the market as a primary institution, and maintaining the market could become the legitimising cause for the war on terrorism.

The question of the US is at the time of writing the more worrying because it is a concrete development, whereas terrorism, despite September 11, is still a hypothetical one in terms of its ability to change the development of global international society. In a nutshell, the question is whether or not the US is turning its back on the pursuit of a multi-lateralist liberal international order, and restyling itself in more imperial mode. As one observer puts it: 'There is hardly a single international institution that has not been questioned, undermined or outright abandoned by the United States in the name of its need to protect its sovereign interests' (Barber 2001: xxii). The empirical evidence for such a turn is mixed, and vulnerable to the success or failure of the US's attempt to reconstruct Iraq as a liberal democracy. It is also unclear whether present developments represent the peculiarities of the second Bush administration, or some deeper turn in US politics which has been reinforced by 11 September. Also unclear is whether this turn is driven primarily by the logic of a 'unipolar' structure (the US being effectively unbalanced in a military sense by the other great powers), or whether it arises from the domestic character of American exceptionalism, with (to oversimplify somewhat) its extreme demands for national security, its claim to own the future, and its uncritical belief in the essential goodness and rightness of American society. The causes for concern are visible in several directions: the Manichaean, 'with us or against us' rhetoric associated with the 'war on terrorism'; the attack on the framework of secondary institutions that the US was instrumental in building up over the last half-century; the claim to a unilateral right to pre-emptive war, and its exercise against Iraq; and the general undermining of multilateralism by its preference for unilateral action and *ad hoc* coalitions.

A serious and sustained move by the leading power along these lines could, if sustained, alter the present shape and direction of the international social structure. It could reverse the decay of war as an institution, and halt or reverse the rise of multilateralism and international law. *In extremis*, it could put a huge strain on sovereignty and non-intervention by asserting a right to change regimes on grounds either of support for terrorism or attempting to acquire weapons of mass destruction that might be used against the US or US allies such as Israel. It could revive the institution of anti-hegemonism by casting the US more in the role of a threat rather than as a carrier of acceptable universal values. If Europe and Japan begin to fear, or oppose the US, some extremely hard choices would follow. Should they begin to distance themselves from the US, rethinking their bandwagoning posture, and weakening the West as a coherent core? Or should they accept a more naked, less Gramscian, form of hegemony, with implications of suzerainty in the requirement to acknowledge that American exceptionalism (here defined in terms of the requirement of the single superpower role) legitimates the US standing outside and above the secondary institutions and international laws that form the framework of multilateralism for the rest of interstate society? Could the EU survive if its close association with, and dependence on, the US became a central point of controversy? Perhaps not, as suggested by the splits over the Iraq war. Reactions against a more imperial US could also change the balance between the global and the sub-global levels of social structure, with the former weakening back to a more bare-bones pluralism, and the latter becoming more differentiated and more self-contained, a scenario close to that of a world of blocs.

The interplay amongst primary institutions provides a useful way of thinking about this scenario. It could be argued that the rise of multilateralism and the market as primary institutions are closely linked (OECD 1998: 80–1). It could be argued further that their associated network of secondary institutions has been a critical factor in the downgrading of the role of balance of power, alliances, anti-hegemonism and to a lesser extent, war. If multilateralism is itself downgraded by sustained US attacks on it, then a resurgence of these older institutions is a likely result. In this sense the accumulation of empirical evidence by neoliberal institutionalists that secondary institutions do facilitate cooperation under anarchy is highly relevant. Those secondary institutions have been the front line of a deeper primary institution of multilateralism that has defined what constitutes normal practice in managing international society. It is not clear that the Bush administration recognises this fact, and therefore understands the probable cumulative consequences of its actions. Nor is it clear how far the US can go in downgrading multilateralism without beginning to jeopardise the market, and whether US interests in sustaining the market therefore act as a brake on its unilateralism. Needless to say, the adoption of a more imperial posture by the US would necessarily change the balance among the binding forces of interstate/international society. One of the remarkable features of US hegemony over the past half-century was its ability to build a consensual international order that was increasingly held together by calculation and belief rather than coercion, and which operated multilaterally through a host of mediating secondary institutions. Empires do not work that way. Coercion is their first tool, and loyalty their first demand. If the US turns strongly and durably in this direction, then the consequences for interstate and international society will be large.

The second sense of 'where to from here?' concerns the direction of the research project implied in this book, and its implications for those who work in, or listen to, the English school tradition. What should be the research priorities of those who want to pursue a more social structural approach to English school theory, and what are the implications for those within the more Wightian and Vincentian normative traditions?

To the extent that this book is an opening rather than a closing, a provocation rather than a definitive rendering, more (probably much more) needs to be said about the framework set out here. I know that I have not fully mastered the subject of primary institutions, and since this is the key to the English school's claims, more work needs to be done on both the conceptualisation of primary institutions, and on linking this conceptualisation more systematically to the neoliberal institutionalist and regime theory studies of secondary institutions. One question that may be central to exploring this linkage is: 'where are the limits of constitutive effects in international society?' Is the boundary between primary and secondary institutions understandable in terms of the difference between constitutive effects and regulatory practices defined and created by preconstituted actors within a preconstituted game? I rather suspect not, but this question needs to be addressed. A more coherent understanding of institutions also needs to be read into the historical account. As implied in this chapter, I think that the concept of primary institutions offers considerable scope for revising the English school's accounts of the expansion and evolution of international society. The same could be said of pluralism and solidarism. I have set out what I think is a clearer rendition of the pluralist–solidarist spectrum, but it is not one with which I expect everyone to agree. I hope that those who disagree will take it as a challenge to revisit their own conceptions and see how they stand up to the points raised. Among other things, those interested in solidarism need to face up to the issue of convergence, and the question posed by Vincent as to whether the only way of making solidarist development compatible with sovereignty and its derivatives is for states to become more alike internally. What are the implications for this way of thinking of the wider arguments about homogenising forces that can be found in the IR literature? In particular, I hope those in the solidarist tradition will think hard about why they have excluded the economic sector, and what the implications are of bringing it on board. It seems to me that there are interesting opportunities to bring English school thinking and International Political Economy work into closer contact, not least in thinking about the interplay of the market and multilateralism with other institutions. In thinking about all of this it is important to recognise that solidarism, like society, is not necessarily nice. Solidarity is about shared interests and sympathies, and can encompass a wide range of values.

Also, to those in the solidarist wing, and as well the historical Wight/Watson one, there is the challenge to make more explicit the role of binding forces, both in evaluating the historical record, and in advocacy of solidarist developments in human rights and other areas. If vanguardism is to be accepted as a key mechanism for advancing international society both historically and in the present, then the question about the role of coercion in the pursuit of the market and human rights cannot be evaded. How are we to deal with the tension between moral doubts about means, versus historical evidence that coercion can work as a way of implanting primary institutions on the global level, and the moral imperative to 'do something' now? How do advocates of solidarism deal with the reality and the legitimacy of second-order pluralism versus the push towards global homogenization implied in the pursuit of 'universal' values?

I have given the concept of world society an empirically marginal role describing an extreme form of liberal development, and replaced its present main functions with the idea of the interplay amongst the interstate, interhuman and transnational domains. Wighteans may not want to give up the idea of world society as that which is in opposition to interstate society, or based on political programmes with an alternative foundation to the sovereign state, and I have no problem with that usage continuing in the normative discourse. But present usage of world society covers so many meanings as to sow more confusion than clarity, and this weakens the structural potential of English school theory. If my solution is not liked, perhaps it will stimulate other suggestions about how to deal with this problem.

More straightforwardly, the framework in this book invites much more study of sub-global international social structures and the way in which they interact with the global level. Some ideas here might be gleaned from work I have done with Ole Wæver (Buzan and Wæver 2003), which confronts the global–sub-global problem in the context of regional security complexes and global polarity. Bringing in the sub-global also requires retelling the story of the expansion and evolution of international society. It opens up prospects for linking English school thinking to regionalist work, particularly the study of the EU. More work needs to be done on the particular characteristics of liberal international societies, and this would be helped if it could be contrasted with more specifically theoretical understandings of the non-liberal possibilities for interstate, international and world societies.

In sum, there is scope for an English school research programme that takes the particular qualities and characteristics of second-order societies as its subject, the pluralist–solidarist spectrum as its basic benchmark, and primary institutions as its principal object of investigation. Such a programme would focus on mapping and explaining the evolution of primary institutions in second-order societies. Its investigations would take systematically into account the role of socio-political geography, the interplay among the interstate, interhuman and transnational domains, and the effect of binding forces. This programme offers research opportunities of both a macro and a micro kind. Macro in the sense of studying the evolution of interstate/international society as a whole, micro in the sense of studying the evolution of particular primary institutions, or particular sub-global interstate/international societies. Although some might think that the argument in this book takes it (and me) outside the English school, that is not how I see it. My own conclusion at the end of this work is that the English school does indeed have the potential for grand theory that I suspected at the beginning. I hope I have shown at least some of the ways in which it can be developed so as to claim its rightful place in the pantheon of IR theories.

References

Abbott, Kenneth W. and Duncan Snidal (2000) 'Hard and Soft Law in International Governance', *International Organization*, 54:3, 421–56.

Abbott, Kenneth W., Robert O. Keohane, Andrew Moravcsik, Anne-Marie Slaughter and Duncan Snidal (2000) 'The Concept of Legalization', *International Organization*, 54:3, 401–19.

Adler, Emanuel and Michael N. Barnett (eds.) (1998) *Security Communities*, Cambridge University Press.

Ahrne, Göran (1998) 'Civil Society and Uncivil Organizations' in J. C. Alexander (ed.), *Real Civil Societies*, London: Sage, 84–95.

Albert, Mathias (1999) 'Observing World Politics: Luhmann's Systems Theory of Society and International Relations', *Millennium*, 28:2, 239–65.

Alderson, Kai and Andrew Hurrell (2000) 'International Society and the Academic Study of International Relations' in Kai Alderson and Andrew Hurrell (eds.), *Hedley Bull on International Society*, Basingstoke: Macmillan, 20–53.

Alexander, Jeffrey C. (1998) 'Introduction – Civil Society I, II, III', in J. C. Alexander (ed.), *Real Civil Societies*, London: Sage, 1–19.

Almeida, Joao de (2001) 'The Origins of Modern International Society and the Myth of the State of Nature: A Critique', paper presented to the ECPR Pan-European International Relations Conference, University of Kent, September 2001, 39 pp.

  (2002) 'Pluralists, Solidarists and the Issues of Diversity, Justice and Humanitarianism in World Politics', unpublished ms., 21 pp.

Anderson, Benedict (1983) *Imagined Communities: Reflections on the Origin and Spread of Nationalism*, London: Verso.

Anheier, Helmut, Marlies Glasius and Mary Kaldor (2001) 'Introducing Global Civil Society' in Helmut Anheier, Marlies Glasius and Mary Kaldor (eds.), *Global Civil Society 2001*, Oxford University Press, 3–22.

Armstrong, David (1999) 'Law, Justice and the Idea of a World Society', *International Affairs*, 73:3, 643–53.

List of references

Ashley, Richard K. (1987) 'The Geopolitics of Geopolitical Space: Towards a Critical Social Theory of International Politics', *Alternatives*, 12:4, 403–34.

Barber, Benjamin R. (2001) *Jihad vs. McWorld*, New York: Ballantine Books.

Barkin, J. Samuel (1998) 'The Evolution of the Constitution of Sovereignty and the Emergence of Human Rights Norms', *Millennium*, 27:2, 229–52.

Boli, John and George M. Thomas (eds.) (1999) *Constructing World Culture: International Nongovernmental Organizations since 1875*, Stanford University Press.

Bozeman, Adda (1984) 'The International Order in a Multicultural World' in Hedley Bull and Adam Watson (eds.), *The Expansion of International Society*, Oxford University Press, 387–406.

Brown, Chris (1995a) 'International Theory and International Society: The Viability of the Middle Way', *Review of International Studies*, 21.2, 183–96.

(1995b) 'International Political Theory and the Idea of World Community' in Ken Booth and Steve Smith (eds.), *International Political Theory Today*, Cambridge University Press, 90–109.

(1998) 'Contractarian Thought and the Constitution of International Society Perspective' in David R. Mapel and Terry Nardin (eds.), *International Society: Diverse Ethical Perspectives*, Princeton University Press, 132–43.

(1999) 'An "International Society" Perspective on World Society', paper for World Society Workshop, Darmstadt, November, 26 pp.

Bull, Hedley (1966a) 'The Grotian Conception of International Society' in H. Butterfield and M. Wight (eds.), *Diplomatic Investigations*, London: Allen and Unwin, 51–73.

(1966b) 'Society and Anarchy in International Relations' in H. Butterfield and M. Wight (eds.), *Diplomatic Investigations*, London: Allen and Unwin, 35–50.

(1977a) *The Anarchical Society. A Study of Order in World Politics*, London: Macmillan.

(1977b) 'Introduction: Martin Wight and the Study of International Relations' in Martin Wight, *Systems of States*, Leicester University Press.

(1979) 'Natural Law and International Relations', *British Journal of International Studies*, 5:2, 171–81.

(1982) 'Civilian Power Europe: A Contradiction in Terms?', *Journal of Common Market Studies*, 21:1, 149–64.

(1984) *Justice in International Relations*, Hagey Lectures, Ontario: University of Waterloo.

(1990) 'The Importance of Grotius in the Study of International Relations' in Hedley Bull, Benedict Kingsbury and Adam Roberts (eds.), *Hugo Grotius and International Relations*, Oxford: Clarendon Press, 65–93.

(1991) 'Martin Wight and the Theory of International Relations' in Martin Wight, *International Theory: The Three Traditions*, edited Brian Porter and Gabriele Wight, Leicester University Press/Royal Institute of International Affairs, ix–xxiii.

Bull, Hedley and Adam Watson (1984a) 'Conclusion' in Hedley Bull and Adam Watson (eds.), *The Expansion of International Society*, Oxford University Press, 425–35.

(eds.) (1984b) *The Expansion of International Society*, Oxford University Press.

Burke, Patrick (forthcoming) 'European Nuclear Disarmament (END): A Study of its Successes and Failures with Particular Emphasis on its Work in the UK', Ph.D. thesis, University of Westminster.

Burton, John W. (1972) *World Society*, Cambridge University Press.

Bush, George W. (2002) *The National Security Strategy of the United States of America*, Washington, DC: White House, September.

Buzan, Barry (1991) *People, States and Fear*, London: Harvester Wheatsheaf.

(1993) 'From International System to International Society: Structural Realism and Regime Theory Meet the English School', *International Organization*, 47:3, 327–52.

(1996) 'International Security and International Society' in Rick Fawn, Jeremy Larkin and Robert Newman (eds.), *International Society After the Cold War*, London: Macmillan, 261–87.

(2001) 'The English School: An Underexploited Resource in IR', *Review of International Studies*, 27:3, 471–88.

(2003) 'An English School Perspective on Global Civil Society' in Stefano Guzzini and Dietrich Jung (eds.), *Copenhagen Peace Research*, London: Routledge.

Buzan, Barry and Richard Little (1996) 'Reconceptualizing Anarchy: Structural Realism Meets World History', *European Journal of International Relations*, 2:4, 403–38.

Buzan, Barry, and Richard Little (2000) *International Systems in World History: Remaking the Study of International Relations*, Oxford University Press.

(2001) 'Why International Relations has Failed as an Intellectual Project, and What to Do About It', *Millennium*, 30:1, 19–39.

Buzan, Barry and Gerald Segal (1998a) 'A Western Theme', *Prospect*, 27: February, 18–23.

(1998b) *Anticipating the Future*, London: Simon and Schuster.

Buzan, Barry, and Ole Wæver (2003) *Regions and Power: The Structure of International Security*, Cambridge University Press.

Buzan, Barry, Charles Jones and Richard Little (1993) *The Logic of Anarchy*, New York: Columbia University Press.

Buzan, Barry, Ole Wæver and Jaap de Wilde (1998) *Security: A New Framework for Analysis*, Boulder, CO: Lynne Rienner.

Carr, E. H. (1946) *The Twenty Years' Crisis 1919–1939: An Introduction to the Study of International Relations*, London: Macmillan, 2nd edition.

Clark, Ann Marie (1995) 'Non-Governmental Organizations and their Influence on International Society', *Journal of International Affairs*, 48:2, 507–25.

Cohen, Raymond (1998) 'The Great Tradition: The Spread of Diplomacy in the Ancient World', Jerusalem: Hebrew University, unpublished ms, 17 pp.

Cox, Robert (1986) 'Social Forces, States and World Orders: Beyond IR Theory' in Robert O. Keohane (ed.), *Neorealism and its Critics*, New York: Columbia University Press, 204–54.

(1994) 'Global Restructuring' in Richard Stubbs and Geoffrey Underhill (eds.), *Political Economy and the Changing Global Order*, Toronto: McClelland and Stewart, 45–59.

Cronin, Bruce (1999) *Community Under Anarchy: Transnational Identity and the Evolution of Cooperation*, New York: Columbia University Press.

(2002a) 'The Two Faces of the United Nations: The Tension Between Intergovernmentalism and Transnationalism', *Global Governance*, 8:1, 53–71.

(2002b) 'Multilateral Intervention and the International Community' in Michael Keren and Donald Sylvan (eds.), *International Intervention: Sovereignty Versus Responsibility*, London: Frank Cass, 147–68.

Cutler, Claire A. (1991) 'The "Grotian Tradition" in International Relations', *Review of International Studies*, 17:1, 41–65.

Deutsch, Karl W., Sidney A. Burrell, Robert A. Kann, Maurice Lee Jr, Martin Lichterman, Raymond E. Lindgren, Francis L. Loewenheim and Richard W. van Wagenen (1957) *Political Community and the North Atlantic Area: International Organization in the Light of Historical Experience*, Princeton University Press.

Diez, Thomas (2000) 'Cracks in the System, or Why Would I Need Luhmann to Analyze International Relations', Draft paper for ECPR workshop on Modern Systems Theory and International Society, COPRI, April, 16 pp.

Diez, Thomas and Richard Whitman (2000) 'Analysing European Integration, Reflecting on the English School: Scenarios for an Encounter', *COPRI-Working Papers 20/2000*, Copenhagen Peace Research Institute.

(2002) 'Comparing Regional International Societies: The Case of Europe', paper presented to ISA Conference, New Orleans, March, 13 pp.

Donnelly, Jack (2002) 'The Constitutional Structure of Ancient Greek International Society', paper presented at BISA Conference, London, December, 39 pp.

Douglas, Mary (2001) 'Poverty and the Moral Vision', paper presented at the Encounter with Mary Douglas, London, Centre for the Study of Democracy, University of Westminster, June, 19 pp.

Dunne, Tim (1995) 'International Society – Theoretical Promises Fulfilled?', *Cooperation and Conflict*, 30:2, 125–54.

(1998) *Inventing International Society: A History of the English School*, London: Macmillan.

(2001a) 'New Thinking on International Society', *British Journal of Politics and International Relations*, 3:2, 223–44.

(2001b) 'International Society', unpublished ms. presented at the English school workshop, Bristol, June, 109 pp.

Dunne, Tim and Nicholas Wheeler (1996) 'Hedley Bull's Pluralism of the Intellect and Solidarism of the Will', *International Affairs*, 72:1, 91–107.

Evans, Tony and Peter Wilson (1992) 'Regime Theory and the English School of International Relations', *Millennium*, 21:3, 329–51.

Fawcett, L. L. E. and Andrew Hurrell (1995) *Regionalism in World Politics: Regional Organisation and International Order*, Oxford University Press.

Fischer, Markus (1992) 'Feudal Europe, 800–1300: Communal Discourses and Conflictual Practices', *International Organization*, 46:2, 427–66.

Fukuyama, Francis (1992) *The End of History and the Last Man*, London: Penguin.

Gellner, Ernest (1988) *Plough, Sword and Book: The Structure of Human History*, London: Paladin.

Gilpin, Robert (1986) 'The Richness of the Tradition of Political Realism' in Robert O. Keohane (ed.), *Neorealism and its Critics*, New York: Columbia University Press, 301–21.

Goldstein, Judith, Miles Kahler, Robert O. Keohane, Anne-Marie Slaughter (2000) 'Introduction: Legalization and World Politics', *International Organization*, 54:3, 385–99.

Gong, Gerritt W. (1984) *The Standard of 'Civilization' in International Society*, Oxford: Clarendon Press.

Gonzalez-Pelaez, Ana (2002) 'Basic Rights In International Society: R. J. Vincent's Idea of a Subsistence Approach to the Practical Realisation of Human Rights', Ph.D. Thesis, CSD, University of Westminster.

Guzzini, Stefano (1993) 'Structural Power: The Limits of Neorealist Analysis', *International Organization*, 47:3, 443–78.

Guzzini, Stefano, and Anna Leander (2001) 'A Social Theory for International Relations: An Appraisal of Alexander Wendt's Theoretical and Disciplinary Synthesis', *Journal of International Relations and Development*, 4:4, 616–38.

Haas, Peter M. (ed.) (1992) 'Knowledge, Power and International Policy Coordination', Special Issue of *International Organization*, 46:1.

Halliday, Fred (1992) 'International Society as Homogeneity: Burke, Marx, Fukuyama', *Millennium*, 21:3, 435–61.

Hanks, Patrick (ed.) (1986) *Collins Dictionary of the English Language*, London: Collins.

Hansen, Birthe (2000) *Unipolarity and the Middle East*, Richmond: Curzon Press.

Harris, Ian (1993) 'Order and Justice in "the Anarchical Society"', *International Affairs*, 69:4, 725–41.

Hart, H. L. A. (1961) *The Concept of Law*, Oxford: Clarendon Press.

Hassner, Ron E. (2003) 'Radical Constitutive Change in International Relations: A Short History of Chess', http://www.standford.edu/~rony/chess.htm (6 February 2003), 21 pp.

Held, David, Anthony McGrew, David Goldblatt and Jonathan Perraton (1999) *Global Transformation: Politics, Economics and Culture*, Cambridge: Polity Press.

Helleiner, Eric (1994) 'Regionalization in the International Political Economy: A Comparative Perspective', *Eastern Asia Policy Papers No. 3*, University of Toronto–York University Joint Centre for Asia Pacific Studies, 21 pp.

Herz, John H. (1950) 'Idealist Internationalism and the Security Dilemma', *World Politics*, 2:2, 157–80.

Hill, Chris (1996) 'World Opinion and the Empire of Circumstance', *International Affairs*, 72:1, 109–31.

Hollis, Martin and Steve Smith (1991) *Explaining and Understanding International Relations*, Oxford University Press.

Holsti, Kalevi J. (2002) 'The Institutions of International Politics: Continuity, Change, and Transformation', paper presented at the ISA Convention, New Orleans, March, 62 pp.

Huntington, Samuel P. (1996) *The Clash of Civilizations and the Remaking of World Order*, New York: Simon and Schuster.

Hurd, Ian (1999) 'Legitimacy and Authority in International Politics', *International Organization*, 53:2, 379–408.

Hurrell, Andrew (1991) 'Regime Theory: A European Perspective', paper presented to conference on The Study of Regimes in IR, Tübingen, 28 pp. A revised version was published as 'International Society and the Study of International Regimes' in Volker Rittberger (ed.), *Regime Theory in International Relations*, Oxford: Clarendon, 1993, 49–72.

(2002a) 'Norms and Ethics in International Relations' in Walter Carlsnaes, Thomas Risse and Beth A. Simmons (eds.), *Handbook of International Relations*, London: Sage, 137–54.

(2002b) 'Foreword to the Third Edition: *The Anarchical Society* 25 Years On' in Hedley Bull, *The Anarchical Society*, Basingstoke: Palgrave, vii–xxiii.

Ikenberry, G. John (2001) *After Victory: Institutions, Strategic Restraint and the Rebuilding of Order after Major Wars*, Princeton University Press.

Jackson, Robert (1990) *Quasi-States: Sovereignty, International Relations and the Third World*, Cambridge University Press.

(1992) 'Pluralism in International Political Theory', *Review of International Studies*, 18:3, 271–81.

(2000) *The Global Covenant: Human Conduct in a World of States*, Oxford University Press.

James, Alan (1978) 'International Society', *British Journal of International Studies*, 4:2, 91–106.

(1986) *Sovereign Statehood: The Basis of International Society*, London: Allen and Unwin.

(1993) 'System or Society', *Review of International Studies*, 19:3, 269–88.

(1999) 'The Practice of Sovereign Statehood in Contemporary International Society', *Political Studies*, 47:3, 457–73.

Jones, Roy E. (1981) 'The English School of International Relations: A Case for Closure', *Review of International Studies*, 7:1, 1–13.

Jung, Dietrich (2001) 'The Political Sociology of World Society', *European Journal of International Relations*, 7:4, 443–74.

Kagan, Robert (2002) 'Power and Weakness', *Policy Review*, 113, 1–29.

Kapstein, Ethan B. (1999) 'Does Unipolarity Have a Future?' in Ethan B. Kapstein and Michael Mastanduno (eds.), *Unipolar Politics: Realism and State Strategies After the Cold War*, New York: Columbia University Press, 464–90.

Keane, John (2001) 'Global Civil Society?' in Helmut Anheier, Marlies Glasius and Mary Kaldor (eds.), *Global Civil Society 2001*, Oxford University Press, 23–47.

Keck, Margaret E. and Kathryn Sikkink (1998) *Activists Beyond Borders: Advocacy Networks in International Politics*, Ithaca: Cornell University Press.

Kedourie, Elie (1984) 'A New International Disorder' in Hedley Bull and Adam Watson (eds.), *The Expansion of International Society*, Oxford University Press, 347–56.

Keene, Edward (2000) 'The Dualistic Grotian Conception of International Society', paper presented to BISA Conference, Bradford, December, 20 pp.

(2002) *Beyond the Anarchical Society: Grotius, Colonialism and Order in World Politics*, Cambridge University Press.

Keohane, Robert O. (1988) 'International Institutions: Two Approaches', *International Studies Quarterly*, 32:4, 379–96.

(1995) 'Hobbes' Dilemma and Institutional Change in World Politics: Sovereignty in International Society' in Hans-Henrik Holm and Georg Sørensen (eds.), *Whose World Order?* Boulder, CO: Westview Press, 165–86.

Keohane, Robert O. and Joseph S. Nye (1977) *Power and Interdependence*, Boston: Little Brown.

(1987) '*Power and Interdependence* Revisited', *International Organization*, 41:4, 725–53.

Knudsen, Tonny Brems (1999) 'Humanitarian Intervention and International Society: Contemporary Manifestations of an Explosive Doctrine' (ms., 432 pp.), Aarhus: Department of Political Science, University of Aarhus.

Krasner, Stephen (1983) 'Structural Causes and Regime Consequences: Regimes as Intervening Variables' in Stephen Krasner (ed.), *International Regimes*, Ithaca: Cornell University Press, 1–21.

(1995) 'Power Politics, Institutions and Transnational Relations' in Thomas Risse-Kappen (ed.), *Bringing Transnational Relations Back In*, Cambridge University Press, 257–79.

(1999) *Sovereignty: Organized Hypocrisy*, Princeton University Press.

Kratochwil, Friedrich (1989) *Rules, Norms and Decisions: On the Conditions of Practical and Legal Reasoning in International Relations and Domestic Affairs*, Cambridge University Press.

Kratochwil, Friedrich and John Gerard Ruggie (1986) 'International Organisation: A State of the Art on an Art of the State', *International Organization*, 40:4, 753–75.

Linklater, Andrew (1981) 'Men and Citizens in International Relations', *Review of International Studies*, 7:1, 23–38.

(1996) 'Citizenship and Sovereignty in the Post-Westphalian State', *European Journal of International Relations*, 2:1, 77–103.

(1998) *The Transformation of Political Community*, Cambridge: Polity Press.

(2002) 'The Problem of Harm in World Politics: Implications for the Sociology of States-systems', *International Affairs*, 78:2, 319–38.

Lipschutz, Ronnie D. (1996) 'Reconstructing World Politics: The Emergence of Global Civil Society' in Rick Fawn and Jeremy Larkin (eds.), *International Society After the Cold War*, Basingstoke: Macmillan, 101–31.

Little, Richard (1995) 'Neorealism and the English School: A Methodological, Ontological and Theoretical Reassessment', *European Journal of International Relations*, 1:1, 9–34.

(1998) 'International System, International Society and World Society: A Re-evaluation of the English School' in B. A. Roberson (ed.), *International Society and the Development of International Relations Theory*, London: Pinter, 59–79.

(2000) 'The English School's Contribution to the Study of International Relations', *European Journal of International Relations*, 6:3, 395–422.

Luard, Evan (1976) *Types of International Society*, London: Macmillan.

(1990) *International Society*, Basingstoke: Macmillan.

McKinlay, R. D. and Richard Little (1986) *Global Problems and World Order*, London: Pinter.

McLean, Iain (1996) *Concise Dictionary of Politics*, Oxford University Press.

Mann, Michael (1986) *The Sources of Social Power Vol. 1: A History of Power from the Beginning to AD 1760*, Cambridge University Press.

Manners, Ian (2002) 'Normative Power Europe: A Contradiction in Terms?', *Journal of Common Market Studies*, 4:2. 235–58.

Manning, C. A. W. (1962), *The Nature of International Society*, London: LSE/ Macmillan.

March, James G. and Johan P. Olsen (1998) 'The Institutional Dynamics of International Political Orders', *International Organization*, 52:4, 943–69.

Masters, Roger D. (1964) 'World Politics as a Primitive Political System', *World Politics*, 16:4, 595–619.

Mayall, James (1982) 'The Liberal Economy' in James Mayall (ed.), *The Community of States: A Study in International Political Theory*, London: George Allen & Unwin, 96–111.

(1984) 'Reflections on the "New" Economic Nationalism', *Review of International Studies*, 10:4, 313–21.

(1989) '1789 and the Liberal Theory of International Society', *Review of International Studies*, 15: 297–307.

(1990) *Nationalism and International Society*, Cambridge University Press.

(2000) *World Politics: Progress and its Limits*, Cambridge: Polity.

Mayhew, Leon H. (1968) 'Society' in *International Encyclopedia of Social Science*, vol. 14, 577–85.

Meyer, John, John Boli and George M. Thomas (1987) 'Ontology and Rationalization in the Western Cultural Account' in George M. Thomas, John Meyer, Francisco O. Ramirez, John Boli (eds.), *Institutional Structure: Constituting State, Society, and Individual*, Newbury Park, CA: Sage.

Meyer, John W., John Boli, George M. Thomas, Francisco O. Ramirez (1997) 'World Society and the Nation-State', *American Journal of Sociology*, 103:1, 144–81.

Miller, J. D. B. (1990) 'The Third World' in J. D. B. Miller and R. J. Vincent (eds.), *Order and Violence: Hedley Bull and International Relations*, Oxford: Clarendon Press, 65–94.

Milner, Helen (1991) 'The Assumption of Anarchy in International Relations Theory: A Critique', *Review of International Studies*, 17:1, 67–85.

(1997) *Interests, Institutions and Information*, Princeton University Press.

Mosler, Hermann (1980) *The International Society as a Legal Community*, Alphen aan den Rijn: Sijthoff and Noordhoff.

Nardin, Terry (1998) 'Legal Positivism as a Theory of International Society' in David R. Mapel and Terry Nardin (eds.), *International Society: Diverse Ethical Perspectives*, Princeton University Press, 17–35.

Nau, Henry R. (2001) 'Why "The Rise and Fall of the Great Powers" Was Wrong', *Review of International Studies*, 27:4, 579–92.

Neumann, Iver B. (2001) 'To Know Him Was to Love Him. Not to Know Him Was to Love Him from Afar: Diplomacy in Star Trek', unpublished ms., Norwegian Institute of International Affairs.

Noortmann, Math (2001) 'Non-State Actors in International Law' in Math Noortmann, Bas Arts and Bob Reinalda (eds.), *Non-State Actors in International Relations*, Aldershot: Ashgate, 59–76.

Noortmann, Math, Bas Arts and Bob Reinalda (2001) 'The Quest for Unity in Empirical and Conceptual Complexity' in Math Noortmann, Bas Arts and Bob Reinalda (eds.), *Non-State Actors in International Relations*, Aldershot: Ashgate, 299–307.

Nye, Joseph S. (1990) 'Soft Power', *Foreign Policy*, 80, 153–71.

OECD (Organisation for Economic Co-operation and Development) (1998) *Open Markets Matter: The Benefits of Trade and Investment Liberalisation*, Paris: OECD.

Onuf, Nicholas (2002) 'Institutions, Intentions and International Relations', *Review of International Studies*, 28:2, 211–28.

Onuma, Yasuaki (2000) 'When Was the Law of International Society Born? An Enquiry of the History of International Law from an Intercivilisational Perspective', *Journal of the History of International Law*, 2:1, 1–66.

Osiander, Andreas (1994) *The States System of Europe 1640–1990*, Oxford: Clarendon.

Paul, Darel E. (1999) 'Sovereignty, Survival and the Westphalian Blind Alley in International Relations', *Review of International Studies*, 25:2, 217–31.

Peterson, M. J. (1992) 'Transnational Activity, International Society and World Politics', *Millennium*, 21:3, 371–88.

Ratner, Stephen R. (1998) 'International Law: The Trials of Global Norms', *Foreign Policy*, 110, 65–80.

Rengger, Nicholas, (1992) 'Culture, Society and Order in World Politics' in John Bayliss and N. J. Rengger (eds.), *Dilemmas of World Politics*, Oxford: Clarendon Press.

(1992, 1996) 'A City Which Sustains All Things? Communitarianism and International Society', *Millennium*, 21:3, 353–69.

(1999) *Beyond International Relations Theory? International Relations, Political Theory and the Problem of Order*, London: Routledge.

Reus-Smit, Christian (1997) 'The Constitutional Structure of International Society and the Nature of Fundamental Institutions', *International Organization*, 51:4, 555–89.

Richardson, James L. (1990) 'The Academic Study of International Relations' in J. D. B. Miller and John Vincent (eds.), *Order and Violence: Hedley Bull and International Relations*, Oxford: Clarendon Press, 140–85.

Risse-Kappen, Thomas (1995a) 'Bringing Transnational Relations Back In: Introduction' in Thomas Risse-Kappen (ed.), *Bringing Transnational Relations Back In: Non-State Actors, Domestic Structures and International Institutions*, Cambridge University Press, 3–33.

(1995b) 'Structures of Governance and Transnational Relations: What Have We Learned?' in Thomas Risse-Kappen (ed.), *Bringing Transnational Relations Back In: Non-State Actors, Domestic Structures and International Institutions*, Cambridge University Press, 280–313.

(2002) 'Transnational Actors and World Politics' in Walter Carlsnaes, Thomas Risse and Beth A. Simmons (eds.), *Handbook of International Relations*, London: Sage, 255–74.

Rosenau, James N. (1966) 'Pre-theories and Theories of Foreign Policy' in R. Barry Farrell (ed.), *Approaches to Comparative and International Politics*, Evanston: Northwestern University Press, 27–92.

(1990) *Turbulence in World Politics: A Theory of Change and Continuity*, London: Harvester Wheatsheaf.

Ruggie, John (1983) 'Continuity and Transformation in the World Polity: Towards a Neorealist Synthesis', *World Politics*, 35:2, 261–85.

(1993) 'Territoriality and Beyond: Problematizing Modernity in International Relations', *International Organization*, 47:1, 139–74.

(1998) *Constructing the World Polity*, London: Routledge.

Scholte, Jan Aart (2000) *Globalisation: A Critical Introduction*, Basingstoke: Macmillan.

Searle, John R. (1995) *The Construction of Social Reality*, London: Penguin.

Shaw, Martin (1992, 1996) 'Global Society and Global Responsibility: The Theoretical, Historical and Political Limits of "International Society"', *Millennium*, 21:3, 421–34.

(1994) *Global Society and International Relations*, Cambridge: Polity.

Smith, Anthony D. (1992) 'National Identity and the Idea of European Unity', *International Affairs*, 68:1, 55–76.

Snidal, Duncan (1993) 'Relative Gains and the Pattern of International Cooperation' in David Baldwin (ed.), *Neorealism and Neoliberalism*, New York: Columbia University Press.

Sørensen, Georg (1999) 'Sovereignty: Change and Continuity in a Fundamental Institution', *Political Studies*, 47:3, 590–604.

Strange, Susan (1988) *States and Markets: An Introduction*, London: Pinter.

Suganami, Hidemi (1989) *The Domestic Analogy and World Order Proposals*, Cambridge University Press.

(2001) 'Alexander Wendt and the English School', *Journal of International Relations and Development*, 4:4, 403–23.

(2002) 'The International Society Perspective on World Politics Reconsidered', *International Relations of the Asia-Pacific*, 2:1, 1–28.

Thomas, George M., John Meyer, Francisco O. Ramirez, John Boli (eds.) (1987) *Institutional Structure: Constituting State, Society, and Individual*, Newbury Park, CA: Sage.

Tilly, Charles (1990) *Coercion, Capital, and European States AD 990–1990*, Oxford: Blackwell.

Tönnies, F. (1887) *Gemeinschaft und Gesellschaft*, Leipzig: Fues's Verlag.

Underhill, Geoffrey (2000) 'State, Market, and Global Political Economy: Genealogy of an (Inter-?) Discipline', *International Affairs*, 76:4, 805–24.

Vincent, R. J. (1978) 'Western Conceptions of a Universal Moral Order', *British Journal of International Studies*, 4:1, 20–46.

(1986) *Human Rights and International Relations: Issues and Responses*, Cambridge University Press.

(1988) 'Hedley Bull and Order in International Politics', *Millennium*, 17:2, 195–213.

(1992) 'The Idea of Rights in International Ethics' in Terry Nardin and D. Mapel (eds.), *Traditions of International Ethics*, Cambridge University Press, 250–69.

Wæver, Ole (1992) 'International Society – Theoretical Promises Unfulfilled?', *Cooperation and Conflict*, 27:1, 97–128.

(1996) 'Europe's Three Empires: A Watsonian Interpretation of Post-Wall European Security' in Rick Fawn and Jeremy Larkin (eds.), *International Society After the Cold War*, London: Macmillan.

(1998) 'Four Meanings of International Society: A Trans-Atlantic Dialogue' in B. A. Roberson (ed.), *International Society and the Development of International Relations Theory*, London: Pinter.

Wallerstein, Immanuel (1984) *The Politics of the World-Economy*, Cambridge University Press.

Waltz, Kenneth N. (1979) *Theory of International Politics*, Reading: Addison-Wesley.

Warner, Caroline M. (2001) 'The Rise of the States-System in Africa' in Michael Cox, Tim Dunne and Ken Booth (eds.), *Empires, Systems and States: Great Transformations in International Politics*, Cambridge University Press, 65–89.

Watson, Adam (1987) 'Hedley Bull, States-Systems and International Studies', *Review of International Studies*, 13:2, 147–53.

(1990) 'Systems of States', *Review of International Studies*, 16:2, 99–109.

(1992) *The Evolution of International Society*, London: Routledge.

Weller, Christopher (2000) 'Collective Identities in World Society' in Mathias Albert, Lothar Brock, Klaus Dieter Wolf (eds.), *Civilizing World Politics:*

Society and Community Beyond the State, Lanham, MD: Rowman and Littlefield, 45–68.

Weller, Marc (2002) 'Undoing the Global Constitution: UN Security Council Action on the International Criminal Court', *International Affairs*, 78:4, 693–712.

Wendt, Alexander (1992) 'Anarchy Is What States Make of It: The Social Construction of Power Politics', *International Organization*, 46:2, 391–425.

(1999) *Social Theory of International Politics*, Cambridge University Press.

Wheeler, Nicholas (1992) 'Pluralist or Solidarist Conceptions of International Society', *Millennium*, 21:3, 463–87.

(2000) *Saving Strangers: Humanitarian Intervention in International Society*, Oxford University Press.

Wheeler, Nicholas J. and Tim Dunne (1998) 'Hedley Bull and the Idea of a Universal Moral Community: Fictional, Primordial or Imagined?' in B. A. Roberson (ed.), *International Society and the Development of International Relations Theory*, London: Pinter.

Whelan, Frederick G. (1998) 'Legal Positivism and International Society' in David R. Mapel and Terry Nardin (eds.), *International Society: Diverse Ethical Perspectives*, Princeton University Press, 36–53.

Wight, Martin (1966) 'Western Values in International Relations' in Herbert Butterfield and Martin Wight (eds.), *Diplomatic Investigations*, London: Allen and Unwin, 89–131.

(1977) *Systems of States*, ed. Hedley Bull, Leicester University Press.

(1979) *Power Politics*, ed. Hedley Bull and Carsten Holbraad, London, Penguin, 2nd edition.

(1987 [1960]) 'An Anatomy of International Thought', *Review of International Studies*, 13:3, 221–7.

(1991) *International Theory: The Three Traditions*, ed. Brian Porter and Gabriele Wight, Leicester University Press/Royal Institute of International Affairs.

Williams, John (2001) 'New Spaces, New Places: Territory and Change in International Society', paper presented to the ECPR Pan-European International Relations Conference, University of Kent, September, 14 pp.

Woods, Ngaire (ed.) (2000) *The Political Economy of Globalisation*, Basingstoke: Macmillan.

(WSRG) World Society Research Group (1995) 'In Search of World Society', Darmstadt/Frankfurt/M.: World Society Research Group Working Paper No. 1. Updated version as 'Introduction: World Society' in Mathias Albert, Lothar Brock, Klaus Dieter Wolf (eds.) (2000) *Civilizing World Politics. Society and Community Beyond the State*, Lanham: Rowman & Littlefield, 1–17.

Zhang, Yongjin (1998) *China in International Society since 1949*, Basingstoke: Macmillan.

(2001) 'System, Empire and State in Chinese International Relations' in Michael Cox, Tim Dunne and Ken Booth (eds.), *Empires, Systems and States: Great Transformations in International Politics*, Cambridge University Press, 43–63.

(2002) 'Towards a Regional International Society? Making Sense of Regionalism(s) in Asia', paper at ISA Convention, New Orleans, March, 15 pp.

Index

CAMBRIDGE STUDIES IN INTERNATIONAL RELATIONS